CHARACTERISTICS of COMPASSION

Portraits of
EXEMPLARY
PHYSICIANS

HELEN MELDRUM

Associate Professor of Psychology
Program in Health Sciences and Industry
Department of Natural and Applied Sciences
Bentley University
Waltham, Massachusetts

JONES AND BARTLETT PUBLISHERS
Sudbury, Massachusetts
BOSTON   TORONTO   LONDON   SINGAPORE

World Headquarters
Jones and Bartlett Publishers
40 Tall Pine Drive
Sudbury, MA 01776
978-443-5000
info@jbpub.com
www.jbpub.com

Jones and Bartlett Publishers
Canada
2406 Nikanna Road
Mississauga, ON L5C 2W6
Canada

Jones and Bartlett Publishers
International
Barb House, Barb Mews
London W6 7PA
United Kingdom

Jones and Bartlett's books and products are available through most bookstores and online booksellers. To contact Jones and Bartlett Publishers directly, call 800-832-0034, fax 978-443-8000, or visit our website www.jbpub.com.

Substantial discounts on bulk quantities of Jones and Bartlett's publications are available to corporations, professional associations, and other qualified organizations. For details and specific discount information, contact the special sales department at Jones and Bartlett via the above contact information or send an email to specialsales@jbpub.com.

Copyright © 2010 by Jones and Bartlett Publishers, LLC

All rights reserved. No part of the material protected by this copyright may be reproduced or utilized in any form, electronic or mechanical, including photocopying, recording, or by any information storage and retrieval system, without written permission from the copyright owner.

The authors, editor, and publisher have made every effort to provide accurate information. However, they are not responsible for errors, omissions, or for any outcomes related to the use of the contents of this book and take no responsibility for the use of the products and procedures described. Treatments and side effects described in this book may not be applicable to all people; likewise, some people may require a dose or experience a side effect that is not described herein. Drugs and medical devices are discussed that may have limited availability controlled by the Food and Drug Administration (FDA) for use only in a research study or clinical trial. Research, clinical practice, and government regulations often change the accepted standard in this field. When consideration is being given to use of any drug in the clinical setting, the health care provider or reader is responsible for determining FDA status of the drug, reading the package insert, and reviewing prescribing information for the most up-to-date recommendations on dose, precautions, and contraindications, and determining the appropriate usage for the product. This is especially important in the case of drugs that are new or seldom used.

Production Credits
Publisher: David Cella
Associate Editor: Maro Gartside
Production Director: Amy Rose
Senior Production Editor: Renée Sekerak
Production Assistant: Jill Morton
Senior Marketing Manager: Barb Bartoszek
Manufacturing and Inventory Control Supervisor: Amy Bacus
Composition: Auburn Associates, Inc.
Cover Design: Scott Moden
Cover and Title Page Image: © Patricia Hofmeester/ShutterStock, Inc.
Printing and Binding: Malloy, Inc.
Cover Printing: Malloy, Inc.

Library of Congress Cataloging-in-Publication Data

Meldrum, Helen.
  Characteristics of compassion : portraits of exemplary physicians / by Helen Meldrum.
      p. ; cm.
  Includes bibliographical references and index.
  ISBN-13: 978-0-7637-5733-5
  ISBN-10: 0-7637-5733-0
  1. Physicians—United States—Biography. 2. Physicians—Awards—United States. I. Title.
  [DNLM: 1. Physicians—Biography. 2. Empathy—Biography. 3. Physician's Role—Biography. 4. Physician-Patient Relations—Biography. WZ 112 M518c 2010]
  R153.M45 2010
  610.92—dc22
  [B]
                                                                                              2008054197

6048

Printed in the United States of America
13 12 11 10 09   10 9 8 7 6 5 4 3 2 1

Praise for *Characteristics of Compassion: Portraits of Exemplary Physicians*

A truly inspirational collection of physician profiles. I would highly recommend this book to anyone contemplating a career in medicine, to those just starting in practice, and to any physician in need of refreshing his spirit and sense of meaning and purpose in life.

Joan Waldron Huppi, MD
Medical Director
United Healthcare, Vienna, VA

Dr. Meldrum has written a wonderful book about true heroes in medicine. These are physicians who make a daily difference in the lives of their patients by selflessly volunteering their time, effort, knowledge, and resources to improve people's health and well being. This book makes one realize that the practice of medicine is truly a noble calling.

Jean Howard
President
American Medical Association Foundation, Chicago, IL

Dedication

So many of the physicians profiled here mentioned that their parents taught them about treating people with respect and consideration. I have also been fortunate to have parents who modeled decency and kindness. This book is for:

Anne Libbey Meldrum
and
Philip Hingston Meldrum

Foreword

Having served on the admissions committee of the Pritzker School of Medicine at the University of Chicago for 15 years, I have read a great number of personal statements from applicants who attempt to fill the reader with hope that the next generation of physicians will be the most altruistic, humanitarian, and compassionate that ever evolved. I read the applications and am truly inspired by the ideals that these young people want to bring to the profession; I believe that some will indeed make a difference with their careers. However, over and over, I watch as something diverts that idealism in each class of new doctors. A fortuitous Board score; the realization of staggering educational debt; or some blend of learned practicality, stereotyping, and cynicism convert these overtly well-intended individuals into pragmatic decision makers who too often choose personal concerns over those of society at large. As an academic physician, I have pondered just how we have done this to the next generation. Where did the optimism and community-directed focus go? That is why I found it rejuvenating to read about the undiminished passion evident in the physicians gathered together in *Characteristics of Compassion: Portraits of Exemplary Physicians*.

The urge to make a difference in people's lives through medicine must be nourished if it is to survive the harsh realities and pressures of such a demanding field. Many students, particularly those from disadvantaged backgrounds, have obvious humanistic tendencies to give to others, but they just do not know how they can contribute. For the past few years, I have gathered a number of essays from applicants to the Minority Scholars Award and permitted some of my students to read them. It was as if their whole perspective changed on what was important in society. This book gives me another such resource to offer. To be able to read about the philosophies and beliefs of distinguished physicians in a variety of practices such as the honorees profiled here will be such a gift for my students. Many of them have never before heard anyone articulate what they could do to address health disparities and maintain their own humanity at the same time.

Young physicians in training hear the rumblings of their older colleagues who are leaving the practice and cannot help but wonder what they have gotten themselves into. But that negativity can be counteracted by the stories of the doctors in these pages who use their talents to serve individuals and programs; who give of their own funds to open clinics or start movements; who enter retirement only to return to work to build resources for communities. As the President of The Chicago Medical Society, I believe that even doctors with many years of practice will be inspired by the everyday heroism displayed by the indefatigable physicians in these pages. The true altruistic spirit of the medical profession is embodied by these men and women who go the extra mile to serve others. I sincerely hope that this book will find its way to experienced doctors who may be thinking that they are too busy to volunteer their time at a local clinic, but just need to glimpse the lives of peers finding ways to help neighbors as well as those in need half a world away. The American Medical Association Foundation's Pride in the Profession Award recipients profiled in *Characteristics of Compassion: Portraits of Exemplary Physicians* exhibit in their daily work that spirit of other-directedness on a grand scale through their efforts to change policies, develop talent, build infrastructure, and of course provide care to individuals.

These physicians are role models not just for our young doctors, but for all physicians. When my residents and students read of these exploits on behalf of humanity, they will be reminded of the caring that they themselves originally brought to their pursuit of medicine. The lives of these physician heroes and heroines in these pages are real, and this makes all the difference to those who read about them. Although it may seem impossible to do some of the things they do, it is incontrovertible that someone is doing it. This means that every doctor has the capacity to step up as well. So read *Characteristics of Compassion: Portraits of Exemplary Physicians* and be touched by these wonderful examples of our physician colleagues who go above and beyond practice norms for the betterment of humanity, thereby upholding the highest ideals of the medical profession.

William McDade, MD, PhD
Associate Professor and Associate Dean for Multicultural Affairs
Pritzker School of Medicine at The University of Chicago
Chair, The American Medical Association Foundation
Excellence in Medicine Awards Selection Committee

Contents

Foreword vii

Preface xi

Chapter 1　Introduction and Overview .1
　　　　　　Choosing the Profession 4
　　　　　　Professional and Personal Identity 14
　　　　　　The Wellspring 22

Chapter 2　The Woman Who Answered More Than
　　　　　　One Calling 35
　　　　　　Dr. Anne Brooks

Chapter 3　Supporting This Small and Sickly World 49
　　　　　　Dr. Michael VanRooyen

Chapter 4　Finding Peace on the Other Side of Trauma 61
　　　　　　Dr. Sylvia Campbell

Chapter 5　The Doctor Who Flunked Retirement 75
　　　　　　Dr. Jack McConnell

Chapter 6　A Voice for the Urban and Rural Poor 89
　　　　　　Dr. Bruce Gould

Chapter 7　Making Common Ground for Faith and Health . .103
　　　　　　Dr. G. Scott Morris

Chapter 8　Listening to Many Truths 115
　　　　　　Dr. Coleen Kivlahan

Chapter 9	Inheriting a Commitment to Service ....127 *Dr. Mark Asperilla*	
Chapter 10	What Is Harder Than Brain Surgery? Mobilizing the Healthcare Community ....141 *Dr. Gary VanderArk*	
Chapter 11	His Rx: Spiritual Healing ....153 *Dr. Gerald G. "Jerry" Jampolsky*	
Chapter 12	Living from Mission to Mission ....165 *Dr. Jeannette South-Paul*	
Chapter 13	Having an Impact on Health in the Small City and Leaving a Bigger Legacy ....179 *Dr. Leonard Morse*	
Chapter 14	Have Compassionate Care, Will Travel ....191 *Dr. Wendy Ring*	
Chapter 15	The Kindest Cut: Surgery with Soul ....203 *Dr. William Schecter, with Dr. Gisela Schecter*	
Chapter 16	A Summation of What Was Shared 217	

Acknowledgments 253

About the Author 255

References and Resources 257

Index 267

Preface

". . . we should be concerned not only with our own welfare but also with that of others, and with human society as a whole." [1,p. 9]

Albert Schweitzer
Physician, Philosopher, Theologian, and Humanitarian[2]

". . . we can work for a world of solidarity, in which people from different backgrounds mobilize resources and build the foundations of a dignified life for all . . ." [3,p. xxiii]

Paul Farmer
Physician, Medical Anthropologist, Healthcare Activist, and Humanitarian[4]

These are the voices of true luminaries. Albert Schweitzer has been gone from the earth for almost half a century, while Paul Farmer has yet to live through his 50th year, and he has already contributed so much to our world. Many aspiring healthcare professionals know about these towering figures and have been inspired by them. Both physicians are members of a rarified small group, so it might be difficult for a doctor in training or even one at midcareer to easily identify with the magnitude of their impact. Yet so many of the healthcare professionals that I have had the privilege to work with over the past 25 years articulate a true contentment with the scope of their much more modest outreach efforts. A growing number, unfortunately, while not expressing outright regret, now find themselves advising the next generation of premedical students to possibly reconsider their vocational choice. A sad few go as far as to suggest that just about any other profession is bound to be more rewarding than practicing medicine in 21st-century America.

What would it take to tip the balance back in favor of those who believe that excellence in medicine can be more regularly approached, if not perfected? Could younger and older physicians alike be inspired by peers who maintain a vision for their daily practice that includes a focus on hopefulness and determined perseverance? I was at a loss for where I might find these everyday healthcare heroes until the spring of 2007. That is when I happened to notice a full page advertisement in a national newspaper announcing the annual winners of the American Medical Association Foundation Pride in the Profession Award (cosponsored by the Pfizer Medical Humanities Initiative). The nominees were said to reflect the highest standards of integrity, commitment to service, community involvement, altruism, and leadership in the medical profession. The awards honor physicians whose lives encompass the true spirit of being a medical professional—caring for people. They practice medicine in areas of challenge or crisis or devote their time to volunteerism or public service. This group of physicians serves as the collective voice of patients in the United States who otherwise might not be heard.

These doctors sounded exactly like the exemplars I sought. Given the prestige and knowledge repository of the American Medical Association Foundation, it seemed a reasonable assumption that the award honorees would represent the finest in the field. I contacted the foundation and was greeted with gracious enthusiasm. In discussions with the executive staff, I learned that the call for nominations goes out to both American Medical Association members and nonmembers, medical societies, physician volunteer groups, and beyond through advertisements and Web postings. The composition of the selection committee is refreshed each year with an eye toward diversity. The response varies year to year, but often hundreds of names can be forwarded for all of the excellence in medicine awards combined (there are four separate honors). Typically, three to four doctors from that pool are singled out to receive the Pride in the Profession Award. The honorees are evaluated on merits and accomplishments that go beyond their scientific and medical expertise, and the committee is open to lauding doctors who show ingenuity and sometimes an unorthodox creativity.

As someone who has worked nationally and internationally for over two decades as a consultant and researcher in the field of health communication, I have come to know many talented and empathic physicians. But had I attempted to select my subjects personally, through my own contacts, my own biases and subjective assessments would have affected the results. Using the awards selection process to identify my exemplary physician group allowed me to proceed with a sample independent of my own personal preferences.

I gained access to the award archives back to 2002 (the annual tradition was started in 2000) and attempted to contact each winner listed through the spring of 2008. I arranged to conduct taped interviews with as many of the recipients as I could reach, because I felt they might provide firsthand insights into what mind-sets and motivations served to set them apart from so many of their peers. About half of the winners of the award agreed to be part of this project (14 total out of a possible 27). I am pleased that those participating physicians represent some diversity in terms of ethnicity and gender, come from different regions of the country, and also provide a bit of variety in practice and research specialties.

I should make clear that I promised each physician that the information that I would make public would be a summary of what led them toward the finest hours of their life's work. I did not dig for evidence of the types of blemishes and wrinkles that appear on the life of any of us complex human beings. My interests were in what choices they felt served them well. Being a total stranger as I approached each interviewee, I was asking for their trust. Putting myself in their shoes, I think I might have turned down the offer to talk to an unknown college professor if she told me that she wanted to formulate a rigorous psychological critique of my character. I approached the doctors by telling them that I would like to record their philosophies and beliefs in a text with an accompanying conviction that their words could inspire other preservice and in-service physicians. The fact that they had been recognized as doctors who go above and beyond made them the people whom I really wanted to include. Those interviews have become the basis of this book.

I told the honorees that I recognized the time constraints they live under and promised our communication could be accomplished in a conveniently scheduled taped phone interview, during which I would ask questions about such things as their background, inspirational figures, and any important turning points. I also said that I was interested in what keeps them from becoming burnt out and negative. Finally, I shared that I would have some questions about how they might see a moral or spiritual dimension to their work. To ensure accuracy, all of the honorees were invited to do a prepublication review of the section of the manuscript that focused on their story.

As I undertook this project, I searched the literature to see if there were already books with a similar design but I did not find a comparable volume. I had hoped that scholars might have taken on the task of identifying and providing a rich description of traits or motivations shared by today's leading medical doctors. Nothing similar was to be found. Of course there are many autobiographical books by physicians in training. Individual doctors with more years of experience offer reflections on their practice. There are historical profiles and a few full-length biographies profiling notable physicians.

So I searched again for shorter research reports. The most relevant was a study published almost a decade ago in an issue of the *Archives of Family Medicine*. It presented the results of a brief paper and pencil survey sent to 1200 physicians to inquire about personal values, practice satisfaction, and other factors recorded on a rating scale. However, no rich open-ended data was captured.[5] There are also some private for-profit companies that provide annual recognition to physicians. Still, this ritual seems to be an overly commercial practice of naming "top docs" from regional areas for the purpose of creating glossy advertising in local magazines.

Until 2008, Pfizer Pharmaceuticals maintained a Web site called Positive Profiles that offered descriptions of exemplary practitioners and their work. The brief biographies on that Web site left me wanting to know more. I concluded overall that while there is some research available about motivation, books about caring in medicine, and manuals attempting to define excellence in health care, none could be found that had combined these elements in a single work. That is the reason I contacted these doctors. I thought that by looking more holistically at the lives of outstanding physicians, I could learn more about what makes them tick.

When I think back on my own earliest fascination with the study of lives, I think of my graduate school professors who have dedicated so much of their work to profiling rare and inspiring individuals. Developmental psychologists Lawrence Kohlberg, Carol Gilligan, and Robert Kegan all graced my life as teachers in a key period that shaped my interests. William Damon (who taught me at Clark University) and Anne Colby (who lectured at Harvard in my years there) have assembled an amazing catalog of figures in so many of their books and articles that continue to influence my thinking. *Some Do Care: Contemporary Lives of Moral Commitment*[6] traces the life stories of moral leaders who made significant contributions to their communities. Bill Damon's *Noble Purpose: The Joy of Living a Meaningful Life*[7] further identifies the benefits of dedicating one's life to a cause. This book owes a great intellectual debt to the methods I absorbed during my time with these fine educators and from following their later work.

One hot summer day as I took a short break from finishing my final entries to this text, the universe offered me another opportunity to reflect on the current state of the art in the physician–patient relationship. I ran out on an errand to my insurance agency. The clerk there knew that I was a college professor and launched into the "it must be nice to have the whole summer off" speech that makes me unreasonably defensive. So I offered up that I had been working very hard, actually, writing a book about exemplary physicians. She looked at me with wide eyes and responded with what can only be described as a combination snort, giggle, and harrumph. "They exist?" she howled "I didn't know there was anybody still around that was an outstanding physician!" Her comment was in line with what I had been hearing from other friends who liked to kid me that my text would be a very short book indeed. These encounters made me think about one of the most famous exchanges in the history of editorial journalism. Just over a century ago, *The Sun* newspaper (New York) writer Francis Church[8] responded to the poignant inquiry of Virginia O'Hanlon, an 8-year-old whose little friends had told her that there really was no Santa Claus. "Please tell me the truth," Virginia wrote at the urging of her father, a hard-nosed New York City surgeon and deputy coroner employed by the police department. The response was printed. "Your little friends are wrong. They have been affected by the skepticism of a skeptical age. They do not believe except what they see...." Several critics have interpreted the writer's response as chiding the adult readership for losing faith in faith itself.

It can certainly be said that in this era of managed care, medical tourism, and healthcare disparities, many Americans have lost faith in the delivery system and their practitioners. Church's point, that some people only believe what they can see, really resonated with me. The physicians in this book constitute the proof for those who have grown cynical. During my conversation with Dr. Coleen Kivlahan, one of the award honorees, we came to speak of both Albert Schweitzer and Paul Farmer and acknowledged how truly big and perhaps intimidating their life stories could seem to some physicians. Many doctors or medical students who feel uncertain about the depth and breadth of their own commitments might have trouble identifying with those who make such huge personal sacrifices routinely and without complaint. Coleen said she was happy that I was collecting the smaller stories of physicians who make meaningful contributions without gaining big entries in the history books. I am also pleased that doctors who embody the best values of the medical profession through leadership, service, and integrity have shared their stories with me. It is plain to see that through their dedication, they enrich their patients' lives, colleagues' work, and shared communities.

What follows is an overview in which I discuss some of the sources and ideas that sparked my questions for the physicians; readers will then have the privilege of "meeting" each doctor. In a summary chapter I offer commentary and thoughts that struck me after I collected the stories. In addition to traditional references, I have also included a resources section on each chapter that is offered to fill in some details related to my background search on each honoree. I hope the good doctors' words of wisdom and discernment will make a real difference to working physicians and to the next generation to come.

CHAPTER 1

Introduction and Overview

We no longer have doctors in America; we have *healthcare providers*. We aren't patients; we're *consumers*. The healthcare system has turned the art and science of healing into big business, and many doctors can no longer devote the greater part of their working hours directly to patient care, faced as they are with reams of insurance- and legal-related paperwork, the constant threat of malpractice, and a burgeoning patient population. Despite this, some physicians still enter the profession with deeply held convictions, hopes, and idealism, and go on to excel not just as medical doctors, but as human beings. Some volunteer their time and expertise mentoring others or volunteering their services. Some found or fund organizations devoted to good works. Some spend their off hours lost in research or tinkering with tools and ideas for theories or devices whose only profits may be measured in lives saved. Many do this on a volunteer basis and some in addition to their very full-time jobs as medical doctors.

Why? Let us consider two fictional doctors—Dr. Smith and Dr. Jones. Why does Dr. Smith go to the office, treat patients, and go home in time for dinner, while Dr. Jones goes to the office early, plugs away at some pet research project, treats patients, stops at the hospital to check a patient's progress, goes to the board meeting of a charitable group, types up extensive notes about each patient of the day, and picks up take-out on the way home to a dark house? Why are some people just so . . . *good*?

This is no small question. It is universally acknowledged that the healthcare system in the United States is ailing. What is less clear is what is causing the problems and how to effect a cure. As the life expectancy and overall health of Americans have increased, patients' levels of respect and trust for the doctors sworn to prevent, diagnose, and treat illness have decreased. People question the quality and course of their care, suspicious that the doctors' tests and treatments are based less on what is best for the patient than on what is allowed by the insurance companies. Most of the suggested cures for the healthcare system focus on finance, as though the medical expenditures growing uncontrollably and metastasizing at every level of the system are the cause of the ills. But what if the cause goes deeper than that? What if there's something much more basic we need to make healthy before we can hope to take care of the upward-spiraling costs?

In 1996, one doctor suggested a different root cause of our healthcare system's ailing state. "Medicine's profound crisis," he wrote in *The Lost Art of Healing*, "is only partially related to ballooning costs, for the problem is far deeper than economics. In my view, the basic reason is that medicine has lost its way, if not its soul. An unwritten covenant between doctor and patient, hallowed over several millennia, is being broken" (Lown, 1996, p. xi). Who is this doctor to be suggesting that there might be something not quite right at the human level? Surely he must be some obscure, radical scientist to put forth a view so contrary to common wisdom. No, this doctor is none other than renowned cardiologist and Harvard Medical School professor Dr. Bernard Lown—the man who developed a version of the defibrillator that resuscitated hundreds of thousands of patients. He is also one of the founders of Physicians for Social Responsibility, and cofounder of the International Physicians for the Prevention of Nuclear War. Doctor Lown was a recipient of the 1985 Nobel Peace Prize because of his work to prevent nuclear war. More recently, Lown and his colleagues founded the Alliance to Defend Health Care, a physicians' group dedicated to the patient advocacy and reform of the U.S. healthcare system. Clearly he has spent considerable time taking the pulse of the system, so his words deserve close attention.

What does he mean, "Medicine has lost its way, if not its soul?" Lown's essential message is that the vital connection of trust between doctor and patient—a bond that held fast through 3000 years of medical tradition—has broken. In other words, there is not enough caring in health care.

"Healing is replaced with treating, caring is supplanted by managing, and the art of listening is taken over by technological procedures. Doctors no longer minister to a distinctive person but concern themselves with fragmented, malfunctioning biologic parts," he wrote. "The distressed human being is frequently absent from the transaction" (Lown, 1996, p. xii).

As I pondered Lown's words in view of my own question of why there were so many Dr. Smiths (good, possibly even great doctors) and so few Dr. Joneses (exemplary physicians *and* praiseworthy people), it struck me that if I were to examine the lives of a sampling of Dr. Joneses, I might be able to identify some common denominators that led them to excel, and perhaps this information could be used to lend insight into our current healthcare system.

So I decided to interview Pride in the Profession Award Honorees, and I proceeded to think about what I would like to ask these doctors. I found that my interview questions fell into three general areas. I am reluctant to reduce these areas as some bulletized list of catchphrases with somewhat similar meanings but perhaps different connotations (e.g., goals, dreams, milestones, plans). Inevitably the themes would overlap as well; since the original purpose of categorizing the types of information was to facilitate my own analysis after the fact. I decided to forgo any organizational labeling until after I had completed all the interviews and begun to study them in earnest, and only then determine whether the results themselves suggested logical groupings. I approached the interviews with three broad descriptions of information I wanted to gather; these can best be relayed as questions.

The first general area of questioning explored those things that led each interviewee toward a medical profession. This encompassed a range of topics—everything from parental guidance and childhood heroes to pivotal moments and synchronistic events. I asked such questions as these: Do you recall any single moment or event, or several related incidences, when as a child or adolescent you consciously decided to become a doctor? Were you encouraged or discouraged by anyone such as family, friends, counselors, or others, and did this have any effect at all on your decision or specific plans?

The second general area of questioning concerned the actual experience of being a doctor and what part that played in the interviewee's sense of self. My intention was to find out, if at all possible, to what degree the role of physician informed the individual's personal credo and identity—and vice versa. These questions were less dependent on memory and more dependent on reflection, as these sample questions suggest: In what ways does your current medical practice differ from what you once imagined it might be? Have you accomplished any or all of your major life goals, and if not, what have been the obstacles? Have you experienced burnout? If not, how have you prevented it, and if so, how have you dealt with it?

The third general area of questioning was an attempt to assess the interviewee's inner strengths (and perhaps weaknesses) in terms of such abstract constructs as character, principles, and motivation or inspiration. My purpose in delving into these topics was to analyze in which ways, if any, the interviewees shared characteristics in common and identify any possible correlation between these and the doctors' acknowledged outstanding achievements. To this end, I asked such questions as these: Have you ever found yourself in a situation as a doctor where the correct course of action concerning a patient conflicted with your sense of what was the right thing to do? What is the most important reason you get out of bed each morning? What enables you to persevere in the face of resistance?

Choosing the Profession

The initial questions were designed to tease out any and all of the details of what might have contributed to an interviewee's pursuing a life in the medical profession. A natural starting point seemed to be the traditional life story, with an emphasis on anything that contributed to the doctors' choice of career and to the achievement of that goal. "Life stories—our chosen form of narrative—tell us much about individual and collective, private and public, structural and agentic and real and fictional worlds. Stories occupy a central place in the knowledge generated by societies" (Goodley, Lawthom, Clough, & Moore, 2004, p. ix). Notwithstanding the vagaries of memory, any milestones or turning points in the physicians' lives would very likely emerge from such biographical narratives.

The process of collecting and analyzing life stories sounds deceptively simple, but in fact that very process could affect the quality, quantity, and interpretation of the findings that result. Foos and Clark (2003, p. 207) quote gerontologist Peter G. Coleman (1999, pp. 133–139) and his definition of four lenses that can be used to view life stories. They emphasize that the same lenses must be used for all interview data to ensure comparability—namely, *coherence* (the linking thread); *assimilation* (interpretation of events); *structure* (beginning, middle, and end); and *truth* (the reality perceived by the storyteller). Coleman noted that when telling life stories, people with a greater sense of perceived control were more apt and better able to recollect and relate their personal histories in an orderly and meaningful narration rather than as a haphazard reporting of nonsequential and perhaps even inconsequential vignettes. Perhaps this can be attributed to the fact that, as professor of psychology Charles R. Snyder has said, a solid understanding of oneself makes goal-directed thinking an easier task, since "personal coherence serves to clarify the important goals of one's life; in turn, having specified goals increases the probability that the adolescent has the necessary will- and way-related thoughts to pursue these goals" (Snyder, 1994, p. 102).

One might expect the exemplary physicians interviewed to have this "solid foundation of self-hood" (Snyder, 1994, p. 102) and to have a proficiency, if not mastery, in the area of goal-directed thinking. Given their stellar achievements in multiple areas of their lives, and given the likelihood that they would consider themselves to have a relatively high degree of control in their lives, the interviewees seemed likely to present logically structured tales with relevant detail during their interviews. This proved, most often, to be true. Perhaps the public attention paid to their achievements contributed to their apparent ability to recollect and comment on memories from their formative years.

In 2006, National Public Radio began a show entitled *This I Believe*, a series of audio essays in which people both famous and unknown expounded on their personal belief systems and how these developed. Inspired by the original 1950s radio series of the same name and produced by Edward R. Murrow, *This I Believe* examines life lessons gleaned from both monumental and mundane events and observations, and how these shaped the present and future for the respective tellers. In the introduction to the printed book version of the 80 audio essays, Studs Terkel summed up his own thoughts in this way: "My credo consists of the pursuit and the act. One without the other is self-indulgence. This I believe" (Allison & Gediman, 2006, p. 5).

That the interviewees in this book must have followed a similar philosophy I knew by virtue of the selection process—it was their *actions*, not their *desires*, that qualified them for nomination—and it was my pleasure to be allowed to elicit from them the same sorts of memories of epiphanies, turning points, encouragements, and inspirations as those captured in the essays. To tell the full story, I had to be concerned not just with the act but with the pursuit that shaped the doctors' lives.

To that end, I approached the physicians' personal histories from two directions. First, I simply asked, with a minimum of guides and prompts, that they tell me their life stories. This allowed the respondents, rather than me, to decide what elements might or might not have been significant and thus warrant inclusion. As British biographer Gordon Bowker (1993, p. 19) said, biographies are in a "constant state of becoming," which suggests that a self-appraisal of one's achievements and circumstances in the present might have a noticeable effect on the tenor and content of a life story. We have entered the age of biography (Bowker, 1993) with our growing fascination for reality television, celebrities' behaviors, 24-hour event coverage; exposure to the barrage of information about important life stories no doubt affects people's sense of what to add, or leave out, when telling one's own personal narrative. Examining the approaches and concerns regarding the process of studying life stories, the authors of *Researching Life Stories: Method, Theory, and Analyses in a Biographical Age* (Goodley et al., 2004, p. ix) argued that "notions of identity are linked into projects by which people write their own lives in varying conditions of alienation and empowerment." That is, people tend to select narrative elements to fit a particular context—in this case, the life of an exemplary physician engaged in additional humanitarian endeavors.

To say that memory can be flawed is only to repeat what we all know to be true. Not only is selective memory a common occurrence, but it is also common for the memories themselves to be factually inaccurate—two events are conflated in recollection as one, stories we know only second-hand transform over time into memories, and contexts and continuities become muddled over time. I do not mean to suggest that life stories, including those told by the physicians interviewed here, are in any way untrue or deliberate misrepresentations of fact. My intention in raising the idea that narrators may not be 100% reliable and that every detail recounted may or may not be true in the actual, provable sense (and I as interviewer would be none the wiser) is merely to acknowledge the necessity of accepting the life stories as they are told. Ultimately, it may not matter. American scholar of autobiography Timothy Adams said, "Autobiography is the story of an attempt to reconcile one's life with one's self and is not, therefore, meant to be taken as historically accurate but as metaphorically authentic" (Adams, 1990, p. ix). Thus, while I did gather such facts as specific years and locations, it seemed more important to note whether the interviewee mentioned them at all than to determine if they were correct.

Few people have personal biographers. Since the self-narratives rely so heavily on memory, it's necessary to discuss, in brief, some of the research that had been done concerning life stories and memory. Much of it confirms what many already know, namely that it is not uncommon to retell stories in such a way as to cast a particular light on the subject, whether positive or negative. What is not so well known is that this can happen without the narrators' intent. Studies have shown that personality can affect not only what is included or excluded from a life story but also the way in which such stories are recounted. McAdams (1982, as cited in Fivush & Haden, 2003, p. 197) suggested that the brain processes motive-related events differently than it does events that do not relate to the narrators' personality motives. He also found that people with high agentic motives more often included in their life stories memories that emphasized action and choices (e.g., mastery, achievement) and told their stories in such a way that they were always central. This contrasted with people with high communion motives, who recalled events and experiences that included and featured others, and their stories often emphasized similarities and interdependence among people. More specifically, autobiographical memories are dependent on the kinds of situations that precipitate the emergence of the memory, the personality motives that are characteristic of the individuals reporting the memory, and the methods used to measure motives (p. 198). In essence, some people star in their own life stories, whereas others prefer to be part of a larger ensemble cast. Would this difference correlate with the difference between good doctors and exemplary physicians? Does it all come down to seeing oneself as part of a large, interconnected network and a bigger plan?

Other subconscious factors can affect the telling of life stories such as the circumstances that precipitate the story (e.g., a formal interview versus a first-date introduction) (Nakash & Brody, 2006). These might include unintentional conflation of separate events, selective memory, telescoping timelines, and simple faulty recall. Of course, retrospective interpretation and conscious editing can color the stories as well; as the adage says, hindsight is 20/20. As mentioned earlier, in the case of the exemplars, I had to make the conscious decision to accept what was offered as true, without any attempt to substantiate or verify the data. Nevertheless, I couldn't help wondering if our doctors found it easier to retrieve positive memories of events and circumstances or negative ones. I was also curious whether they recalled positive and negative memories with equal facility, yet chose to recount more of one than another. I wondered if the exemplars would tell stories that did not relate one misfortune after another, but rather would string together a series of happy choices, lucky coincidences, and supportive people.

My second approach to collecting personal histories, once the interviewees had told the whole story, was direct questioning. I asked an identical set of questions of each of the physicians with the goal of establishing a framework of common denominators that I might later compare (e.g., background, family influence). I queried each about their home lives as children and adolescents, and how they were raised and who might have led them to their career choice. I asked if they had known people who inspired, encouraged, or helped them work toward their goal when they were young—and similarly, if anyone had tried to dissuade them or alter their career paths. Included would be not only real people in direct contact such as parents, extended family, peers, teachers, or other social contacts, but also media celebrities and even fictional characters from books, television, or movies.

Some developmental theories are pertinent in examining these various influences in the physicians' early lives, and I touch lightly here on the issues of nature/nurture; continuity/discontinuity (gradual versus abrupt change); self-activity/passivity (self-determination versus change through external forces) (Sigelman & Rider, 2006, p. 29). These developmental issues might conceivably affect not only the specific career choice but the level of commitment—the amount of energy devoted to and joy extracted from that profession. For example, someone who decides to become a doctor more out of some instilled sense of duty or tradition may not embrace the field with the same vivacity as one who makes the same decision based on having seen the local doctor help an ailing relative back to health. Additionally, ". . . some adolescents prefer not to work at all for a while rather than be forced into an otherwise promising career which would offer success without the satisfaction of functioning with unique excellence" (Erikson, 1968, p. 129). Would these doctors have come to their work without some type of moratorium?

Similarly, the concept of personality—traits, behaviors, ways of thinking, motives and emotions—would likely affect career choice. Weiten and Lloyd (2006, p. 34) called personality "an individual's unique constellation of consistent behavioral traits." Would consistency play a major role in choosing a profession? It would certainly be rare to make such a decision without deliberation over time.

Russell Muirhead, who writes on the moral meaning of work, has argued that while it is true that personality affects the work we choose to do, the reverse may also be true. For those who dedicate the bulk of their waking hours to their professions, the work can also affect personality, making them "more compassionate or more stern, more decisive or more resentful, more deft or more argumentative" (Muirhead, 2004, p. 28). Because of its power to communicate to others an established place in the social hierarchy, given others' preconceptions, biases, and even stereotypes, a job itself has significance beyond just a means of income. It can be, for many, an important and integral part of self-description. The most commonly asked question from strangers making small talk is, "What do you do?" In this day and age, the underlying question people really want to ask is, "Who are you?" The listeners' reactions will almost certainly vary according to the answer given: factory worker, stay-at-home mother, astronaut, or pediatrician. For people with certain personalities, the right to identify as a physician may fulfill some important need, and the anticipation of such fulfillment and the accompanying satisfaction and pride could easily drive career choice. For such people, "work cannot be merely another of life's routines but is rather a key source of their identity" (Muirhead, 2004, p. 28).

This book is not the proper forum for an in-depth examination of the nature of personality and psychoanalytic theory; it should suffice to note any personality-related similarities or differences among the interview subjects, both as observed and documented by others, and as perceived by the physicians themselves. Foos and Clark (2003, p. 179) quoted mystery writer Dame Agatha Christie: "We are the same people as we were at three, six, ten, or twenty years old. More noticeably so, perhaps, at six or seven because we were not pretending so much then." The physicians' viewpoints on Christie's belief and whether they felt that they personally have changed much or not over time drew out some useful insights, particularly with regard to such things as motivation and dedication. Foos and Clark maintained that while traits remain relatively stable as people age, their concerns do change—as do their coping strategies (Foos & Clark, 2003). Some studies have suggested that the period during which people's personalities show the greatest degree of change is during their 20s (Clausen & Jones, 1991, p. 209). This is also the age at which most students must make a commitment if they intend to pursue medical careers.

There is no consensus among personality theorists regarding the degree to which people are actively involved in their own development; some assert that individuals contribute in an active way through the natural curiosity of the species that drives people to explore and absorb cues from their environments, whereas others argue that human nature is essentially passive, and that circumstances and settings play a much larger role in personality development than an individual's innate traits (Sigelman & Rider, 2006). Either way, it appears that similar environments do not guarantee similar development. Psychologist John Chirban (2004), for example, wrote that children growing up in environments that are less than ideal often become adults who may share certain characteristics but whose outward characters vary significantly, and noted that "turbulence in the home often pushes us to extremes" (p. 35). He cites two people with similar backgrounds, noting that both "wrestled with loneliness, depression, and self-loathing while exhibiting powerful charisma" (Chirban, 2004); although both became professional actors, one constantly sought to forge strong emotional connections while the other shunned affection and personal relationships. A child growing up in a tumultuous environment may very well go on to become an exemplary physician. Would such a person have powerful charisma and—even more pertinent here—would the physician be emotionally distant or restrained, or would he or she be warm and intimate? Chirban (2004) used the term *true self* to describe what in common parlance is called the authentic person deep down and argued that "if parents or society ignore rather than celebrate the qualities of a child's true self" (p. 35) it can be difficult if not impossible for that child to reach personal fulfillment. In examining the self-narration by the exemplary physicians, it would be useful to be able to gauge whether the interviewees felt that in living their exemplary lives they were embracing their true selves.

Formal institutional settings also appear to play a role in career choice in general and might well influence the decision to pursue a career in medicine, as well as what kind of physician someone may become. Schools, for example, are just one area where the seeds of such aspirations may be sown, then nurtured or left to wither away. The United States has seen a broadening in the spectrum of school structures and teaching styles—charter, private religious, coed, home-school, magnet—in addition to the obvious differences such as class size, electives, or the availability of extracurricular activities. Of the many options, could any one of these be more apt to produce exemplary physicians? The interviews were designed to touch on details about the physicians' education. For example, did the physicians, as students, add sports, clubs, church groups, committees, and volunteer work to their busy high school and college years?

"Both organizational features within schools and differences between schools shape the distribution of educational outcomes having implications also for career outcomes (Lee, Bryk, & Smith, 1993, p. 43). Education professor Duane Brown, who specializes in career development issues, has said that the traditional U.S. educational system relies heavily on grouping, most often by perceived ability to learn, which is known as tracking. Students are funneled into distinct programs in which the content, teaching style, and ultimate educational goals differ drastically from one another. In effect, the students are labeled as one of these: vocational, general, college prep, remedial, honors, special needs, gifted, etc. (Brown, 2002, p. 44). Critics argue that tracking creates an inequitable system. I wondered if the exemplary physicians shared a common label early on.

This importance of role models in the physicians' life stories begged exploration. During the interviews, I tried to discover in each case who had the most influence on shaping their character and preparing them for life in general from birth until they entered medical school. The interviews were also designed to help paint a picture of the events and environments they encountered during that same time period—places, years, current events, significant occurrences, personal tragedies or triumphs, and other possible factors.

Among those life stories, would it be common to hear mention of a favorite relative or friend who was a healthcare professional and whom the interviewee sought to emulate, consciously or otherwise? There were also references to role models from movies or media. Since the 1950s, television has had a love affair with the medical profession, most often portraying doctors as heroic, if sometimes imperfect figures in these programs: *Ben Casey, Dr. Kildare* (1960s), *Medical Center, Marcus Welby, Quincy, M*A*S*H* (1970s), *St. Elsewhere, Doogie Howser, M.D.* (1980s), *Chicago Hope, ER* (1990s), and *Nip/Tuck, House, Grey's Anatomy* (2000s). Doctors on the big screen have been equally ubiquitous. For most people, the first sustained exposure to such often-idealized visions of doctors comes at a time of life when they are struggling to establish their own identity. They are likely moving from what Erikson called *latency* (around ages 6 to 12 years), with its conflicts between industry and inferiority, on their way to *early adulthood* (around ages 18 to 34 years), with its conflicts between intimacy and isolation, and commitment. The interim *adolescence* (ages 12 to 18 years) is fraught with the conflicts of identity and role confusion as people explore their individuality—a key part of which is making choices in preparation for a career (Erikson, 1950). George Vaillant described a similar stage in which the conflicts are between career consolidation and self-absorption. The question of what might differentiate a job from a career, he answered with four words—commitment, compensation, contentment, and competence. This shift represents the "transformation of preoccupation with self, of commitment to an adolescent's hobby, and (as Shakespeare put it) of 'seeking the bauble reputation' into a specialized role valued by both self and society" (Vaillant, 1993, p. 149). The interviews were structured to encourage revelations on how and when the physicians recognized their career-related talents and abilities and made a conscious commitment to enter the medical profession.

Even now the majority of positive media role models of doctors are more often men. Male doctors on the small and big screen vastly outnumber female doctors, and the women who are represented often showcase the traditional working woman work/life conflicts, whereas it is exceptionally rare for a portrayal of a male doctor to question how that doctor can successfully balance family life with professional life. In light of gender stereotype differences in the era the interviewed doctors came of age, the ratio of male-to-female Pride in the Professions award winners (approximately 2:1) should not be surprising. Although the numbers have risen significantly in the past 4 decades (only 7.6 percent of physicians were female in 1970), male doctors still outnumber their female counterparts by almost three to one (American Medical Association, 2006). The importance of role models and mentors in this cannot be overstated. Successful scientists almost invariably were once chosen by esteemed researchers to be assistants or protégés (Zuckerman, 1977). The absence or presence of a strong mentor figure has a direct correlation to the attrition rate in students in the sciences, with women being especially prone to change fields if they find no such mentor (Subotnik, Stone, & Steiner, 2001). What do our good doctors say about this phenomenon?

Sigelman and Rider (2006) addressed the role of mentors in occupational development. Ideally this mentor would be part counselor, part coach, part role model. In particular, mentors should pass along invaluable tips about the unwritten rules that drive professions. Good mentors do not feel threatened by their protégés; rather they applaud and promote them. Our doctors were asked about key lessons from relationships with mentors, the cultivation of the work together, and their separation or ongoing connection. Erik Erikson wrote frequently about the concept of generativity, "everything that is generated from generation to generation: children, products, ideas, and works of art" (Erikson & Evans, 1967, p. 51). He held that established middle-age professionals have a need to pass on their wisdom and experience to the next generation. The caveat, of course, is that the emerging generation needs to be receptive to such mentoring.

Working or studying with scientists who share one's race or gender also has a positive effect on the career goals of science students (Hill, Pettus, & Hedin, 1990). Parents in the field can provide a dual benefit, as mentors/ role models within the profession as well as the primary architects of such ethical foundations as respect for humanity, honesty, morality, commitment, and similar virtues. Irrespective of professional field, in the course of good parenting, children also learn important life lessons crucial to socialization, including conflict resolution, empathy, mutual respect, obligation fulfillment, listening skills, resilience, responsibility, and discipline, among others (Bolt, 2004; Snyder, 1994). I was interested to learn the percentage of exemplary physicians for whom one or both parents also worked in the medical profession.

Strong mentor relationships after medical school also play a positive role in professional development, with advantages to both protégé and mentor; similarly, having a poor mentor has been shown to be worse than having no mentor at all (Kail & Cavanaugh, 2007). In the interviews, the exemplary physicians are invited to speak to their experience of mentoring relationships.

Many well-known and highly respected doctors readily credit teachers, research partners, and advisors for their success. Take, for example, the aforementioned cardiologist and Harvard Medical School professor Dr. Bernard Lown. Although Lown is not among the current list of Pride in the Professions awardees, he would certainly meet the qualifications. A man of many great accomplishments, he nevertheless opens his book, *The Lost Art of Healing*, with characteristic humility. "Great teachers and extraordinary institutions enabled me to forge ahead in medicine and to evolve a philosophy of healing" (Lown, 1996, p. vi). Lown became a mentor as well; one of his children (Beth Lown) became a physician leading the movement to humanize medicine.

Professional and Personal Identity

The second series of questions sought to determine to what extent the daily reality of being a doctor informed the physicians' sense of self, and how much of a role it played in their identity. While elements of the life stories could not be completely separated from the development of the physicians' sense of self, chronologically speaking the emphasis was no longer on what they wanted to be when they grew up, but concerned essentially everything after the physicians entered medical school up to and including the present. Additionally, this series of questions added a layer of reflection as I probed beneath events and circumstances to discover the physicians' perceptions and insights.

Earlier I mentioned Lown's notion of a philosophy of healing, which is nurtured in part by the practitioners' early professional experiences, interactions, and life lessons. This suggests a fully realized personal credo that speaks directly to a physician's sense of purpose. The greatest database of literature outlining doctors' stated reasons for entering the medical field would have to be a collection of medical school applications and interview transcripts. Such a database would no doubt be filled with heartwarming and inspirational anecdotal introductions to hundreds of thousands of idealistic altruists. Most premed students declare that they want to enter medical school so that they can remain in a scientific field and help people while doing so. A relative few mention inspirational doctors they have known. Almost none cite parental pressures, prestige, or money (Coombs, May, & Small, 1986).

Once they have earned their medical degrees, however, it may be that at least part of the difference between the ordinary and the extraordinary practitioners comes from the answer to this simple question: What gets you out of bed in the morning and off to work? Regardless of the field in question, it is possible to distinguish between the concept of a job and a calling. Williams (1999, p. 99) gave these very clear, distinctive definitions. A job, he said, is "mechanical, with a job description; we are measured to see how well we have performed this function, and rewarded accordingly. . . . True work, on the other hand, comes from within us, and is about being engaged; it is where we choose to channel our life's energy." He summed up the distinction thus: "A job is a what, not a why . . . . Good work contains a *why*, not just the *what*" (Williams, 1999, p. 99). Since the exemplary physicians in question have been cited for more than simply doing their jobs, as it were, it seems likely that their interviews would reveal a belief that medicine is more than a job but true work—a calling.

Calling in this sense has nothing to do with religious matters. It has everything to do with one's personal philosophy and self-image, or identity—a continuing and coherent sense of self over time (Foos & Clark, 2003). It also has much to do with one's major life goals. Many a young child, when asked, "What do you want to be when you grow up?" will answer, "doctor" without any thought or realization of what that truly entails, merely responding to the environmental cues from books, television, toy manufacturers, family, and peers. Most do not go on to be doctors. Erikson suggests that an adolescent's choice of a future occupation represents a key part of establishing an identity, not because of the profession itself but because of the exercise of free will, imagination and self-discovery it requires ". . . it is the ideological potential of a society which speaks most clearly to the adolescent who is so eager to be affirmed by peers, to be confirmed by teachers, and to be inspired by worthwhile 'ways of life.'" (Erikson, 1968, p. 130).

During medical school and in the early years following graduation, most physicians appear to have, for the most part, already established their identity, and while this will continue to evolve over time, their essential sense of self has settled into place. As they eased into their professional lives, the new physicians would unavoidably come to reflect on how the actual fact of being a doctor compares with their anticipatory imaginings. The prolonged training would have left them minimally familiar with the mechanics of being a doctor—for example, the basic routines of hospital rounds or private appointments, or the specific tasks of reading an X-ray or making an incision—yet as with any job, the new doctors no doubt encountered surprises. Some of these have been welcome. Others may have been rude introductions to the disparity between practicing under the aegis of the educational safety net and being the ultimate authority in what could be a life or death situation. From the moment they received their medical degrees, the physicians would have another opportunity to reflect on their decision to enter the field. Weighing their daily routines and experiences against their ideals and life goals, they might find that the greater the difference between the two, the less satisfaction they would derive from their professional lives.

Suppose that after a year or 2 or 5, a physician finds that the practice does not fulfill those life goals set down in youth, or conflicts with long-held ideals and visions. There would seem to be three main avenues of recourse: emotional resignation, professional recalibration, or external engagement. Many healthcare professionals that I have worked with seem to typify the first response, emotional resignation. In this situation, a variety of reasons from financial constraints to personal inertia might lead to a gradual shutting down. Expectations dim, excitement fades, and the profession becomes little more than a mantle worn for 40-plus hours a week and then shrugged off at quitting time. It becomes, in short, just a job.

Job satisfaction depends in large part on how well expectations and actual conditions coincide. During the late 1990s, an extremely popular bumper sticker read, "I owe, I owe so it's off to work I go." Statistics have shown that more heart attacks occur on Monday morning—the traditional start of the workweek—than any other time in a week (Murakami et al., 2004). No one has named a restaurant chain T.G.I.M. (Thank God It's Monday). Clearly many people have a love–hate relationship with work; the questions become which outweighs the other, and how should one address the imbalance? As people age, some professional options fall by the wayside. There are plenty of starting over career stories, but the fact remains that some jobs require the energy, resilience, health, and fitness most often found in youth. In addition, as people take on families or other responsibilities and commitments, such requirements as extensive travel or relocation can seem onerous.

The anticipation of job dissatisfaction seems to be increasing; when I asked at what age they would like to be retired, almost every one of my students in an introductory psychology class pledged their intentions to try to set aside enough money so that they could retire by age 40. That's 27 years shy of the current age required to receive full Social Security benefits. It was as if they had decided in advance that whatever career they chose could not possibly hold their interest or provide longstanding satisfaction. The intrinsic motivation for the work itself seemed to be lacking, and they were looking ahead at their professional lives as merely a means to an end, as something to endure on the way to life *after* work.

Joshua Halberstam (2000) discussed this distinction in depth, and concluded that when we are lucky enough to do what we are meant to be doing, we automatically have a career, not a job. Williams (1999) used the word *engaged* to describe the determining factor, and called the feelings that pull us toward a certain rewarding profession a "calling," albeit in a secular sense. Levoy (1997, p. 137) suggested that hearing a true calling requires one to connect the dots between signals and starting points that come through many different channels, including dreams, fantasies, cravings and ambitions, persistent symptoms, fears, and resistances—channels whose messages are related by seeming synchronicity. Recognizing and tallying these synchronistic events and coincidences requires an attitude of openness. The "union of objective needs and subjective meaning [happens] consciously for many people" (Hopcke, 1997, p. 101), allowing them to recognize when they have found the work they were meant to do, and to pursue it wholeheartedly.

Whereas the first series of interview questions were designed to capture the bare bones of a life—names, places, achievements—the second set of inquiries aimed to flesh this information out with the kind of retrospective percipience that is sometimes possible only in hindsight. It could easily happen that someone could experience what Levoy (1997) called "messages" without recognizing them at the time as part of a larger synchronistic calling, and yet still heed the call itself to become a physician. To elicit or perhaps even discover such moments required a more open-ended questions such as: How did you become aware that your interests or hobbies—e.g., biology, puzzle solving—might coalesce into a vocation? What were your life goals as a child, a teen, and as a young adult, and if they have changed, do you know why? Hopcke (1997, p. 101) has said that rigidity can blind us to synchronicities, and that the way to allow "meaningful coincidence to change the story of [one's] life [is to] wander the world randomly and be willing to listen to whatever life presents." The random wandering is not intended literally, of course, but suggests an openness to experience and possibility outside the realm of the expected. This prompted questions like: Do you recall a point in your life where things clicked, prompting you to choose a career in medicine? Now that you've practiced medicine for years, would you consider medicine your true calling? If not, what is your true calling, and is being a doctor a part of that?

The second way that a physician can react to the realization that being a doctor may not be living up to expectations is professional recalibration. By *recalibration,* I mean resetting expectations or trying to change the status quo. The latter could mean changing professions entirely, of course, or it could mean addressing the reasons that reality falls short of satisfaction, such as cutting back on hours, leaving private practice for a hospital post (or vice versa), or narrowing a specialty. To do so, the physicians would have to consciously assess the parts of their professional lives that were not satisfying and perhaps rethink certain choices. Erik Erikson

(1968) thought everyone would benefit from this type of certain self-directed therapy. As mentioned earlier, he called these earnest reflections "moratoriums," and argued that under such conditions people's sense of self emerges more fully and their identity becomes clearer. A physician who is recalibrating must make choices, including the choice to remain in the status quo.

A choice, of course, is not the same as a commitment. Character and commitment will always be measured by actions. Wanting to help people is not the same as actually stepping outside one's comfort zone to work with AIDS patients or opening a private practice. As theologian Margaret Farley (1986) pointed out, even commitment can have less-than-straightforward meaning, and it appears in many nuanced forms, including what she calls "prereflective commitments"—those commitments people make prior to any explicit recognition of them. Typically, however, we think of commitments as conscious outward actions, pledges we make to others or to ourselves—that is, giving our word about something.

Often we think of commitment as the intention to work toward a single goal, but that need not be the case. Catherine Bateson (1989, p. 9) spoke of "the creative potential of interrupted and conflicted lives, where energies are not narrowly focused or permanently pointed toward a single ambition." Not only must physicians adapt and keep current if they have made a professional commitment, but they may also have to revisit their wider visions and occasionally renew or add commitments. Farley (1986) made a distinction between intellectual, *abstract* commitments—for example, the pursuit of truth and other types of value commitments such as justice—and *action* commitments, whether specific momentary undertakings or lifelong plans. Did our exemplar physicians find the need for a major recalibration, or did they subconsciously make minor adjustments, internally and externally, to maintain job satisfaction? Are they explicitly aware and conscious of the depth of their own commitments?

A key part of satisfaction with an ongoing professional commitment is a healthy work–life balance. Psychiatrist Robert Coles (1993) argued that people who respond to a call or mission are especially susceptible to depression and burnout. In his frequent interviews with people who performed long hours of volunteer work, the word *burnout* surfaced repeatedly. People with exceptional dedication are often highly self-critical, or perhaps more likely to discuss their sense of their own impending burnout more openly. Dr. Coles recounted an exchange he shared with

Dr. Martin Luther King at a conference in the mid-1960s. Coles, King, and a handful of others were discussing burnout—having become all too aware of it both in themselves and in others—when King said, "Burnout is surrender," and then elaborated, "We have just so much strength in us. If we give and give and give, we have less and less and less—and after a while at a certain point we're so weak and worn, we hoist up the flag of surrender. We surrender to the worst side of ourselves" (Coles, 1993, p. 141). Any level of commitment to something physically and emotionally exhausting can take its toll; sustaining such a commitment can exact an exorbitant price. The question is not so much why people suffer from it as it is why some people do not, or are at least capable of overcoming it.

Halberstam (2000) reported that older workers report higher job satisfaction than younger workers, most likely because they have learned to adjust their expectations over time—to recalibrate. Yet how could our exemplary physicians truly excel if they merely adjusted—that is, *lowered*—their expectations? Such behavior might lead to minimal success—doing what needs to be done, and no more—but hardly seems likely to inspire exemplary achievement, although it may help forestall burnout. Even laboratory rats, having found a route through a maze to a pile of food, will retrace that identical route every time, never searching for any alternate—and perhaps shorter—route to their reward. Likewise, people focused on an anticipated reward will be far less likely to try out new ideas or innovative methods (Halberstam, 2000). This suggests that any of the exemplars who might have found the need to recalibrate would not have actually lowered their expectations, but would have instead aimed at changing their environment. This would be analogous to the rats sawing an opening through the wall of the maze to get directly to the food—or perhaps hopping out of the maze in search of different food entirely.

Merely living up to expectations leads to mediocrity; it also can lead to personal malaise. Robin and Dominguez (1992) noted the irony behind the phrase *making a living*, and asked how many people are more alive after work than before, refreshed and energized, ready to spend time with family. "Do we come home from our 'making a living' activity with more life? . . . For many of us, isn't the truth closer to 'making a dying'? Aren't we killing ourselves—our health, our relationships, our sense of joy and wonder—for our jobs" (Robin & Dominguez, 1992, p. 41)? Presumably, the exemplars have escaped this fate. The selection criteria for the awards as well as the actual achievements of these physicians suggests that they *do* have more energy after work, perhaps because they do not view their professional activities as work at all but as something so enjoyable that it is more akin to play. Their varied achievements extend beyond the normal working hours of the physicians into what normally gets called personal time, and they clearly require a great deal of emotional energy and often physical energy as well.

Robert Coles recognized that while burnout can occur in any sort of job, its prevalence within the service professions is especially telling. This includes not just the obvious at-risk professionals such as those in the fields of medicine, education, and counseling, but also those people who expend enormous amounts of time and energy for remuneration that is more emotional and spiritual than financial, such as Peace Corp volunteers, hospice workers, soldiers, and even single parents. The personality and experience people bring with them into their service roles, including their strengths, weaknesses, vulnerabilities, and abilities, must, as Coles phrased it, "yield to human particularity" (Coles, 1993, p. 142). In this view, burnout is not inevitable; the individuals most susceptible are those who have some unresolved psychic injury from early life—some internal, and very likely unrecognized, predisposition toward recreating certain behavior and response patterns from the past. If this is a given, does it dictate that this accomplished group of doctors is somehow better at resolving these types of early life experiences?

Williams (1999) said that to persevere to our true vocation is to know a greater meaning and fullness of life that is deeply satisfying. This level of vocation will always invoke the emotional and spiritual dimensions; the concept of burnout, after all, implies that there was once a flame inside, a burning desire to make a difference. Did our physicians ever find that to keep the spark alive they needed to reinvent themselves? How did they keep nurturing a willing heart?

Gawain (1994) believes that work and play are the same. That is, when we are mindful of whatever we are engaged in at any given time, the result is a fullness and joy in the experience that will be felt by everyone around. The Greeks have the word *amartia* (to miss or fall short of the mark), which describes the loss of personal balance. Although the word is often translated into English (especially in religious works) as *sin*, its true meaning is the emotional state of a person who has gone to extremes and lost proper perspective, which is why Aristotle used the word to describe the character flaw that leads to the protagonist's downfall. It also fits with two simple maxims *meden agan* (no extremes) and *pan metron ariston* (measure is always best) by which the ancient Greeks lived (Chirban, 2004, p. 253). Do our exemplars frame this issue similarly in their own lives?

It is popular to depict people in human service professions as being somehow otherworldly or more saintly than most of us. Williams (1999) debunked some of the myths surrounding such professions, many of which fall into the category of the things that everyone knows and yet turn out to be false, based on stereotypes, old information, and myriad other reasons. Chief among the myths pertinent to this book would be that those who serve must be superhuman, that service does not pay and is best left to those who are already successful and can afford to give, and that it is always better to give than to receive. It seems likely that the exemplar physicians will have seen through these myths and are already fully aware that service, especially excellence in service, does not preclude a normal life.

One attribute commonly found in high achievers that does not appear to be more myth than reality is positive thinking. As with the classic sad sack character Eeyore, the view that life's glass is perpetually half empty seems to hold back otherwise capable people. An overzealous belief that positive thinking will inevitably lead to success and that specific visualizations can actually dictate a course of events is considered a type of magical thinking that fails to differentiate between cause and mere correlation; thousands of people have become millionaires selling self-help books based on this concept, exhorting people to think themselves rich, in love, successful, and healthy. Exploring just this aspect of the exemplars' possible personality and psychological makeup would require delving more deeply into the realm of anomalistic psychology than space and time permit. Anomalistic psychology is the study of "extraordinary behavior and experience, including (but not restricted to) those which are often labeled 'paranormal' " (French, 2007, p. 4), such as placebo effects, dissociative states, hypnosis, synchronicity and the psychology of coincidences—as well as the psychology of deception and self-deception. It is worth examining, however, the role that expectations and attitude might have played in making the exemplars the exceptional people they have become.

Norman Vincent Peale codified the concept in his 1952 classic, *The Power of Positive Thinking*, followed soon after by Maslow's theories of self-actualization and the movements of human potential and self-actualization. Jung defined *guided imagery*, more often known these days as visualization, a type of concentration on a mental picture that develops rich and detailed images. Jung believed that this active imagination enhanced the therapeutic process; decades later it has become a commonly accepted tool in preventive medicine, particularly in self-regulated stress reduction and pain management, as well as a complementary therapy in treatment of illness and disease (Jung, Jaffe, & Saint-John, 1979).

Renowned psychiatrist Karl Menninger is famous for having said, "Love cures people—both the ones who give it and the ones who receive it." In his book *The Vital Balance*, Menninger also weighed in on the power of listening, calling it a magnetic and strange thing and a creative force. The people who listen to us are the ones we move toward. When we are listened to, it helps us know who we are (Menninger, 1963).

The third and final recourse for doctors whose professional lives may not be giving them satisfaction is external engagement. By this I mean extending or going beyond the bounds of their customary role as doctors to seek satisfaction elsewhere and thus regain balance. This may happen unintentionally, for example by discovering or being recruited to a specific cause, but regardless of how physicians engage externally, doing so requires at least a minimum of soul searching lest that engagement conflict with their personal credo or ethics. This brings me to the third series of questions in the interviews.

The Wellspring

My last series of questions during the interviews was designed to answer the obvious question that the first two sets of responses would naturally prompt—namely, How do you do all that—and more? That is, given the time, energy, and emotional dedication that must be invested to be an excellent doctor, how is it that these exemplary physicians were also able to muster the internal resources to invest still more in the humanitarian undertakings that led to their nominations for the Pride in the Profession Award? There are thousands of people, maybe millions, who would love to be able to excel at their professions, raise good families, and still be able to devote themselves to one or more causes, yet most of us find that we cannot do it all. We fall prey to the if onlys—if only I had more time, energy, or money, or if only I had less stress, fewer obligations, and so on and so on—and it is most often our good intentions that fall by the wayside. So how is it that some people are able to do it all—willingly and without ever quenching the fire inside that drives them?

I entered into this project with a hypothesis that, in the end, was substantiated. As I spoke with each physician in turn, I began to realize that even though their answers to my questions seemed on the surface to have little in common, they could be distilled into a few elemental ingredients. That it took me months to perform this distillation seems, in retrospect, nearly inconceivable. I chalk it up to the natural tendency toward tunnel vision when the pursuit heats up; in our impatience to be finished with the data collection and get to the good part—measuring results against hypothesis—we often fail to reflect along the way on the significance of individual answers.

Collecting the data for the third set of queries often took more time than that required for the first two combined, largely because the open-ended questions required the interviewees to do more than recollect; they had to ponder, assess, synthesize. Most knew the answers they wanted to give right away but many were at a loss as to how to express them since they had never consciously done so before. The experience was enlightening for us both, at times, as when I asked such questions as these: What is your greatest regret concerning your life's work? Have you ever been faced with a dilemma in which your personal ethics seemed at odds with your course of action, and if so, how did you handle it? What would you like to see engraved on your tombstone?

Dr. Jerome Groopman wrote in his foreword to *The Soul of a Doctor* (2006, p. xi), "A physician's experience goes far beyond the clinical, because a person is not merely a disease, a disorder of biology. Rather, each interaction between a doctor and a patient is a story." Recognizing this is crucial for physicians, who "can notice, think about, and use what is going on inside and around them. . . . They emerge gradually, along paths marked by a sequence of stages" (Pories, Jain, & Harper, 2006, p. 1) and grow professionally when they break with the antireflective tradition that has long prejudiced medical students against self-examination and questioning the status quo. Self-awareness is a key component of a life lived in an ethical and spiritually evolved manner. Empathy makes it possible to look upon patients as people, not medical problems to be solved. Many of my questions to the exemplars concerned their philosophies of healing—i.e., the nature of their interactions with patients—and encouraged them to reflect.

I started by asking what it was, more or less, that got the physicians out of bed in the morning. The aforementioned cult classic *Your Money or*

Your Life (Robin & Dominguez, 1992) described a world where most people are more "dead" at the end of the workday than they were at the beginning. People get locked into unsatisfactory jobs purely for a paycheck, and often do so because they identify too strongly with the job itself. Presumably, the exemplars have escaped this fate. The selection criteria for the awards as well as the actual achievements of these physicians suggests that they *do* have sustained energy after work, perhaps because they do not view their professional activities as traditional work. Their varied achievements extend beyond the normal working hours of the physicians into what normally gets called personal time, and these endeavors clearly require enormous expenditures of emotional and sometimes physical energy.

How do they do it? Studies have shown that the typical American works 47 hours a week—164 more hours per year than in the 1980s (Schor, 2007). Physicians are not excluded from this phenomenon, so the answer could not lie in the exemplars having copious amounts of leisure time at their disposal. Most were neither rich nor retired. In fact, many of them scoffed at the very idea of retirement.

One possibility was that the exemplars truly enjoyed their day jobs and thought of them not as work but as a chance to spend time doing something they loved. Gawain (1994) said that when we are mindful of whatever we are engaged in at any given time, the result is a fullness and joy in the experience that will be felt by everyone around. The 13th-century theologian Thomas Aquinas said, "There can be no joy of life without joy of work" (Aquinas, 1273). Po Bronson (2002) discussed how his perception that certain jobs were cool and others were not changed when he realized that it wasn't the jobs that inspired passion but passion that inspired joy in a job. "Passion is rooted in deeply felt experiences, which can happen anywhere," he wrote (p. 365). "I used to think that life presented a five-page menu of choices. Now I think the choice is in whether to be honest, to ourselves and others, and the rest is more of an uncovering, a peeling away of layers and discovering talents we assumed we didn't have" (p. 365).

Mindfulness appears to be a key component of enjoying one's work; it would be difficult to feel bored and engaged at the same time. Of course, sometimes the greatest enjoyment can come from those periods when we are *so* fully engaged that we are barely aware of the work. This experience is nearly the opposite of self-examination. Mihaly Csikszentmihalyi (2003,

p. 39) called this "flow," the feeling we get when we are totally immersed in an experience. He chose the term because, as he said, so many people describe the feeling as "being carried away by an outside force, of moving effortlessly with a current of energy, at the moments of highest enjoyment." This mental state is hardly exclusive to physicians but is quite common and has been described by people engaged in a full spectrum of activities from mountain climbing and surgery to farming and parenting. Was the promise of flow possibly what got our physicians going each morning and sent them off to their daily practice? Had they experienced flow before, and if so, what were the circumstances (work, leisure, other)? Perhaps these flow states, like sleep, have restorative properties.

Flow is distinct from autopilot or thoughtlessness. It is not a lack of connection, but a hyperconnection. It is a way of living in the moment with an eye to the future by relying on knowledge gained in the past—the Zen moment. Janet Belsky (2007, p. 315) said that we experience flow as being "energized and alive." She argued that the main criterion that sets the experience apart from simple enjoyment is that flow is intrinsically motivated—intense absorption for its own sake and not because of some expected reward. The lists of achievements of the exemplary physicians, along with the fact that they clearly did not find their medical practices to be energy sinkholes, suggested that "flow" might be a common experience among those interviewed.

Experiencing "flow" does require knowledge gained from the past. Csikszentmihalyi (2003, p. 39) recounted a surgeon's flow experience in which the doctor said that "in good surgery everything you do is essential, every move is excellent and necessary; there is elegance, little blood loss, and a minimum of trauma. . . ." Presumably the surgeon in question must then have had the skills, the tools, the confidence, the knowledge, and the conviction to actually perform the operation at hand. In fact, in an earlier work, Csikszentmihalyi (1997) cited a study in which three generations of villagers in a remote Italian town were asked to report the frequency and timing of their "flow" experiences. The oldest generation reported the greatest number, most of which occurred during some work task; the middle generation reported that half their flow experiences occurred during work and half during leisure; the youngest generation experienced the fewest instances of flow, and these came during leisure activities.

Csikszentmihalyi called flow "a source of psychic energy, neither good nor bad, constructive nor destructive" (1997, p. 60), but said that it was crucial to master the art of using it well. By this he meant that using flow for the sake of feeling good or establishing a good life for oneself was not a bad thing but that one should also channel it toward "goals that will reduce the sum total of entropy in the world." (Csikszentmihalyi, 1997, p. 60). Did the physicians find their work so playlike, so invigorating, that they were able to devote themselves to causes beyond their daily practice. How did they know where best to channel their energies? Did they have a set of standards they used to decide, and how did these standards arise? Just as the surgeon caught up in the flow of an operation should know how to wield a scalpel before making an incision, a good doctor ought to also have knowledge and experience in ethics, honesty, honor, morality, compassion, decency, and standards before making a decision.

The classical Greeks used the word *arête* to mean the quality of virtue that guides one to make ethical decisions. In virtue ethics, people do not make ethical decisions out of duty or even to achieve something good but because "doing the ethical thing is simply part of the most fully human way of living. One does not behave ethically in order to get the benefits of living well, but in living well one performs ethical actions" (Neher & Sandin, 2007, p. 18). In this system, character outweighs rules, and making good judgments are a key component.

If enjoying their work was a primary motivation for them to persevere, and if that enjoyment allowed them to work at making a living rather than making a dying, there remained the question of what led the exemplars to invest themselves in their various causes. Why not spend the time, money, or energy on some more self-serving pursuit like travel or collecting, and benefit those they know—family, friends, personal connections—rather than strangers?

These questions moved me to revisit the concept of character—not the outward gloss of personality but the deeper components such as values and ethics. Richmond (1999) maintained that character is not a genetic predisposition but a product of all the experiences, teachings, and choices made throughout the years. It is, he said, what we rely on in times of crisis. "Under duress, our surface personality falls away. There is no time to think 'What is the right thing to do or say'" (Richmond, 1999, p. 16)? The earliest Greek philosophers believed that practicing virtue ethics could dictate the ethical course of action in any given situation. Could it be that the character beneath the individual personalities of the exemplars had a stronger, more ethical value system that sparked an undying desire to do good? If so, why? What wellspring could provide such abundant motivation?

Virtue ethics, first espoused by Aristotle, is a school of philosophy that focuses on the ethics of right and wrong. This approach relies on character and ethical thinking rather than fixed rules, punishments, rights, duties, or consequences. Since all physicians must demonstrate high character at the time they take their modern-day Hippocratic oath, it seems more likely that virtue ethics could have played a much more important role in making some practitioners into good doctors and others into truly exemplary physicians. The fictitious Dr. Smith, who works a regular shift and then goes home for dinner, is not inherently any less ethical or qualified to decide right from wrong than is Dr. Jones, who works a regular shift yet also devotes time, energy, and money to good causes.

Perhaps there is some element of Dr. Jones's character that cannot be satisfied with personal achievement alone, with simply meeting minimum standards on all fronts, and must always strive for a personal best, or to be part of more sweeping, even universal advancements. The following story illustrates a case presenting to a physician in the mold of Dr. Jones. Rarely do illnesses and diseases follow rules, and while there may be standard treatment protocols, physicians do not have a rule book to dictate the right course of action in any but the most simplistic of circumstances. Perhaps the best example is in the area of diagnostics. While physicians—like most people—come to certain conclusions by following a decision tree of some sort, approaching a patient's condition with a binary mindset can have serious consequences. Groopman cites the example of a young woman who had spent 15 years visiting doctors complaining of intense pain and nausea upon eating. Her general practitioner immediately suspected an eating disorder, but sent her to a specialist to confirm. The specialist dutifully did so, and the patient was treated for anorexia nervosa through medication, therapy, and nutritional monitoring. The problem was, she continued to get sicker, despite the fact that she claimed to be following the prescribed diets and medication schedules. It wasn't until she was sent to yet another specialist to confirm an additional diagnosis, irritable bowel syndrome, that she met the doctor who saved her life. What gastroenterologist Myron Falchuk did that the other doctors did not do was quite simple; he ignored the routine concept of confirming another doctor's diagnosis. Instead he focused on listening to the patient. What he heard led him to correctly diagnose celiac disease; her body was failing to digest the food she ate, and she was slowly starving to death. Falchuk credits his philosophy of healing to his mentor, Sir William Osler, sometimes called the Father of Modern Medicine for having developed the concept of the medical residency program. Falchuk said that it was Osler's view that "if you listen to the patient, he will give you his diagnosis," something Falchuk took to heart. While he embraced the new technology and procedures available, Falchuk believed that "technology had also taken us away from the patient's story. And once you remove yourself from the patient's story, you are no longer truly a doctor" (Groopman, 2007, p. 17).

Had Falchuk followed rules and accepted at face value the previous doctors' diagnosis despite the evidence of the patient's continued failing health, she would have gotten worse. Instead, Falchuk made the ethical decision to not to view her as a patient with anorexia nervosa and irritable bowel syndrome, but as a woman with severe gastrointestinal symptoms. Because of his long exposure to and experience with this sort of empathic approach to patients, Falchuk may even have experienced "flow" as he listened to her story and had the flashes of insight that led him to probe further. While he did not use the terms, Falchuk did report that he was "so excited by this," leading Groopman to characterize him as having "the sweet pleasure of the detective who cracks a mystery, a legitimate pride in identifying a culprit. But beyond intellectual excitement, he showed joy in saving a life" (Groopman, 2007, p. 22).

This delight in a peak experience was something that Abraham Maslow (1954) believed was the driving force of psychological development and part of self-actualization. Self-actualization is the ultimate achievement of one's personal potential, which could only be reached after the fulfillment of a larger hierarchy of needs (physiological well-being, safety, love, esteem, and self-actualization). Both Maslow and Carl Rogers (1961) further ascribed two key traits to self-actualized people. The first was authenticity, or the ability to be spontaneous, alive individuals who believed themselves and their behavior to be ethical and good. The second was empathy, and in particular an empathic interest in problem solving—helping others through emotional conflict in an engaged but nonjudgmental manner. Falchuk exhibited those two traits. Would they also form a central part of the character of the exemplary physicians? These traits would seem ideal for the exemplary physicians, particularly empathy—the ability to imagine what someone else might be feeling and to try to see the world through another's eyes (Bolt, 2004). Kaplan and associates defined empathy as "the capacity to take in and appreciate the affective life of another while maintaining a sufficient sense of self to permit cognitive structuring of that experience" (Kaplan, Jordan, Miller, Stiver, & Surrey, 1991, p. 273). It will be interesting to see if the exemplary physicians manifest these qualities.

Too few medical schools that train doctors in traditional western medicine encourage students in and emphasize the study of empathy. In *The Empathic Practitioner,* Milligan and More (1994, p. 1) noted that many physicians express ambivalence towards the role of empathy in medicine. Western physicians are trained to approach relationships with patients with a kind of find-it-and-fix-it mentality that places the utmost value on empirical objectivity and evidence-based medicine. This approach has eclipsed the notion that interpersonal dialogue with patients could inform their treatment plans. Yet there are doctors who use empathy as a means to empower patients. Will we find a disproportionate number of them among our exemplars?

Many of the preceptors acting as role models for the next generation of practitioners systematically keep themselves detached and self-protective. In the course of my own work in medical settings I have often heard healthcare professionals admonish each other to be professional, which often seems to translate into "Don't have or show feelings about or to your patient." Yet if the aim of a medical interview is to minimize anything personal and subjective, how does the role of the physician in that instance differ from that of a dispassionate journalist pursuing a medical news story? It directs all focus toward the details of disease—on signs, symptoms, and quantifiable evidence rather than on the patients who exhibit those signs and symptoms, and on the patients' perspectives. It removes the human element. Similarly, advances in technology can increase the gulf between patients and their physicians; consider the difference between taking a patient's pulse by laying one's hands directly on a patient's body to personally count beats versus clipping a mechanical device to that same patient's finger. More transpires in this interaction than the accomplishment of a simple task. How do some physicians manage to avoid this distancing and isolation?

As noted previously, illness and disease do not follow rules. What happens when a physician, having developed a philosophy of healing to follow, is suddenly confronted with a situation in which there seems to be a marked difference between the doctor's personal ethics and a suggested response or action? For example, in the 1990s, a directive from the federal government made it illegal for physicians at family planning centers receiving federal funding to discuss abortion with pregnant patients (Milligan & More, 1994). This ran contrary to many doctors' empathic responses and sense of responsibility. Similarly and more recently, certain drugstores came under fire when pharmacists decided not to sell over-the-counter emergency contraceptive pills despite the fact that the prescriptions were legal. I asked the exemplars to describe any similar conflicts they have encountered.

Ethical considerations need not be restricted to general principle but can enter into decisions on the smallest, most human scales (Dan, 1988, p. i). How exemplary physicians approach such instances may be highly instructive. For example, doctors must constantly be aware of more than just the medical implications of their words and actions. Fears of malpractice suits may lead to defensive medicine and may lead to a very different patient–physician relationship and communication style. Doctors are people, too, with doubts and fears that can affect not only physicians' professional lives but perhaps even their choices in extracurricular lives as well, such as where they focus their energy outside the hospital walls— where they volunteer, the causes they work toward, and the goals to which they dedicate themselves.

There are countless cases, too, where the usual course of action in a given medical situation just doesn't feel right to a physician. Groopman (2000) recounted the case of a physicist whose marrow was not producing enough blood cells. A doctor with extensive experience in transplants insisted that the patient undergo a marrow transplant immediately, despite there being no compatible donor available; if his diagnosis of myelodysplasia or aplastic anemia were correct, a transplant would be the best option, but moving forward with an incompatible donor meant that the physicist might die from the procedure or, if he survived, be permanently debilitated by graft-versus-host disease. Groopman's lab, however, found no evidence supporting the first doctor's diagnosis, and talked the patient into waiting while he performed some culturing experiments in the lab. While the cultures were growing, the severely immunocompromised patient nearly died of pneumonia. Along with the antibiotics and transfusion, Groopman suggested trying a white cell growth factor mixed with a red cell growth factor to boost marrow production. The first doctor declared that risky and pointless and was only convinced with great difficulty to try the new protocol. In the end, the intuition of Groopman and his fellow hematologists was validated, and the patient was put on a regular regimen, and no transplant was necessary. Groopman credited a lesson he learned as a student from a highly respected clinician who was not afraid to admit when she did not know the answer to some medical puzzle. Her advice was that in cases where the diagnosis was unclear and the treatment options potentially dangerous, a doctor should stand down and engage in watchful waiting (Groopman, 2000).

Primum non nocere. That Latin phrase means "first, do no harm," and it is one of the first guiding principles a medical student learns. When the danger of an intervention appears to outweigh the possible benefits, the physician has a moral imperative to act in the best interests of the patient, not to do something out of a fear of looking ignorant, out of pride, out of stubbornness, out of habit and reflex, or out of the need to feel useful. During the interviews, uncovering instances in the exemplars' histories where they had to make such decisions could be most enlightening. In a related context, the questions should also elicit the physicians' greatest professional regrets.

How are physicians able to hold out hope without being dishonest at times? How do they cope with feelings of powerlessness when an infant is dying of an incurable condition? Or when—inevitably—an error in clinical judgment is made? How do they keep from reproaching themselves so much that it affects or even paralyzes their ability to care for the next patient? What do they do when patients rebuke them for errors in care? How do they keep themselves from going on the defensive and narrowing their vision for possibilities?

In any discussion of the human capacity for hope, the issue of faith and spiritual beliefs will arise. Csikszentmihalyi (2003) wrote that "flow and religion are different faces of the same quest: to find a reason, a justification for being alive . . . an intimation of what the rapture of life can be, and point toward an existence more imbued with soul" (p. 60). Paul Tillich asserted in the 1950s that faith did not have to be associated with formal religion or belief (Tillich, as cited in Fowler, 1981). Fowler calls faith "a person's or group's way of moving into the force field of life [and] finding coherence in and giving meaning to the multiple forces and relations that make up our lives" (Fowler, 1981, p. 4).

Morality, too, can exist separately from religion, but religions do not exist separately from moral codes. Richmond (1999) said "so much of what passes for 'ordinary life' is, when seen through different eyes, not ordinary at all, but full of potential for spiritual learning" (p. 9). He spoke of questions of a spiritual nature that concern us all, and calls these "koans" after the instructional stories taught by ancient Buddhists. "To practice the koan of everyday life means to confront every situation as though it were a profound spiritual question. In that sense, every koan story is a specific instance of the koan of everyday life" (Richmond, 1999).

In the case of the exemplars, they likely have koans of their own gleaned from a multitude of sources from church, school, medical school, practical experience, and intimate social interaction. To find a set of common koans among the interviews might be tantamount to codifying exactly what it is that is the difference between a good doctor and an exemplary physician.

Colby and Damon (1992) point out that human goodness is both pervasive and fragile. Our sense that we live in an era of increasing large-scale violence might make it more difficult to trust that some professionals can continue to embody strong and genuine goodness that is not diminished or blunted by the tone of the times. In 2007, newly released letters of Mother Teresa widely reported in the news suggest that though she was admired by the outside world, she had many doubts even to the point of doubting the presence of her God. Perhaps we will find some physicians who admit to similar dark nights of the soul while the outside world continues to admire what appears to be a bottomless well of dedication. Those doubts did not cause Mother Teresa to waver in her ministrations, however; she continued her humanitarian efforts despite her temporary skepticism in the existence of her God. After her death in 1997, she was beatified by Pope John Paul II, who bestowed upon her the title of Blessed Teresa of Calcutta. We love to dramatize moral heroes in such a way that sets them apart in mythical terms. Exploring the roots of moral excellence in our physicians might inspire the possibilities for a leap forward by other healthcare professionals who haven't achieved the same public praise.

When Gregg Levoy (1997) wrote about the concept of the true calling, he said that the bewildering effort to determine whether such a calling comes from a higher power or another source is irrelevant. More important is the determination of whether the calling is truly authentic. Will this call provide a feeling of being more alive? Authenticity trumps origination. Furthermore, Levoy does not dismiss the possibility that something less than noble may also contribute energy and drive—unresolved anger at a bitter rival or a scoffing parent, for example.

Many people who belong to no formalized religion, including some who identify themselves as agnostic or atheist, nevertheless would describe themselves as spiritual. Spirituality requires only a fascination with and belief in the intangible, in such unknowns as the nature of the soul. Faith, too, exists easily without an objectified provider in the form of God, Allah, Buddha, or another omnipotent figure; faith is confidence and trust—an unshakable belief in something (or someone) despite the absence of proof. Faith and spirituality motivate us all in our life's work to a greater or lesser extent, from Mother Teresa herself right down to the farmer who plants seeds confident that crops will grow and provide food. James Fowler (1981) said our secret hopes and compelling goals are fueled by faith, and that matters of faith are the dynamic process through which we find meaning in life, which may or may not be religious in content or context. He called faith the way that people see themselves in relation to the force field of life. Dr. Groopman (2003) examined the nature of hope as well, which he defined not as blind optimism ("my cancer will be cured") but as a determination to persevere in full recognition of the odds and obstacles ("I understand that this cancer treatment might actually kill, not cure me, but I have decided that it is my best option"). Many of the physicians who identify as religious will no doubt credit God with being the wellspring of their goodness. How many of the physicians will directly ascribe their actions to a higher power? Of those who don't, how many will see the source as something apart from themselves, such as a feeling of solidarity with other human beings or as an instrument of some universal energy?

Fowler wrote that faith is a universal concern, and it is something that concerns everyone regardless of whether they are religious or not, believers or nonbelievers. His reasoning was that we strive to discover how we should live and what will make life worth living. "We look for something to love that loves us, something to value that gives us value, something to honor and respect that has the power to sustain our being" (Fowler, 1981, p. 5). It is the power to sustain our being that remains elusive—the source of the wellspring.

Fowler (1981) argued that we are all capable of faith, and that moves us to search for that something; the exemplary physicians' something may be what they choose to do beyond the bounds of typical work, and faith that it is meaningful and has value. If we return to our hypothetical doctors, the average Dr. Smith and the exemplary Dr. Jones, the question becomes this: Is the difference between the two the something itself, or simply the faith that moves them to keep looking for it? Is this a mere chance of character—perseverance in the face of resistance, the Sisyphean effort to right wrongs—that drives the exemplars? Or do we all have the capacity to do more, to be more, if we can only divine and tap into our personal something—maybe Csikszentmilhalyi's flow?

If your heart isn't in it, any action becomes work. Mother Teresa said that true wealth is the ability to feel blessed with whatever you have and a willingness to share it. We may feel blessed and grateful, but without the desire to share what we have no matter how much or how little that may be, there is little joy to be found.

And what about people who work happily into their 80s and 90s? Life coaches and psychologists alike all say that the secret to making a living is to do what you love and love what you do. Psychology textbooks had not even included an indexed entry for the word *love* until the past 25 years. It was somehow unscientific to talk about how love underpins creativity, joy, and peace. Yet I suspect our physicians will have focused clearly on the miracles that can occur when love is present, and that if asked what makes the days fly by, a large part of the answer will most likely be a love for the work itself. Did our physicians take comfort from discovering their purpose early in life or did it take time to evolve later over the years? Other, less inspired professionals may have started with clear goals and ideals only to get discouraged or sidetracked into something that devolved into merely a job, a means to a paycheck. What is this magnetic pull? What does it sound like? What does it look like? Most importantly, how did these physicians recognize it? Did they have to go through a special process to learn to listen to their inner selves?

These reflections led to my questions for the exemplary physicians. Is the thing that makes your life worth living specific to you (e.g., your family, your job, your pet cause), or can anyone conceivably share a part of it? Does it all come down to the realization that embracing life itself is the reward, and that it is all about the journey and not the destination? I invite you to listen in with me to the voices of our dynamic doctors as they ponder these questions.

CHAPTER 2

The Woman Who Answered More Than One Calling

Dr. Anne Brooks

Dr. Sister Anne Brooks started her medical mission in Mississippi's Delta region, one of America's least affluent areas, in 1983. She and three other sisters of her order set up the Tutwiler Clinic, an ambulatory care medical clinic dedicated to the idea that quality health care is a right, not a privilege.

Anne Brooks has been a Sister of the Holy Names of Jesus and Mary since 1955. Founded in 1840 and headquartered in Montreal, the congregation is active internationally. For 17 years, Sister Anne taught school in Florida, and volunteered after school at the Clearwater free clinic, an institution for the disadvantaged. She left teaching to start a second free clinic in another Florida community, St. Petersburg. There she lived in a garage behind the clinic with another sister. John Upledger, an osteopathic physician (DO) and founder of the clinics, encouraged Sister Anne to go to medical school. She graduated with the help of a scholarship from the National Health Service Corps. The terms of her scholarship included 4 years of service in a medically deprived area. After completing her internship, she offered her services to cities and counties in impoverished areas. When Tutwiler responded, she reopened a clinic that had been built and abandoned in the 1960s. It still had two waiting rooms, two drinking fountains, and two bathrooms, one for "Whites" and one for "Coloreds."

> One third of the people in Tallahatchie County, where Tutwiler is located, live below the poverty level, and most of the rest live just barely above it. For many years, Dr. Brooks has been the only physician in the western part of the county. Treating illnesses is only one part of the health care Dr. Brooks has provided. Under her direction, the Tutwiler Clinic also established the town's first community center. It includes classrooms to help townspeople earn high school equivalency diplomas as well as a gymnasium for exercise. With 8000 patient visits a year, Dr. Brooks cannot leave the clinic often, but she has developed unique relationships that have resulted in what she calls wonderful gifts: a physician from New York comes for a week during the summer, and an internist from New Jersey comes for a week in the spring and fall. This has allowed Dr. Brooks to attend Continuing Medical Education (CME) meetings and go on fundraising trips.
>
> Tutwiler Clinic and Dr. Brooks have been featured in People Magazine and was the subject of a segment on 60 Minutes. She has been honored by the Caring Institute in Washington, D.C., as one of the most caring people in America. Dr. Brooks graduated cum laude from Barry University, Miami, Florida, and received her Doctor of Osteopathy (DO) from Michigan State University at the age of 44 years.

There have been several phases in Dr. Sister Anne Brooks's life. The first phase, what she calls "a home life of sorts," began in 1938 and ended in 1950. Her father fought in the first World War, and then was deployed again by the navy in 1943 to the Pacific. During that time, Anne was home alone with her mother who began to drink heavily, and dealing with her became very difficult. Anne tried not to do anything that would aggravate her—the classic behavior of a child of addicted parents, which meant learning to walk on eggshells. Anne made a promise to herself that she would never smoke or drink. When her father returned, things went from bad to worse as her parents engaged in physical fights. Anne slept upstairs, and they fought downstairs. Every now and then, she would hear a crash or a thud. She sat the top of the stairs and cried "because I didn't want my parents killing each other."

When her father told her he was going to leave her mother, Anne asked him to take her with him. She was in the middle of sixth grade. They went to Key West, Florida. Because she couldn't stay in the bachelor officers' quarters, her father sent her to a convent boarding school even though she wasn't Catholic and didn't even attend church. When she arrived at the convent, she was terrified by the nuns because of their dress and their unfamiliarity. At age 9, a friend had convinced her that nuns kept little babies hostage in the basements of their convents. A year or 2 later, her beliefs were almost confirmed when a nun who was a librarian picked out a book for her to read called *Murder in the Nunnery*, which now gives Anne a good chuckle.

"It turned out," Dr. Brooks says now, "that nuns were absolutely wonderful people, who insisted that my mother was good, and that my father was good. I didn't believe them of course, because when you are a teenager in the middle of a divorce, you hate both parents." It was the nuns' ability to be substitute parents for Anne and their wholeness in doing so that made her begin to trust them. She also admired their kindness and their willingness to do whatever was asked of them, never saying they couldn't do it, or it was too much, or they were too tired. During that time, Anne became interested in the Catholic faith, but her father refused to let her be baptized.

After her parents' divorce, Anne went to spend the summer with her mother, who had gone further downhill. At least every third day "she'd bring a bottle home and be out of work." Anne discovered that the girl across the street was Catholic and was going to a school taught by the same order as the school Anne had attended in Key West; in fact, one of the nuns from Florida had transferred there. Anne enrolled in that school and signed up to take instruction in the Catholic faith; the pastor of the parish agreed to pay for it. In the midst of the chaos that was her young life, the nuns provided her with a holding place, and what they modeled was extremely influential for Anne. "Happiness was very important to me," she explains, "and to find someone who was happy, content, kind, helpful, and considerate—that was just wonderful." She recognizes that there were insecurities in her own life that led her to find solace with the nuns, but she also believes she has a true calling. She recently celebrated her 50th year in the order.

Dr. Brooks came to medicine through her own medical crisis. She planned to enter her religious community after graduating from high school, and convinced her father, ill with cancer, to let her do it by telling him it was like being in the navy. In training, she began to have trouble with her knees. Well-meaning people told her that she had been kneeling too much to pray. She saw several doctors, and was told that she had arthritis and could not teach a full day, needed to use a wheelchair in the long halls in which she was then teaching, and needed to take 40 aspirin a day. She was to rest in bed the half of the day she wasn't teaching. Despite this arrangement, her pain and debilitation increased. Eventually she ended up in the Brigham Rehabilitation Hospital in Boston for 6 months, getting gold shots to block her immune system, which was attacking her joints.

With the assistance of crutches, Sister Anne went back to teaching, and at one point, served as the principal. She was transferred from an inner-city Black school to a very wealthy White school, which she found quite difficult. She decided to volunteer at a free clinic to feel like she was still doing outreach to the less affluent. The doctor who had started the clinic was John Upledger, a well-known osteopathic physician. He told her that he could make her pain free, and Sister Anne laughed. He had just gotten back from an acupuncture course and was eager to try it on his pain patients. Sister Brooks was quite intrigued. He treated her with acupuncture, nutrition, and general medical and osteopathic treatments, including manipulation under anesthesia for the contractions she had developed from being in and out of a wheelchair or on crutches for 17 years. Finally, she was able to be free of the back brace she had been in for 12 years.

John became a close friend of Sister Anne. Eventually the malpractice insurance became too much for him, and he left Florida and joined the faculty at Michigan State University College of Osteopathic Medicine. On her way to a retreat in Albany, Sister decided to stop and see him. "I got off the plane, and first thing he said was not, 'Hi Anne,' but, 'You've got to be a doctor.' I said, 'You are crazy, I can't even pass chemistry.' " That was the second time he presented her with a major turning point in her life. She stayed with John and his family for a while when she attended premed and medical school. Reflecting on that time, Dr. Brooks sees that these two sections of her life, each with its wonderful people, made her appreciate the gifts that everyone has and the need to give to others.

No one tried to dissuade Sister Anne from becoming a doctor. She was 40 years old when she started medical school, but osteopathic medical schools look for mature students. The University of South Florida told her she couldn't come because she was older than 25; she said, "Well, all right, I'll show you." The residents at Bayfront Medical Center in St. Petersburg invited her to come to their resident talks. One of the doctors at the clinic invited her to observe a thoracotomy. The help she received is one reason she feels so strongly that the patients she sees now need to be cared for, no matter what's wrong with them and whether or not they have any money. She takes her motto from Matthew 10: "Freely you have received, freely give." More than two thirds of her patients have no way of paying for their care.

One person from whom Sister Anne learned her basic respect for humanity is Warner J. "Butch" Anderson. He is a colonel in the army now, but when Sister Anne met him he had just returned, very disillusioned, from Vietnam. He had been a medical corpsman and wanted to go to school to become a physician's assistant. He was the on-site person at the free clinic. The clinic held counseling nights and legal nights for people who were on drugs, and the clinic staff helped them get off drugs. Sister Anne recalls that Butch "didn't care what time of night or day it was; he was there, helping people." Butch's example reinforced for her the need to take all comers.

Anne had some negative experiences with caregivers along the way. When her mother died, she was in the ICU in the city hospital in Washington, D.C. Anne would go there and stand outside the low-walled alcove that was her room. Her mother couldn't talk and didn't know who she was or who Anne was, and young Anne "didn't know what to do with that." None of the nurses seemed to notice; none ever came to stand with her or said anything to her. When she was teaching in Tampa, in the school with the long halls, it was sometimes difficult for her to roll the wheelchair the whole distance, and sometimes people didn't want to take the trouble to push her. Even some of the nuns kept their distance from her.

Her experiences taught her that listening as crucial to the practice of medicine. It means taking into consideration the patient's culture and ability to trust. "When I first came to Tutwiler," she remembers, "the patients would not look me in the eye, because they were Black and I was White, and they knew what happened to people who looked White people in the eye. So I had to completely revise my approach with them." Her patients did not trust her, and they didn't want to tell her anything. However, when she did not leave after a year, as most of the preceding doctors in her position had done, they began to trust her a little bit.

When she showed up at the hospital to see them, their trust in her grew. When they found her coming to their homes when they needed home care or could not get a ride, they began to open up to her. Twenty-five years later, she is able to cajole information out of people, asking them in a way that allows them to give her the information she needs.

Dr. Brooks recalls a particular incident in which listening to a patient was critical. A teacher's aide came in with the complaint of a rash. She was very nervous, and Dr. Brooks listened as she talked about the kids and how hard it was, about being part time and not having any medical benefits, and how glad she was that they were helping her. As she talked, Dr. Brooks noticed that she was catching a breath after every third word. When she listened to her lungs, they were "sopping wet." She took her patient to the hospital for a heart test, and then went to a meeting. She was called out of the meeting when it was discovered that her patient had a clot inside her heart, a rare occurrence, and she was in such terrible cardiac distress that she was only pumping out about 10% of the blood in her heart. In that case, listening to the patient's body language led Dr. Brooks to assess her patient in a way she may not have otherwise.

What gets Sister Anne up in the morning and going strong is that she loves what she is doing. The only times when she wants to stay in bed are when she has had calls every 2 hours through the night or has had to get up and care for a patient who has come to her home in the middle of the night. Although physically exhausted at those times, she does not feel burdened. Rather, she has a sense of her patients' handing her life and wanting her to help polish it up. Although she belongs to a healing profession, she does not consider herself a healer. She specifies: "I am not a healer, I am a facilitator; my job is to empower my patients, and I do that by instructing them and also by loving them to pieces." She realizes that although some of her patients do not care, she has also "got some fellows who are pretty much in love with me . . . If I tell them to do something, they do it. They come in and say, 'Well, doc, you told me I couldn't have my beer, I didn't have any beer all week, and it was really hard, but I did it for you.' " Their attachment to her gives her leverage to move them forward along the health continuum.

It is clear how much Sister Anne loves her patients and staff, so I was happy to hear another story from her that showed me that affection is mutual. "I recently turned 70—and didn't my dear staff put a huge sign on the town fire truck and park it across from the clinic! I didn't know it until they staged a fire drill and we all bailed out of the building. I have a photo of me and a fellow in a wheelchair who drives me nuts with his ability to be uncooperative with the plan of care. He is holding both my hands in his and tears are running down his face and he's saying 'I love you, Dr. Brooks!' What could I say?"

Dr. Brooks finds it a big challenge to help people at times because she is a White person caring for Black people. For example, if they do not have money, they do not have food, but "you can't just hand out food," she says, because that won't enable them to preserve their dignity. What she does is say something like, "Listen, my gutter is a mess—it's full of leaves—can you clean up from here to here, while I finish up getting your medicines ready?" Then she can get them something to eat. Sister explains that the relationships between Blacks and Whites where she is are different than they are in the North, "because we still have plantations down here. We still have people who grew up with the guy who's now the owner of the plantation, and the relationship is a little bit different." She combats these stratified relationships by being present with her care and concern. She visits her patients at home when they are dying, and "people fall over and say, 'She did?'" To Dr. Brooks, it's clear: "Of course I did. That patient was dear to me."

> I am not a healer, I am a facilitator; my job is to empower my patients, and I do that by instructing them and also by loving them to pieces.

Dr. Brooks closed the "Coloreds only" waiting room when she arrived at the clinic. When she hired her first Black employee, the Ku Klux Klan put their newspaper under the windshield wiper of her car. She went on with her work with a knot in her stomach, but luckily nothing happened. One night someone who had been stabbed in the chest was brought to her house. She put him in the dining room. Then the stabber, who had also been stabbed by the man in the dining room, was brought in too. In the meantime, the police were out front, along with about 20 other people, all Black, in a White neighborhood, and Dr. Brooks's next-door neighbor, the deacon of the Baptist church, had gone and gotten his shotgun to protect the nuns. In the end, the patient in the dining room was helping the other patient get his shirt back on, and the police took them both up to the hospital because there was no ambulance service in that part of the county at that time. Dr. Brooks certainly brought changes to the area.

With regard to how her goals are tied into her sense of personal ethics, Sister Anne wants to do her best for people, because that's what was done for her. She is acutely aware that she would not be where she is if other people had not stepped up to the plate and helped her. "It's very strong in my heart that I want to give to people, but I want to give in a way that preserves their dignity and responsibility," Sister Anne says. She adds, "And sometimes they don't take their responsibility, and I yell at them and stamp my foot and make a big scene, and they smile and they say, 'I'll try better, Doctor.' " Dr. Brooks doesn't spend much time thinking about herself. She just keeps on trucking because she has a lot to do. She gets up at 5 a.m. and works until 9 p.m., and sometimes does not pay any more attention to herself than is required to grab lunch and a short nap at noon.

One major obstacle that gets in the way of Dr. Brooks's accomplishing her goals is that, at the time of this interview, she was the only doctor in her county of 14,000. A second doctor is finally coming to join her, now that she is in her 7th decade. The clinic does have a half-time nurse practitioner who also runs their satellite clinic in a town of 283 people. She sees about 1500 people a year there. Sister sees 7500 to 8000 people a year.

Dr. Brooks resists burnout and despair with prayer. "You have to keep your prayer going or you're going to fall on your face," she says. "Part of the prayer is meditation, just jaw-boning with the Lord, and part of it is formal," she explains. She also tries to get to mass a couple of times a week in addition to Sunday. She asserts, "It's easy to dump on the Lord. The shoulders are wide and the wisdom is there." There are also times when she has the weekend off, and she also has doctor friends who come to provide her a few weeks off each year. She spends one of those weeks with friends in the Berkshires. Because Dr. Brooks finds classical music renewing and one of her friends is on the board of the Boston Symphony Orchestra, they go to Tanglewood together. This friend saw Dr. Brooks's clinic on *Good Morning America* in 1985, and she and her husband have supported the clinic in a number of its undertakings ever since. The couple has helped to develop the community education center and outreach program, and participated in Habitat for Humanity. The clinic now has 25 Habitat houses and added the community education center and a gym. "When you see this kind of success and this kind of hope," Dr. Brooks points out, "it's very hard to burn out."

Sister feels that her greatest failure has to do with her own personal time and how she nourishes herself. She was teaching herself how to play the soprano recorder, but ran out of time when she began to accept more nursing home patients because they pay, and the clinic needs money desperately. The clinic's budget is now $2 million. About 73% of that comes from donations, and Dr. Brooks feels she has a huge responsibility to get the money in, so she cuts corners on herself. Her other failure, she thinks, is not ordering the approved tests "like they say in the book," for specific medical problems. For example, if someone comes in with a bad back, she will examine and treat them with hot packs, ultrasound, and osteopathic treatment; she will have them come back every day if they need to for treatment, but she does not order X-rays the first day. Instead, she waits a few days to see if it will settle down, and if it doesn't, then she x-rays. She can do X-rays at the clinic, but with 30 salaried people on staff, paying for an MRI out of donations can be a problem. Not only does she have to do the testing, she then has to find someone who is willing to see the patient for free or for a very limited amount of money. "That's a big hassle coughing up $4000–5000, and sometimes I just can't do it," Dr. Brooks laments. Truly her biggest failure is not being able to duplicate herself.

> You have to keep your prayer going or you're going to fall on your face. . . . It's easy to dump on the Lord. The shoulders are wide and the wisdom is there.

   Dr. Brooks has the support of the three other sisters with whom she lives. They took her off cooking duty because they never knew if she would be home for supper. From different religious communities, they are all roughly the same age, and all work at the clinic. One is a psychologist, one is the clinic coordinator, and the other is the community organizer who runs the community education center. They have been together for 17 or 18 years now, and are each other's family. "We take each other to task if we need to," Sister Anne says. "We do what we can because we love each other; to ease the burden on somebody else . . . It's a whole different thing than having a family with children, where there are squabbles and things that need to be done for your children's sake. It's a whole different level. This celibate life actually has a lot of advantages to it!" They have a rule that anything that's said in the house stays in the house, so they can let their hair down—so to speak. "It's a comfortable feeling," Sister says. They help each other keep a sense of humor. Sometimes at work, Sister will call up the clinic coordinator and for giggles "tell her something absolutely asinine, just to hear her laugh."

The evolution of Dr. Brooks's style of practice has been affected by external circumstances. For the first 10 years she was in Tutwiler, people had no access to the emergency room because there was no transportation. Instead, they came to her house. Many were the nights when she sat up with an asthmatic patient, or checked a baby with a cold, or came over to the clinic and set someone up with a breathing treatment. Occasionally, someone would be so sick that Dr. Brooks and the nurse would drive that person to the emergency room, with one of them doing CPR in the backseat. As time passed, the hospital began to allow its ambulance to come 1 mile into the county. Dr. Brooks happened to live within that 1 mile. She would call the ambulance, and when it arrived she would hop in and say, "Oh, Joe was going to meet us at my house, but he didn't make it, so we gotta go here, there, around the curve, over by the turn-row. The guys would just sort of laugh, and we'd keep on going for another 20 miles, and Joe would get the care he needed at the hospital." No one ever said that Sister is not clever.

Dr. Brooks believes that as she has mellowed, she has learned to practice better and with more confidence. She no longer panics when she sees someone come in with a brown recluse spider bite. She has delivered 18 babies outside the hospital in adverse circumstances—most recently in a car in the backyard of her house; they were twins, the fifth and sixth children of a 21-year-old mother who was 7 months pregnant. With a huge thunderstorm overhead, the RN clinic coordinator was there with Dr. Brooks, handing her umbilical cord clamps, and the counselor was inside warming blankets in the oven. "It was a very interesting experience," Dr. Brooks recalls. "I didn't panic. I would have panicked early on." She notes that, "The mellowness that comes with age and grace and wisdom has played a part in that, also. I no longer have a heart attack when someone comes in with a heart attack." Dr. Brooks has grown into the practice she was put on Earth to do.

> When I'm able to touch a patient, there's a much different connection, because touch can communicate much more than words can. Words have to be interpreted, but touch is direct.

Asked when she has surprised herself with cowardice or courage, Dr. Brooks remembered a woman who caught herself on fire leaning over the stove and refused to go to the hospital. "I was terrified caring for her, but I also respected her wishes. And I think in the end, when she did die, she died without a whole lot of pain and without suffering . . . because we weren't pulling her skin off every day and that sort of thing. It was hard to go with her wishes, but she was steadfast. She was old, she was probably 83, and I think she felt she was finished. I thought she was probably ready to go to God, so I didn't get quite as bent out as shape as I might have when I was younger. I might have not given her a chance to be respected as much. That's something that's been back and forth in my mind. I think that I did contribute to her death by not taking action, but it's like a person who says they're not a code, you gotta respect that, even though it gets to be hard." Sister Anne certainly is equipped to wrestle with the most difficult things in life.

Dr. Brooks does recall a time when she felt the best course of action to take on behalf of a patient was evident, but it was impossible for her to take it. She was chief of staff at the local hospital, and another physician, a surgeon, developed a rare condition. It was sensory, so he could not feel his fingers or his feet. He started self-medicating, and he would go into rages; he became impossible to deal with. One day, the anesthesiologist refused to put his patients to sleep, so Dr. Brooks cancelled his surgeries and went over to his office personally with the CEO to talk with him, and "he beat it out the back door." The next thing Dr. Brooks knew, lawyers were talking to her and litigation was pending. Trying to protect patients from a physician who was clearly incapacitated brought her up against the protections of the legal system.

Sister's biggest regret is that she was not able get her second physician into the clinic sooner. It certainly was not from lack of trying. She talked with every student who had come to do clinical rotations with her, called people, and worked with recruiters "until I was purple in the face."

Finally she met a doctor from Nepal. Born into a Hindu family, he learned about Buddhism, studied Judaism for a number of years, and learned that there is one God for all of us. "He made me cry when he said that," Sister recounts. "If there's one God for all of us, why are we killing each other?" With his broad theology, this new doctor, who, at the time of this interview, had not yet arrived, will most likely fit right in.

Asked about the spiritual component of her work, Sister points to the osteopathic manipulation techniques and the treatments that deal with the craniosacral system. "That cranial rhythm is not just the Qi of the body," Sister contends, "that cranial rhythm is the soul breathing, and you can't tell me it's anything different." Sister believes that when she is able to touch a patient "without being afraid that I'm going to get sued," there's "a much different connection, because touch can communicate much more than words can." Words have to be interpreted, but touch is direct. "It's very easy for me in caring for my patients to be caring for Christ, and it's easy for me to bring people together in prayer. Even in sealing their charts on our computer system after their visit is done, when the computer takes a few seconds to digest the information and confirm the seal, I always pray for that patient." Dr. Sister Brooks's spirituality is fully integrated in her practice of medicine.

From praying and from reading the Scriptures, from reading people like Louis Thomas, Elie Wiesel, and Teilhard de Chardin, and from experience, Dr. Sister Brooks has come to believe that there's a difference between illness and disease. She explains: "Disease is like the biological entity that has assaulted us, or the autoimmune assault, or whatever it is that caused us to break our leg. It's not truly external to us, but it is in a way. On the other hand, illness is how that sickness has affected us at every level of our being." She questions, "What's our relationship with disease in the form of viruses? Are we more susceptible? What's our relationship with the dog? Do I kick the dog because I'm mad at my disease, or mad at God? What's my relationship with the family, and what's my relationship with God?" She believes that, in many cases, a person who has a disease can be cured, but a person who has an illness requires healing.

> Disease is the biological entity that has assaulted us, or the autoimmune assault, or whatever it is that caused us to break our leg. It's external to us, in a way. On the other hand, illness is how that sickness has affected us at every level of our being.

Dr. Brooks points out that she knows a lot of people who have cancer, which she considers a disease, who are in a way healed. They're healed because they've faced their disease and dealt with it. They're not happy to have the disease, but they are at ease with it and able to manage what is happening in their lives. Dr. Brooks thinks that being able to empower people to heal themselves in this way puts "that whole illness thing in control more."

Dr. Sister Anne Brooks hopes that her lasting legacy will be that people remember her as someone who cared and are inspired by her example to go out and do likewise. "If more people cared about each other, for cry-ing out loud, we wouldn't be in the mess that we're in," she asserts. She continually asks herself how to better express her life in a way that will encourage others to do as she has done. Throughout her life, she was inspired by examples of people loving and caring, and she strives to pass that along in the world.

CHAPTER 3

Supporting This Small and Sickly World

Dr. Michael VanRooyen

Dr. Michael VanRooyen has worked extensively in disaster relief and humanitarian assistance in more than 30 countries. In Sudan, he was instrumental in building a new hospital with a major surgical facility and developing community health infrastructure and primary health programs. In the aftermath of Rwanda's horrific genocide, Dr. VanRooyen spent months providing what he calls emergency public health for thousands of refugees. He worked closely with the Rwandan Ministry of Health to help reestablish the country's main central hospital. Dr. VanRooyen also worked in Kosovo to develop emergency services after the war had resulted in displacement and destruction of hospitals. He recently conducted a mission with physicians for human rights to evaluate the characteristics of the genocide in Darfur.

Dr. VanRooyen is acutely aware that emergency medical services are a common need in many countries around the world that are just now emerging from third-world status and seeing large urban populations springing up as a result. People need more than equipment and supplies to reinvigorate their healthcare systems. It is a complicated task that calls for a lot of coordination, and Michael has dedicated himself to improving these processes.

Dr. VanRooyen lectures on disaster management and humanitarian assistance and is widely published on these issues. His research interests include addressing the health and human rights issues that result from war and political crisis. He is currently focused on the issue of gender-based violence in conflicts, particularly in the Democratic Republic of Congo. Prior to joining the Harvard Humanitarian Initiative, Dr. VanRooyen was codirector of the Center for International Emergency, Disaster, and Refugee Studies at Johns Hopkins University, were he also was a professor at the Johns Hopkins School of Medicine. He holds an undergraduate degree from Michigan State University and earned his medical degree from Wayne State University. Dr. VanRooyen completed his residency in emergency medicine at the University of Illinois, Chicago, and earned a Master of Public Health at the UIC School of Public Health and a research fellowship at Harvard. He is a practicing emergency physician at Brigham and Women's Hospital. He is also the founder and codirector of the Harvard Humanitarian Initiative, a Harvard-University-wide program on crisis and conflict.

Michael VanRooyen grew up with a father who had unusual insight into the human condition. His earliest memories are of sitting next to his Dad, a Holocaust survivor, and seeing the numbers tattooed on his arm. "I remember as a boy wrapping my arm around his and looking at those numbers and asking what they were; obviously that was a very big complicated question. He'd tell me some things, not everything, but as I grew up, he would let out more and more about what happened to him in the camps. I became aware of the trauma of war and this huge evil, and it made a great impression on me. My father was my hero." Michael's father, who was not Jewish, was involved with the French underground in Holland, and was captured and imprisoned with Jews and other detainees at Bergen-Belson.

Michael's understanding of the magnitude of the evil his father experienced developed over time. "At first, it was just stories about it, things that happened to my dad, rather than the enormity of it all. I thought of it as things that happened to my father that were horrible and difficult, but I didn't get all of it until much later." It is little wonder that Michael credits his father with being the catalyst for his life's work.

Dr. VanRooyen went on to make a connection between the tragedy of the Holocaust and becoming a physician—a person who would have the power to lessen pain. His participation in a youth service organization, the Boy Scouts, helped him understand the value of service. His mother died when he was 8 years old, and his father remarried a woman with eight children; the resultant merged family was poorly resourced, and Michael's main self-development opportunities came from being in Boy Scouts. Being a scout provided him with a foundation in service, but he did not make the connection to humanitarian assistance and being a physician until much later in life.

Because he did not have a mentor until after his residency, Michael had to feel his way slowly toward the work that became his passion. He recognizes that he could not get there any faster than he did on his own, but he still mourns somewhat that he did not find his vocational path a bit earlier. Now at the vanguard of his discipline, "It took a little while to decide where I wanted to be in this big field."

Although Michael lacked a formal mentor, he did have early supporters. A conversation with the physician father of one of his best friends in high school had an impact. This doctor said very simply, "It's not this unreachable feat; you can do it if you work hard." Young Michael thought, "Oh, I can work hard." That simple comment was a catalyst for Michael. "That's what turned me toward medicine—because he encouraged me, and made it doable."

He also had a high school speech teacher who told him, "Look, you're underestimating yourself, you can do this." Michael bounced things off him, including his thoughts about doing premed. This teacher had a major impact on his believing in himself, and Michael is still in touch with him. As with so many of the other physicians in this text, Michael's earliest cheerleaders were not medical practitioners.

Dr. VanRooyen does not recall encountering any discouraging characters on his journey, but acknowledges that, not growing up in a medical family, "There was not a lot of understanding among my family members about what it took." The difficult parts were applying to college, seeking out scholarships, and setting a premed course with no one coaching him. Once he saw how big the world was, he broke through his sheltered upbringing in a small town and broadened his vision of what he might be able to accomplish.

A vivid experience during junior high school made a powerful impression. Working on a farm and riding in the pickup truck with the farmer, he came upon a boy not much older than he who had flipped a huge tractor on top of himself, and was pinned underneath, folded in half, and conscious. Michael stayed with him throughout the rescue, "completely shocked by the severity of the accident and unable to do anything to help." Ultimately, the boy survived, and his experience unknowingly nudged Michael toward emergency medicine. "I never wanted to feel helpless like that again."

Neither books nor media had a significant influence on Michael. He does recall, a bit sheepishly, watching *Dr. Zhivago* when he was young, and being impressed with "the image of a doctor working in war." At that early phase, however, he did not have a master plan, but was only engaged in trying to expand his world. As he sees it, his frame of reference took a long time to develop, and he wishes that he understood the world at a younger age.

The most compelling and continuous force in Michael's life was his father, who taught him his basic respect for humanity. "My dad was a supremely ethical guy, very friendly and outgoing; he always treated people fairly." An immigrant from Holland, he had a small shoe-repair business, and was well known in town. Observing his father interact with people in a friendly manner and treating them supremely fairly regardless of whether they were men, women, or people of color strongly influenced the way Michael relates to people today. The image Michael draws gives me the impression that much of what he learned about being present with patients came from watching his dad with customers.

When asked about the experience of someone close to him who had had a medical challenge, Michael noted that his mother was hospitalized during the old days of medical practice. In those days, children his age were not allowed in the hospital, and he had to wait in the car or the cafeteria while his father and older brother visited his mother. His experience was of being totally shut out. When he looks back, he feels sad for himself, but even more so for his mother. "Can you imagine," he asks, "37 years old, dying of melanoma, and with her 7-year-old kid waiting in the car because they wouldn't let him up?" He did not fully realize the truly depressing nature of the situation until he became older and had his own children.

Oddly, a few years ago, Dr. VanRooyen's wife was diagnosed with melanoma, at around the same age as his mother had died from the disease. Fortunately however, his wife's melanoma was local and was successfully treated. During his wife's illness, they were at Johns Hopkins, and Dr. VanRooyen especially appreciated being in a medical system that is among the very best in the world. This allowed him to have confidence that anything that was possible would be done.

Noting that this spoke to the medical staff's technical skills, I asked how he had felt about the people relating to his wife at the time. "They were spectacular," he reported. "I was just really impressed with the care and concern of people, the little things, seeing the best of humanity. It was really a great experience to be part of a group of people who care that much." Rarely do I hear people describe their care in such glowing terms.

For Dr. VanRooyen, the role of listening in medical practice is a huge issue, so important that he has developed ways of ensuring that it happens in his practice. He elaborates. "To understand a patient's problem, you need to ask questions about what the problem really is, but at some point you have to stop asking and actively listen. It takes developing habits that allow you to connect with a patient even when the emergency department is going nuts all around you. Habits like, with every single patient you see, pulling up a chair and sitting down beside them. You shake the hand of every single member of the family in the room, and then ask them, 'how can I help you?' You don't interrupt. You give them the time, no matter how busy it is. It's important not only to listen, but also to develop habits that allow you to listen well." Michael's description makes doable what too many harried clinicians have written off as an unobtainable goal.

> To understand a patient's problem, you need to ask questions about what the problem really is, but at some point you have to stop asking, and actively listen. It takes developing habits that allow you to connect with a patient even when the emergency department is going nuts all around you.

Dr. VanRooyen was in Chicago for many years and moved to Johns Hopkins for 7 years as faculty in the emergency medicine department at the medical school and the school of public health. During that time, he managed several international programs, building on his own extensive work abroad. Then he moved to Harvard. He now has an office at the Brigham Hospital, where he works as a physician, and an office at the Harvard University main campus. He travels less now, in large part because of having children, and focuses more on developing programs to get his fellows, residents, trainees, and other faculty working abroad.

Asked what gets him up in the morning and keeps him persevering, he focuses on the big philosophy that motivates him. He thinks that the thing one invests one's life in should be "truly important, because you're going to be spending your most productive days of your life doing it," and he believes that if one has found that thing and has the power to act on it, then that person has a responsibility to act on it. "With the power to act comes the responsibility to act," he asserts and adds, "I feel very much that it's a calling." Dr. VanRooyen considers it an honor to be able to do the work he does. "We all see war and crisis on television or [in] newspapers. We all shake our heads and wish we could do something about it. I'm in a very privileged position to be able to do something tangible. To see a huge need and . . . in some small but meaningful way be able to impact that—it's a gift, a great privilege."

Asked what keeps him in his particular calling, rather than moving toward something easier and perhaps more lucrative, Dr. VanRooyen's answer implies that he thinks his job is the perfect mix of academics and field work. "I have colleagues who have been working in developing countries for 30 years, committed themselves to a life of deprivation to be able to make a difference. They are doing the great work that needs to be done." He thinks those in the field deserve more credit. "I admire greatly my colleagues who work in the developing world. They never get recognized and yet are the ones who are working in some of the world's toughest areas, like in the middle of Congo or a refugee camp in Darfur." Yet this comes from the man who has put himself on the line as an interventionist in more than 30 different countries.

> The thing you invest your life in should be truly important, because you're going to be spending your most productive days of your life doing it.

I inquired about how his goals are tied into a sense of personal ethics. Dr. VanRooyen describes a sense of being responsible for others. The world is not necessarily fair. We live in one set of circumstances and others struggle to survive in places affected by political instability. It is incumbent upon those of us who have resources, intellectual and financial, to work to level the playing field. Having the resources should come with a sense of responsibility. That responsibility drives me to keep doing this work."

As for how this reflects on his own identity, Dr. VanRooyen notes that, "Anyone who does international health draws their identity from it."

Although his work at the Harvard Humanitarian Initiative is building programs that help improve practices on an organizational level, he misses the field work. "Over time, doing less fieldwork can remove you from the work that you identify with." He finds returning to work in the field necessary to keep him motivated.

A seminal event for Dr. VanRooyen was arriving in Somalia as a young physician and a relief worker. It was during this experience that he truly realized his life's work. He was inspired by the massive needs, dedication of those attempting to provide aid, and the complexity of the humanitarian effort. It was clear that although many organizations were attempting to help, much of this work was ineffective and even dangerous. He felt that the world didn't need more organizations doing charitable work; but it needed that work to be more effective in providing appropriate aid that enabled long-term change. As this understanding was confirmed by his experiences in Bosnia, Rwanda, and Kosovo, he realized that his path was to link academics to the practice of humanitarian assistance. His goal became to provide a way to professionalize humanitarian aid by developing the links between academic institutions and organizations working in the field, and to improve research and training.

> It's incumbent upon those of us who have resources, intellectual and financial, to work to level the playing field. Having the resources should come with a sense of responsibility.

Dr. VanRooyen draws an analogy with medical training programs. "It's almost like having hospitals without medical schools," he explains. "When young physicians move from books to start touching patients during their clinical years, the link between practice and medical education is still strong." But, as he notes, prior to the development of humanitarian education, there was no such link. The tens of thousands of humanitarian aid workers and practitioners in the field come from varied backgrounds and have never been trained in the systematized practice. Dr. VanRooyen's interest is in building training programs that teach future aid workers to provide high quality services and produce research that will guide and improve practice. I was reminded of something Michael and his colleague Jennifer Leaning wrote in the *New England Journal of Medicine* in 2005, shortly after the tsunami that struck South Asia in late 2004. They made the argument that relief organizations still have much to learn about shifting from short-term emergency aid work to sustainable longer term interventions that provide the undergirding for localized healthcare systems. Academic connections with field work can lead to a better understanding of this process.

Dr. VanRooyen acknowledges that burnout is a big problem in his field. He attributes his ability to avoid it to the fact that he can balance both worlds. His two worlds are very different; working in a clinical setting in an emergency department has little to do with managing health services in a refugee camp. For him, the "fun of it is to be in high-tech medicine, in a world-class academic facility like Brigham and Women's Hospital, and then, 24 hours later, land in the middle of southern Sudan where there's no electricity, and you live in a grass hut." He finds balancing these two worlds exhausting but also really refreshing. He thrives on the contrast and allows the two settings to support and augment each other.

Dr. VanRooyen identifies his biggest failure to date as his current struggle to get traction around the concept of professionalized humanitarian practice. He clarifies by saying, "I didn't know enough earlier, even a few years ago, how to promote a culture of quality in the field. I didn't have the professional standing or the experience or even the sheer guts to make this case strongly enough, especially to donors. I think my big failure has been to not get major foundations to understand the need to invest in quality. It's the challenge for the next decade to make that happen."

With so much resting on his shoulders, how does he keep from growing discouraged? Dr. VanRooyen's wife does similar work, and she is a great supporter who accepts his extensive national and international travel to speak and work. But it is his three young children who really help him maintain his balance by putting his priorities in perspective. "The trick is to be in Washington, Geneva, or Nairobi and still make it home on time for a piano recital," he comments. He also affirms the value of keeping a sense of humor. He emphasizes the necessity of being able to bond with one's peers, "because the problems we face are so devastating." These problems range from mass displacement, famine, epidemics, and war crimes—"the darkest things in history." In the face of them, he believes, it is necessary to maintain camaraderie with colleagues and maintain optimism. "You have to believe that you can do something to help, because if you don't, then you'll have to leave the field," he states. Among his contemporaries in the field, he thinks the ones who have lasted and really pushed the agenda forward are the ones with persistent idealism and a well-developed sense of humor.

I asked Dr. VanRooyen whether, in thinking about his one-on-one meetings with patients, stateside or elsewhere, there were things that had led him to the type of practice he maintains in the emergency room. He answered, "Part of the adaptability that you have in your professional life comes from your ability to synthesize from all of your different experiences. I believe I can be a better leader at the Brigham and Woman's Hospital because I've run a program in the Congo. They seem to have nothing to do with one another, but the skills that you develop—reading people, understanding them, listening to them, trying to understand core values and barriers, trying to engender support—all those things translate from one setting to another."

Most doctors are said to have a style, and I questioned Dr. VanRooyen as to what had led him to his. He answered, "The emotional intelligence of my father. I watched him. I can close my eyes and see how he stood with people when he interacted. He had a great way with people. I think I developed that very early, listening to people, being friendly with people, disarming them with humor. My style in medicine is to walk into a room and immediately introduce myself to everyone in the room, make them feel at ease, sit down close to a patient, and touch them. When I shake their hand or hold it for a minute, I sit down and stay there and listen, because that's what they come for."

> I can be a better leader at the Brigham because I've run a program in the Congo. They seem to have nothing to do with one another, but the skills that you develop—reading people, understanding them, listening to them, trying to understand core values and barriers, trying to engender support—all those things translate from one setting to another.

Dr. VanRooyen attributes the moments of both courage and cowardice in his life to the circumstances in which he works, commenting, "While we have to stand up for patients and individuals in a clinical setting here in the U.S., my work internationally has led to some powerful events that in my own mind, have enabled me to fail or to do well." He was imprisoned in Zaire during the civil war, right before it became the Democratic Republic of Congo. Held at gunpoint and questioned for several days, he found it fairly intense. "I was scared, but I don't think I acted irrationally. My colleagues and I acted calmly to negotiate our release, but inside, it was quite unnerving." He contrasts that level of fear with the terrifying moment when you are driving a car and someone swerves in front of you. "You're really scared, but then you're okay—you realize wow, that was a close call."

Another time immediately after the war in Rwanda, a group of his colleagues were at a checkpoint and several drunken soldiers were trying to get people to come out of the car, especially the women. He "told the others to stay in the car, then I got out of the car myself and stared those guys down until they backed off and let us go. It's not an unusual moment, especially in that kind of environment, but I realized there's a time to be quiet and do what you're told, and there's a time that it doesn't matter what's going to happen—you have to stand up and face the issue."

Dr. VanRooyen recalls a time when he felt he couldn't follow through on behalf of a patient. "Just a couple of years ago at the Brigham, a colleague of mine had presented to me and asked me, outside of the system, what I thought. She had abdominal pain—turns out she was in early pregnancy—and she developed, right in front of me. She bled into her pelvis and she almost bled out. She went from walking and talking normally to laying down flat, white, passing out, and almost dying on me in the course of a few minutes. I remember it all happening way too fast. I couldn't believe it was happening; it took me way too long." He got the surgeons to take her to the operating room, where it was discovered that she had a ruptured ectopic pregnancy. Michael was frustrated with himself because he was stuck in thinking of his colleague as a healthy person and was, he believes, delayed in making the adjustment to thinking of her as someone seriously ill. He was thoroughly shaken. I imagine how a worse outcome for the woman would be the type of thing that would keep Michael awake at night for years.

I asked Michael whether he had any disappointments about his choice of careers, and he responded, "I don't have any regrets when it comes to this. I remain very grateful to be in this business, and looking back on all the things I could have done with my career, nothing comes close to this. I think that when we retire, and look back on our life's work, I wish for anybody that they could have done something that is really valuable, that their life could count for something important. I'm sure I will not have accomplished everything I would have liked to, but you just try to make some change for the better."

Dr. VanRooyen grew up Catholic and was very active in his church throughout high school and college and even in medical school and beyond. He points out that like others "who have a lot of life experience and especially a variety of cultural experience, many people's religious views, and mine are no exception, get more universal. I've always had a very strong spiritual component to what I did. It all stems back to the sense of equity in the world, and while my religious views have evolved over the years, the basic premise of contribution and social justice is pretty strong." His words reminded me of the great tradition of Catholic activists like Fathers Phil and Daniel Berrigan.

Michael hopes that his legacy will be "improving this humanitarian industry of providing relief in conflict and crisis." He acknowledges that it is a young field that is evolving, and he hopes to have a hand in the positive development of the discipline. He wants to make sure that survivors always "have a positive image of the assistance that they get, so that they see it as a good thing, rather than something that is flawed or corrupt."

At the end of our discussion, I asked Dr. VanRooyen to go back to the question of cowardice, which he had asked for time to think about earlier. He spoke of a feeling he has experienced that was not patient related. "I can remember circumstances where I felt like I was abandoning my post. I felt the most strongly about that in Bosnia, because I was in a war hospital and I was only working there for a little while. So I remember packing it up and leaving when they had to stay. Here I am at this war hospital and they're being bombarded and there's more patients coming in all the time, and the local staff is exhausted and malnourished. I come in to help them for a few weeks, but then I leave, and I can leave, and I always could leave. It's similar to what we saw in *Hotel Rwanda* [a major motion picture]. The conflict deteriorates in a humanitarian crisis that threatens civilians, but the international staff gets evacuated. In the past I've evacuated out of Somalia or Bosnia, in the middle of really horrible circumstances with tremendous guilt. I feel like I'm one of them, but the fact is that I always knew that I could come home." He knows many aid workers who have experienced the guilt and ambivalence of leaving an area of deteriorating security.

Dr. VanRooyen keeps much of his experience to himself. "I found that trying to talk to people at home was often difficult. It's hard to explain,

> My style in medicine is to walk into a room and immediately introduce myself to everyone in the room, make them feel at ease, sit down close to a patient, and touch them. When I shake their hand or hold it for a minute, I sit down and stay there and listen, because that's what they come for.

and after a while, I'd stopped trying to tell people about the details. People can ask me, and I'll tell them a little bit, but they don't really know the context, so it's hard for people outside of this world to understand, and I'm not going to try. Perhaps I also have the lingering guilt of leaving when there was so much more to do and that my efforts were inadequate. I went there and I came back and I'm in the paper, or something nice like this interview happens, but I didn't do anything of significance. . . .

I can imagine the enormity of difficulty of trying to help in such horrific circumstances, but I am left feeling that even though Dr. VanRooyen has traveled with many medical missions, he feels that he can never do enough.

Michael was influenced early by such a powerful figure in his life, his father, a Holocaust survivor. As he matured he developed a deep understanding of the impact of war and its effects. From the confines of his small town, he drew on the support of others who had a wider vision of what was possible for him, ultimately finding his life's work a world away. Dr. VanRooyen feels his opportunities created a responsibility for him to continue in his field, and he feels privileged to be able to help in a meaningful way in the most extreme human experiences.

CHAPTER 4

Finding Peace on the Other Side of Trauma

Dr. Sylvia Campbell

Dr. Sylvia Campbell began volunteering at the Judeo Christian Health Clinic while she was a surgical resident at Tampa General Hospital. Her commitment to the clinic has grown over almost 3 decades as a volunteer, a board member, and as president of the board of directors. At the free clinic she treats patients with breast cancer, obstructed gall bladders, renal failure, and more—patients who have been forced to delay seeking medical treatment due to lack of insurance. Sylvia believes it is incumbent upon organized medicine to be part of the solution and she is very aware that having little or no insurance carries frighteningly similar consequences—delayed treatment and poorer outcomes. Her heart goes out to the people who have fallen through the cracks of the healthcare system.

The Judeo Christian Health Clinic had a modest beginning in 1972 in a Sunday school classroom on a 1-night-per-week basis. By 1999, the clinic had raised $1 million within the community to build a new 8000-square-foot facility with 12 examining rooms, a laboratory, a licensed pharmacy, 3 complete dental operatories, and an optician's dispensing lab. An ongoing affiliation agreement with the University of South Florida College of Medicine enables the clinic to provide in-depth family practice clinics. Although Dr. Campbell has cared for thousands of patients as a surgeon, belonging to a truly ecumenical board of directors representing

Catholic, Jewish, and Protestant faiths enables her to impact clinic policy and take on an additional role recruiting other volunteers and raising funds to support its mission.

In addition to this extraordinary level of commitment in her own community, Dr. Campbell has volunteered her services annually in Haiti for many years. She also has been involved in efforts to build and sustain a school in Uganda as well as an HIV clinic for children there. Sylvia traveled with the Florida Department of Health to Mississippi to provide care immediately after Hurricane Katrina for 9 days. She has written extensively on her numerous medical missions and on domestic violence, injury, and trauma. Dr. Campbell was awarded the American College of Surgeons Humanitarian Award in 2007.

In addition to her private practice in surgery in Tampa, Dr. Campbell has served as clinical faculty in the department of surgery at the College of Medicine, University of South Florida. Sylvia earned an undergraduate degree at Emory University, where she also completed an MS in molecular genetics. Her MD is from the University of South Florida, where she did her general surgery residency.

Two events in Dr. Campbell's early life influenced her to become a physician. The first occurred during the 1950s when she was 6 years old, at her family's summer lake house in Orlando. There were five children there; her younger brother was two. One day, one of the neighbor children asked, "Where's Troy?" They found him at the bottom of the lake, not breathing. Dr. Fraser, a local urologist who was nearby, saved him with a knee-and-back CPR technique. Sylvia remembers "waiting down the road for the ambulance for hours . . . going to the hospital, seeing him in the oxygen tent." The memory stuck with her as an example of the impact of lifesaving medical skills that the physician was able to bring to bear in a crisis.

The second event that influenced Sylvia's career direction occurred when she was 13 years old and had a friend visiting at the lake for the summer. They were out on a boat, some young men were driving their boats recklessly, doing figure eights and trying to look cool, and Sylvia's friend fell off the front of the boat. The boat turned, the rudder hit her arm, and "the whole lake turned red." "Everyone just froze," Sylvia remembers, but she jumped in and pulled her friend out and took care of her; she was rushed to surgery and was fine. "Those were probably the two events that had the biggest impact on me in life . . . ." They seem to her as having somehow ordained that she would go into medicine by making her realize how tenuous life is, and what a difference "being someone who can change the direction one way or another" can make.

With this affinity for being by the water at crucial times, it somehow makes sense that Sylvia met her husband at a swimming pool; they were both lifeguards. He became her first major supporter in her life's work, encouraging her from the start to be a surgeon. She had planned to be a marine biologist, but he realized that she probably was not going to be happy working in a lab. "He encouraged me from the first time I met him," Dr. Campbell recalls. He wanted her to do whatever it was she wanted to do, even though medicine, particularly surgery, wasn't a very common field for women to pursue at the time. During her childhood, Sylvia was never told that she couldn't do something just because of her gender. Instead, the message she received was, "If it's something you want to do, if you work hard enough, it could happen." The combination of this message and her husband's encouragement propelled her toward her goal.

Dr. Campbell recalls only one person who ever opposed her life plan—a physician at a hospital where she was clerking before she returned to school. His response to her expressed desire to go to medical school was, "What do you want to do that for? Just be a nurse; my sister's a nurse. You can't go to medical school; you'll never do that." Sylvia didn't listen to him. She believes that if people listen to others who tell them "no," they will never do anything. She realizes that it may be easier to accept what people say but thinks it is better in the long run to make it happen, because then people end up doing what they want to do. "It'd be horrible to live a life where you couldn't live your dream," she contends.

The Vietnam War had a significant impact on Sylvia. It was the first war brought right into civilians' faces by the media. Seeing "all the atrocity and horror" made her want to do something that would make things different. War continues to affect her. The night the United States declared war in Iraq, she wrote a letter to include in the journals she keeps for her children, questioning, "What have we done? What kind of world are we creating for you? What are we giving to you? What are the ramifications of this horrific thing that we're doing?" Many of the war's polytrauma victims are being sent to the VA hospital in Tampa. "You go on that ward and there are all these young kids," Sylvia describes, "and the worst part of it is, a lot of those kids shouldn't live. But we've got the capability of keeping them alive now." Sylvia believes that the amount of psychological, emotional, and physical damage that is going to be done by the Iraqi War is "going to make Vietnam look like nothing.... Why can't we learn from history?" she laments.

Sylvia's mother taught her respect for humanity by modeling kindness and by being "a good human being." She also stressed to Sylvia the importance of a faith community, and the church was very important to Sylvia as she was growing up. She continued attending even when she was older and her family no longer went to church. She was always asking, "God, what is it you want me to do?" She believes that she did take the path God intended for her. Her faith also taught her a basic respect for humanity. "I believe that we're all brothers on this earth," she contends. "None of us are better or worse, we just happen to be planted in different places ... If you're given a lot in life, you have to help people who don't have as much as you do." This belief has been strengthened by her mission trips to third-world countries.

Sylvia experienced a serious medical crisis when her fourth child was stillborn. "It was horrible," she remembers. One of the things she realized through this experience, and something that she shares with her cancer patients today, is that "the only thing you can really control in your life is how you react to things that happen to you. When your life is totally shattered, the only thing you can control is how you put the pieces back together." The stillbirth of her child was one of Sylvia's life-shattering events, and she acknowledges that although it was not an experience she ever wanted to have, she grew and learned from it. "The people who walked that part of my journey with me were wonderful, both in the medical and other spheres," she recalls. One of her colleagues, a friend, delivered her stillborn child, which Sylvia recognizes was difficult. Another friend cancelled her appointments to sit with her in the hospital, and another friend gave her a book that helped her enormously. The message Sylvia got from the book was, "When you're hurting, you're going through this horrible time, but the people who are walking down the street, those other people have to go on with life. You want to scream at them, 'Don't you know what I'm going through right now?' and yet they're just going on with their lives. But a lot of times we forget that." Sylvia has used her painfully gained knowledge to develop a better understanding of her patients' experience.

Another health-related crisis that influenced Sylvia was her mother having Alzheimer's disease. Not only was it very difficult watching someone she loved disappear, but for her there was another level of despair in not being able to help her. "You spend your whole life trying to be a healer and you can't do anything to stop it. It was so hard," Sylvia explains. She did find it healing in a way, though, when her Mom died, because she realized that her Mom was finally free. She describes her mother's passing as "a very peaceful thing for her after a long time of chaos." Her mother's experience has made her wonder, "Where is the soul of someone with Alzheimer's? Are they in between places? Because they're not there . . ." Sylvia brings this level of thoughtfulness to her practice.

> "I believe that we're all brothers on this earth. None of us are better or worse, we just happen to be planted in different places. . . . If you're given a lot in life, you have to help people who don't have as much as you do.

Surgeons, Sylvia asserts, tend to be people who do things. This characteristic is part of her makeup too, but has been tempered by taking care of people who have cancer. She's learned that, "to sit in there and listen to people is in many ways more healing than the things I can do with a knife." She listens to more than her patients' words. "You have to listen to everything they're saying . . . you have to listen to their body language, their aura of how they are when they come in." She follows her patients for a long time, and over time she creates a safe place for them, such that they can come in and tell her what it is in their lives that is affecting them. She recognizes that this may not be normal for a surgeon. Nonetheless she considers it so important to listen and "not really tell them what to do, but ask the questions that help them figure it out." Listening, she knows, is one of the more human things we can do. She finds other ways to be human with her patients as well. She appreciates that being a surgeon allows her to touch her patients; as she changes their dressings and looks at their wounds, and she has a big sign in her office that says, "Hugs are healing."

Refusing to focus on the negative enables Sylvia to persevere. She focuses instead on how much she gets back. She feels fortunate to be able to interact with people every day "in a way that some people never experience in their whole lives." She believes that being able to be a physician is a gift, and she needs to use that gift in the right way. She admits to getting tired, but when she does, she reminds herself that she would be much more tired if she were working two or three jobs or doing something she hated, as some of her patients must. Growing up, Sylvia was taught to persevere. Her father ingrained in her an old saying, "Remember, once a job has begun, never leave it 'til it's done," and she strives to do just that.

Sylvia believes that if she commits to a task, she needs to do the best she possibly can with it. At the same time, she doesn't want to lose her soul. Many times in her life, she remembers what she learned long ago from reading Steinbeck's *Winter of Our Discontent*—that "once your light goes out, you can't get it back." What helps keep her moral compass pointing true North and going in the right direction is reminding herself that, "once you fall out, once you take the easy road, even if it's just a little bit maybe not quite right, even if you gain from it financially, you've really lost everything."

Sexism might have gotten in Dr. Campbell's way had she allowed it to. Instead, she "chose not to be bothered by the sexist stuff, not to participate in that, not feel like I had to do it better because I was a woman." She feels that by, in essence, rising above it and moving forward steadily she learned to work around barriers. Dr. Campbell keeps her eye on her long-term goals no matter what gets in her way, "whether it's managed care or HMOs or all the changes in health care that have occurred over the past 25 years I've been practicing." She asserts, "People have been practicing the art of medicine for thousands and thousands of years, and they'll continue to do it. All these obstacles are just temporary changes that go along with society. But if you can just keep your focus on what you're doing and do it the best way, usually you can get around most of the obstacles." She concedes that it is more difficult than it used to be, but contends that there are ways to get around the bureaucracy, especially in this country. "It's easy to complain about things here until you go somewhere where they have nothing." Her work in Haiti demonstrated this to her, and she thinks that if everyone worked in a third-world country for awhile, the issues here would seem much more surmountable.

Sylvia admits that there are "a lot of horrible problems with our insurance system," but in this country, she asserts, "you can always get care." While "it may not be the kind of care [or] be gold standard of care," she believes that the difference between this country and other places is that here, "no one will be left to die in the streets." She notes that she has recently reviewed AMA foundation grant applications for free clinics around the country, and found that everywhere, from big cities to little towns, people are trying to take care of people who do not have any way of being taken care of. "People want to help people," Sylvia insists, "if you just show them how." Dr. Campbell points out the example of one of her patients who had fallen through the cracks, having been denied health insurance because of a prior condition but being unable to receive free care because she had assets. Many people in the community came forward to help her. Sylvia is one of those people who perpetually sees the glass as half full.

Sylvia resists burnout and despair by learning from her patients and by giving to them. Helping them "to walk through times that are devastating to them and their families," and making it "easier than it would have been if you hadn't been with them," keeps her from getting discouraged. "That and prayer," she says. She advocates listening to one's inner self and intuition and having some private time and space. "Whether it's doing exercise, listening to music, gardening—whatever it is, it's really important that everybody, in any life situation, has a sacred place that they can go to. It may not be outside yourself, it may be inside yourself. But you have to have it," Sylvia concludes.

She has activities outside of medicine that keep her balanced. Physical challenges are important to her. She has run marathons, has her third-degree black belt in tae kwan do, and thinks walking is an interesting, Zenlike experience, especially by the water in the early morning. In fact, on the morning we had our conversation, she had just come back from a very long charity walk held on the causeway to Tampa Bay. Sylvia loves to work in the yard and plant things and watch them grow. Whenever anything horrific happens in her life, she goes out in the garden and plants things. She does what is healing for her own spirit, knowing that "you can't continually give, or you'll empty out. You have to fill yourself back up." She knows that healers have to heal, too.

Dr. Campbell's husband and children help her keep her sense of humor. Her husband jokes with her and makes everything laughable. Sylvia gains perspective by watching the cardinals in the back yard; they remind her of her place in the world, and not to make herself too important. "I think we always continually need to realize how unimportant we are, in a way that's easy and kind of humorous," she offers.

Among Sylvia's greatest successes are her three wonderful children. She describes them as "people who will give back to society." If this is so, then it is because she has shown them how. About 6 years ago, she received an e-mail from a 15-year-old girl in Uganda who had a hole in her heart. The girl could not walk across a room anymore, because she was so short of breath. Sylvia arranged to bring her over to the United States, and the girl and her uncle stayed with her and her family for 6 weeks. The girl had her surgery, and now she is finishing college. Dr. Campbell's efforts snowballed. She and her family took the girl and her uncle to their church, and the whole congregation became involved. They developed a scholarship fund for kids in the village so they could go to school and college; they had 18 homes built for widows; and they helped extended family members raise children who had lost their parents to AIDS, as the young girl had. They built 8 wells, a preschool, and a primary school, and now are trying to build a medical clinic. Even the people Dr. Campbell surrounds herself with seem indefatigable.

> It's really important that everybody, in any life situation, has a sacred place that they can go to. It may not be outside yourself, it may be inside yourself. But you have to have it.

Sylvia remarks that she has not done anything special; she just has not said no to the special requests that come her way. She recalls Patrick, a little boy who got run over by a truck right before she got to Haiti; it took 3 years for them to get him to the United States for surgery. She also recalls a little boy, 18 months old, who was brought to the clinic when she was there. He had been caught in a fire and had a 40% total body surface burn. "We were up in the middle of nowhere, we didn't have anything, we didn't have satellite, we didn't have e-mail, all we had was a CB radio," Sylvia remembers. "We said, this little boy is going to die if we don't get him to a burn unit. That's the kind of thing you don't say you can't do. You just say, yes you can; you make it happen." A United Nations helicopter came to the village to take him to the burn unit, and now he is healed and in the first grade. "This is the kind of thing you look at and say, it's a joy and privilege to have been a part of that, but it would have been so easy just to say, 'oh well.' What a lesson to me!" Sylvia says. Dr. Campbell has clearly carried this lesson into other areas of her life; at the free clinic where she volunteers, they see 25,000 patients a year. She is very proud to be a part of that.

Sylvia started out as the only female surgeon in the county. It was an interesting journey from there to her current practice. She had done a lot of trauma work as a resident and got very involved in the practice where she is now, covering three emergency rooms (ERs) at once. At that time there was no trauma system or major center, or even a concept of one. A surgeon could be in the operating room of one hospital and get a call for an emergency in another hospital, and have to go. So Sylvia did a study in which she reviewed all of the deaths over a year and determined which ones could have been prevented had there been a major trauma center up and running. She published the paper and then took it to the board of county commissioners. From there an agency was established, and as a result, a designated trauma center was developed.

Other than on mission trips, Dr. Campbell doesn't do trauma surgeries anymore. No one with whom she currently works realizes how she was involved in laying the groundwork of developing the trauma system. Reflecting on this, she remarks, "It's nice to sit back and see the system working." Friends from college who were involved in the Caribbean trauma system helped her, but, again, "It's one of those things where you can't say 'no,' you've just got to do it."

Sylvia recalls a time when she had to summon her courage. It was Christmas day, her children were all young, and they were on their way to her in-laws' house. She had her jingle bell earrings on. As they exited the interstate, they saw a car wreck. She made her husband pull over and stop. "There were these little girls who had been thrown out of the car. One of them had her head between the wheel and the fire hydrant, and there was a lady underneath the car," Sylvia remembers. "I went into surgeon mode and had the guys pick the car up off the lady and get the little girl stabilized." By the time the paramedics got there, she was covered in blood. When Dr. Campbell tried to intubate the girl, it became obvious that she had a dislocation. "Her mother was outside screaming and her little Christmas shoes were lying on the ground," Sylvia recalls the surreal scene. "It was one of those things where you have to have it together. You can't be emotional at that moment; you have step back and be totally unemotional." Sylvia was successful at doing so. Then everybody left, and they went to their Christmas dinner. Just like the doctor who was nearby to save her little brother in childhood, she had made herself ready to make the ultimate difference.

Another incident that required Sylvia to have courage and put her emotions aside occurred the day after Christmas when her son was a year old. She was on ER duty and got a call—a gunshot wound to the chest.

They brought the patient in, and it was a 1-year-old baby who was shot during a drug deal that went bad. "Everybody was just sad," Sylvia explains. "It was a little tiny baby. We weren't expecting it." She had to say to herself, "Don't think about your son, who's the same age, just get in there and get everybody moving and hope that he survives." He did survive, but for Sylvia it was one of those moments when "you have to be not a mother; not a woman; not a caring, kind person; you just have to function."

These are the occasions she thinks back on and realizes she was courageous only in retrospect. Dr. Campbell believes that it is one reason medical training is the way it is, so that physicians can simply take action when necessary. Part of the process is to leave emotions aside and step in and make decisions, "and then step back out and let the emotions come." Sylvia probably departs from the thinking of many doctors in that she firmly believes that being able to let the emotions come forth eventually is critical to being able to continue the work.

Dr. Campbell acknowledges that tough judgment calls are a part of medicine, and it happens to everyone. "If it doesn't happen to you," she says, "then you're probably not being true to yourself." She also admits that there have been times when she has known the right course of action for a patient, but has not been able to follow through. "Sometimes people just don't want to do what you know is right," she laments. Yet she understands that what she may know is right because of her training may not be right for the person who is her patient. "When they choose not to do it, it's difficult not to get angry," she concedes. "You want to say, how can you do this? How can you not do this?" She sometimes wonders whether if she'd explained things differently, her patient would have made another choice. Yet she realizes that it is not black and white. Her true regret would be "if I ever got to be too black and white, instead of being gray."

> Judgment calls are a part of medicine, and happen to everyone. If it doesn't happen to you, then you're probably not being true to yourself.

Sylvia recalls one case—a laparoscopic surgery. When a laparoscopic surgery is going to be done, the patient is told that the surgeon may need to open, because it is not known positively whether the information is going to be obtainable from the laparoscopy alone. One young girl got very angry about this, and because of this was refusing to sign the permit.

Sylvia "went to talk to her and she was okay once I explained it to her. I think if you just take time and listen to what they're really saying, she was really afraid. I think my biggest regret would be if I let being tired or having a long day get in the way of that, of taking the time to go back and explain things, because usually it's a communication problem." Sylvia adds, "You forget that because you've done this 5 million times, but for that person that day, it's their first and only case; they've never done it before. It's a huge life-changing event for that person. It's so easy to forget that, because it's the same old thing for you; it's routine. But it's not the same old thing for the person on the operating table, or in the hospital bed. It's a huge thing, and we forget that." Dr. Campbell thinks that lessons in these important practices need to be taught more in medical school.

> You may have done [a procedure] five million times, but for that patient, that day, it's a huge life-changing event. . . . It's a huge thing, and we forget that."

On the other hand, Sylvia has had patients whose minds no amount of communication could change. She recalls a patient who was a Jehovah's Witness, whose wife would not allow him to receive blood, and the patient died as a result. "You can't change that; you can't think, 'Can I change their thinking?'" Sylvia expresses. "It's a hard lesson to learn. You present to people what you think is the best thing for them and let them make the decision that they have to make for themselves. It takes a lot of years to get to that point; you have to kind of get beaten up a little along the road before you can reach that point." Sylvia has reached this point of realization and is able to accept that she does not have the power to change minds.

Dr. Campbell believes that "if you heal the body alone, you haven't really healed somebody. You have to heal their spirit as well." She thinks this is not emphasized enough in medicine today. "I think that everybody has some kind of spiritual component to them, and you need to receive that, and accept whatever is there, and include that in what you're doing when you take care of someone . . . We don't do things by ourselves," she attests. "I think we're given the ability to do things to help people heal better, but I think there's another dimension to it that I certainly don't understand, but I know it's there." Sylvia wants to work with this element, in whatever form it presents itself to her patients, so that she can help them heal holistically.

> If you reach out and give of yourself, then you're the one who's really received. If you reach out and try to nourish others, you're really the one who's fed. By being able to reach out and do that, you're touched, you're healed, you're the one who's really allowed to grow and be the person you're supposed to be.

Sylvia hopes that her lasting legacy is about reaching out to other people to heal them. "I think that we leave a little part of ourselves with every person we touch, and we take a little part of them with us, and that continues on," she states. "If you reach out and give of yourself, then you're the one who's really received. If you reach out and try to nourish others, you're really the one who's fed. By being able to reach out and do that, you're touched, you're healed, you're the one who's really allowed to grow and be the person you're supposed to be. If we could all try to understand that, what a better world it would be." Sylvia hopes that her legacy is a significant contribution toward a greater understanding of this human connection.

Dr. Campbell also hopes that the legacy she leaves to colleagues and coworkers is one that emphasizes interdependence. "It's a team effort," she reports. "You can't do anything without the other people there. Each person has a job and role that's just as important as everyone else's. Just because you're the one holding the knife doesn't mean that you're any more important than anyone else. Everyone in that room is important, and everyone involved in the care of the patient is important, and they need to be respected and honored for that." Sylvia hopes that this respect for everyone on the team is a contagious force that spreads throughout healthcare organizations.

Sylvia worries about the state of the medical profession. "It's so easy to get discouraged; it's so easy to listen to all the negatives . . . nobody talks about the good things that happen on a daily basis to all of us, like the little old lady who held your hand and said thank you, or about the patient that says God bless you, or the person who brought you a thank-you card, or a little patient from the free clinic who doesn't have anything, but brought you a little angel from the dollar store. Those are the kind of things. . . . Being able to walk out to the waiting room and say to somebody, 'They're going to be all right.' And see the family and the reaction that they have. Those are the things that people need to think about, you know, not, oh, we have to fight the HMOs and all the insurance paperwork. That's just part of life. Life's not pretty or fun all the time, but that's just the way it is." Sylvia does not consider medicine a job, but a life. She compares it to the work of a friend who is a minister. "A lot of what we do is similar. He doesn't work 9 to 5, and I don't either. It's a life." Indeed, so many lives are enriched because Dr. Campbell answered this calling.

CHAPTER 5

The Doctor Who Flunked Retirement

Dr. Jack McConnell

Throughout his career, Dr. Jack McConnell made widespread contributions to medicine that would affect the quality of many lives. A nationally recognized scientist, Dr. McConnell has served as corporate director of advanced technology at Johnson & Johnson Laboratories, as vice president of new product development at McNeil Laboratories, and as director of clinical research at Lederle Laboratories. He played a leadership role in the development of an early version of the polio vaccine, the tuberculosis tine test, Tylenol in pill form, and the first commercial M.R.I. system used in the United States. He also coauthored the U.S. Senate bill authorizing the Human Genome Project and is a founding trustee of the Institute for Genomic Research. By anybody's standards, Dr. McConnell had a stunningly successful career, but it turned out that there was something at which he was a spectacular failure—retirement. He moved to Hilton Head, South Carolina, thinking that he might get to play a bit of golf, but just could not keep himself from responding to people's needs.

Jack noticed that a large number of the resort island's low-income residents had no health care. To serve them, he started a free medical clinic, luring recently retired physicians and nurses back to work by offering them a way to practice medicine in the fashion of days gone by—an unhurried, personal approach that predates managed care. When he founded the first Volunteers in Medicine Clinic in 1994, Dr. McConnell persuaded South Carolina lawmakers to waive the typical licensing procedures, obtained blanket malpractice coverage for a fraction of the normal rate, and even coaxed local contractors to donate their construction services. Now, the national Volunteers in Medicine Institute is using McConnell's model to build a network of free clinics nationwide; so far it has opened over 65 clinics from coast to coast. Because of McConnell's tireless efforts, the U.S. Congress passed a law that gives volunteers in free medical clinics federal malpractice protection.

Jack's postretirement career has made such a difference for so many people that the American Medical Foundation has honored him by creating the Jack B. McConnell, MD Award for Excellence in Volunteerism, which recognizes the work of senior physicians who provide treatment to U.S. patients who lack access to health care. But perhaps Jack McConnell's greatest contribution to quality of life worldwide is found in his concept of a circle of caring. He calls this concept the spiritual foundation of Volunteers in Medicine.

Dr. McConnell attended undergraduate studies at the University of Virginia, Charlottesville, and earned his medical degree from the University of Tennessee School of Medicine, Memphis. He continued his postgraduate training in pediatrics at Baylor College of Medicine, Houston, Texas. He also attended business school programs at Harvard University and Columbia University.

Jack McConnell began thinking about becoming a doctor when he was 6 or 7 years old, the youngest of seven children, and the only one still at home during the day with his mother, who suffered from a respiratory illness. He began to take care of her. "She directed me and gave me feedback. I spent so much time with her that I began to say, this taking care of people is not a bad idea." He also admired her physician, a crusty old fellow who sat down and answered Jack's questions. "It was then that I determined that I would become a physician." That very same curmudgeonly doctor gave Jack one of his first jobs in high school, working at his office. Yet surprisingly, Jack is credited with having a warm and empathic bedside manner.

Jack recalls being outside the doctor's office early one morning, waiting for the office to open. As the doctor was coming up the bottom stairs, a woman was struggling up the steps, taking short breaths. "He said, 'What's wrong, Agnes?' She said, 'I'm just sort of out of breath.' And he said, 'Are you taking that medicine that I gave you?' She replied, 'Yes.' 'How did you get here?' 'I walked.' He replied, 'Well, if you walked 4 miles here, you can walk 4 miles back. And when you get home, take that medicine!'" Dr. McConnell notes that, however harsh and inappropriate, the doctor had a sense of humor too, and "was also very giving. You could call him any time of the day or night and he'd be there in 10 minutes. He was an old-style physician." Since Dr. McConnell describes himself as a soft touch, it seems he was able to take the very best qualities from his role model, while leaving behind what he did not want to replicate.

Perhaps his patience with patients was learned at home. Dr. McConnell describes his family as close knit. His first supporter was his mother, "but my dad was right behind her." His mother and father were born and raised in log cabins that their parents had built. She became a schoolteacher. He was a farmer, "a bright sort of fella, but a bit of a roustabout. He courted my mother, and she said, 'I will consider marrying you, but no promises, mind you, until you get a college education.' He had not finished high school. So he crammed his 6′3″, 200-pound frame into a desk and finished high school. Then he alternately rode and walked his mule a distance of about 75–80 miles to a small Methodist college in southwest Virginia. He was looking around for a place to enroll when he came to a sign that said, 'President's Home.' He was not a shy fellow, so he tied the mule to the fence and knocked on the door. The president opens it and my dad says, 'Good morning, I'm Enoch Luther McConnell, and I want to attend Emory and Henry College.' The president asks, 'Have you registered?' And he says, 'That's what I think I'm doing right now.' The president continued, 'Do you have any money?' He replied, 'No I don't have any.' The president took a second look at him and asked, 'Have you had breakfast this morning?' My father replied, 'No, nor supper or dinner yesterday either.' He went in and had breakfast. The outcome was the president decided my dad could sleep in his basement, take care of the furnace in the wintertime and the yard in the spring and the fall, and that would be his tuition." Dr. McConnell continues, "He finished the 2-year course, which was all that Emory and Henry provided in 1906. He then went back home to see my mother and said, 'Mattie I've done what you want me to do, but you may not wish to marry me now, because I have found Christ and I intend to be a Methodist preacher.' She threw her hands up and said, 'Thank God, my prayers have been answered.' They were married shortly afterwards." Dr. McConnell recalls, "I never heard a cross word between them. They were very gentle and kind with each other." Dr. McConnell clearly incorporated the sweet qualities he learned from his parents into his approach with patients.

Dr. McConnell is clear that he learned his basic respect for humanity from his mother and father. "It was around the table where we ate and talked and in the examples they set for us. Every night my father would say the blessing, and then he would look up and ask us, 'Well, what have you done for someone today?' If you had nothing to say, that was okay. You could just say pass the gravy and get on with your eating. But if you did something, you were the hero of the night, and everyone around the table knew it. We always wanted to be the only one to have a project. If you did, our dad would ask us, 'Where do you plan to do it? How big do you think it's going to be? How much is it going to cost? Who around the table would you like to work for you?'" Clearly, Jack's dad showed him early in life what skills are needed to do strategic business planning.

> Every night my father would say the blessing, and then he would look up and ask us, 'Well, what have you done for someone today?' If you had nothing to say, that was okay. You could just say pass the gravy and get on with your eating. But if you did something, you were the hero of the night, and everyone around the table knew it.

Jack remembers when his dad assigned him a project. Jack had been working at a small shoe repair shop and noticed a pile of shoes that had been repaired but seemed to have been there a long time. After a period of time, he asked the owner of the shop if he could have the shoes to give to people who were in dire need. The owner said yes. When Jack mentioned at the supper table that he had several shoes to give away, his father assigned two of his older siblings to help him with the project. "It was one of the best memories of my life. My father not only taught us the joy of giving, but how to organize it for success." Teamwork learned from his father enabled Dr. McConnell to open his clinics many decades later. "I owe him the credit for the Volunteers in Medicine Clinic here on Hilton Head and all the clinics that we've opened." It is clear how much Jack himself loved and respected his father and how he has taken on his legacy and made it grow.

Although Jack knew early on that he wanted to be a physician, his path was not linear. When he graduated from high school, he had planned to enlist and become a pilot for the length of his military service. In the course of going through the medical exam for basic training, the X-ray machine malfunctioned. The examiner said, 'You are okay except for the X-ray. We cannot give you an assignment now but when you go for your induction they will take an X-ray there and if it is okay, you will be in the air force.' I went back and told my father of the experience." But mysteriously, 2 months later, Jack received word that he was assigned to the navy V-12 program at University of Virginia. Dr. McConnell has no idea how the decision was made. "But," he says, "I wouldn't be at all surprised if Daddy contacted a congressman regarding the issue. To this day I don't know how I was placed in the program. "I can believe I had earned it as I was near the top of my class." Whether his father or fate intervened, Dr. McConnell made the most of his opportunity.

> I never let obstacles get in the way of a good project that had merit and worth. You have to know who you are and what you believe in order to succeed. Otherwise you're just lost in the palm of someone else who is leading you astray.

At University of Virginia (UVA), Jack took every course he could find to prepare himself for medical school. But he did not graduate from college. "I still don't have a bachelor degree. I went 2 years straight, 24 months, which would equate pretty much to 4 years of college today." But he did not take the humanities requirements needed to fill his liberal arts credits, and he did not care. And neither did the navy. He continued marching, going to class, working in the labs, and studying. Dr. McConnell focused on what was important to him.

Jack was confident his good grades in the sciences would get him into medical school. It helped that there was one chemistry teacher who expressed pride in Jack. "That just sets a fire in a boy who is trying hard." Years later, when Jack was in business, that same teacher came to the pharmaceutical company seeking a grant for one of his projects. Jack did not know he was coming, but happened to be walking by the president's office when his former teacher called out his name. "I was delighted to see him again. He said, 'I have had you on my mind several times.' We chatted for awhile and then I escorted him into the president's office and introduced him to the president with the highest recommendation. He received the grant." To help someone who had supported him when supporters were rare was obviously very gratifying for Dr. McConnell.

Jack does not remember anyone keeping him from his progress. Perhaps this is because he learned a lot about diplomacy along the way. "There were those who saw things differently, but I never allowed a relationship to implode because of a friendly difference. I managed somehow to work things out so everyone was on board." There were those who opposed what Dr. McConnell wanted to do, however, he says, "I never let it get in the way of a good project that had merit and worth. You have to know who you are and what you believe in order to succeed. Otherwise you're just lost in the palm of someone else who is leading you astray." Because he knew himself so well and his own goals were so clear to him, neither the lack of supporters nor the different thinkers forestalled Dr. McConnell.

Like so many young physicians in training during the World War II era, Jack admired Dr. Albert Schweitzer. "My thought at one time was that, like Schweitzer, I would be a missionary in Africa. I read lots of books about it and consulted with my pastor, and he encouraged me to wait until I finished medical school—which was probably very good advice." Dr. McConnell continued to read Schweitzer's books and articles and to view him as a role model. One of his few regrets to this day is that he did not travel to Africa as a medical missionary.

As a young man, Dr. McConnell endured a medical challenge that changed the direction of his career. He had just finished his training program, internship, and residency when he was inducted back into the navy. The medical examination revealed a cavity in the right upper lobe of his lung. With the techniques then available, they suspected tuberculosis but could not confirm it. The hospital where he had trained put him on total bed rest so he did not get a chance to go directly into practice. Instead, he spent a year flat on his back. "My feet never touched the floor, and whatever I did during the day, I had to do in bed." All of the doctors with whom he had trained left, and his remaining friends were busy with residencies and starting practices. The room in which Jack was placed was a cell that had been designed for prisoners. "I became claustrophobic and shouted for them to get me out of there." They finally moved him to a corner room with windows, and that made it a little better. Yet Dr. McConnell describes his caregivers during that time as consistently wonderful.

The year that Dr. McConnell spent in bed recuperating from TB was another turning point in his life. The only thing he could do was read. He read every journal he could lay his hands on from cover to cover, many of which he would not have read otherwise—the *American Medical Association Journal*, several science journals, internal medicine journals, and all of the specialties. One friend collected outdated journals and brought them to Jack. Another asked how he could help. He built what Jack asked for: a rack that would fit across his lap on which his books could rest. Then he could read without having to hold his hands up all day. "It was a handsome little thing. I wish I still had it, it meant a lot to me, but I gave it to another patient when I left."

Jack had been thinking about being a pediatrician, but from his reading, he realized that he did not want to follow that path. He did not think it would be stimulating enough after he learned what else was going on in the world of medicine. "I realized I wanted to go into the scientific world where the new drugs were being discovered. The world of practice didn't seem as challenging anymore. It seemed too confining and limited. So I set out to learn all the science I possibly could that was being done by the pharmaceutical industry." When he was released from the confinement of total bed rest, he signed on to sail as a ship's doctor on cruises through the Caribbean. A few months later, he joined the pharmaceutical industry. Dr. McConnell was able to use the unexpected moratorium that his illness offered to find the scale of work he wanted to pursue.

> I don't get angry or frustrated. It is the wrong way to use your energy. . . . If you're not calm and confident within yourself, you're not going to be able to convince anyone else of the merit of your project.

Asked what gets him up every morning and keeps him going, Dr. McConnell recalls that when he first moved to Hilton Head, he thought, "Great! I'm free now. I can play golf and travel and eat in good restaurants." But he had never been so bored in his life. His father's words came back to him: "What have you done for someone today?" He realized he could spend his time more wisely. As a board member of the local hospital, he began to make rounds to see the hospital patients, trying to see if they were pleased by the care they had received, and, if not, how to improve it. He noticed there were no African Americans in the hospital, and mentioned that to the chairman of the board. He said, "No, they don't like to come here; they prefer to go elsewhere." When Jack asked why not, the chairman said, 'They don't feel comfortable here.'" Jack sensed there might be a prejudice toward African-Americans and he just let the subject drop for the moment.

To assess the situation, Jack began picking up workers who were hitchhiking at the end of their day's work and driving them to their destination. He asked where they got their health care. "And they all said the same thing, 'We don't get any.' I asked, 'what if you were to break your leg?' And they said, 'Oh, well, they'll set it and send us home the next day.'" It was then that Jack was determined to help.

At church the next Sunday. he noticed there were a half a dozen retired doctors, and two or three retired nurses. Suspecting there were more on the island, he realized that he had been handed what he needed—retired medical professionals. "I committed to using retired doctors and nurses to provide the care at the free health clinic I wished to develop." He invited the retired healthcare providers on the island to a meeting to hear an influential and nationally known speaker in the field of medicine. Twenty-seven showed up. Jack told them what he wanted to do, and after going into some detail, he asked each of them for help. Eighteen physicians said yes. The others had valid reasons not to continue practicing. All of the nurses in attendance said yes. Dr. McConnell's initiative, begun in the early 1990s, was a forerunner and inspiration to many of the church-based nursing ministries in this country as well.

> When we first opened the clinic, the people would come in and sort of slide in quietly as if they were trying not to be seen or heard and did not belong there. Now we greet them, shake their hand and those we have known for a long time give a big hug. There is a place for the children to play while their mothers and fathers go into the examining rooms. This is the way medicine ought to be practiced.

What keeps Dr. McConnell going today is his belief that his idea has not spread as widely as it can. "I will not stop," he vows, "until it is a national organization." He is also inspired by the "joy of walking into our clinic and talking to the people who come in there and need our help . . . We are starting clinics all across the country. If you get a good idea rolling, others will want it for their community. That is encouraging." His determination, his experience of joy, and the encouragement that comes from the appreciation of communities that have had success with his ideas are the driving forces behind Dr. McConnell's continuous work on behalf of others.

Dr. McConnell's goals with Volunteers in Medicine are tied to his personal sense of ethics through his religious beliefs. "It is my service to Christ. I help the poor, the hungry, the thirsty, the sick, and the lonely, and provide them with care. That's a large part of my personal ethic. It is an outgrowth of what I learned around our dinning room table when I was a child growing up. It is one of the most satisfying and rewarding things I can think of to do in life. It gives me a sense of satisfaction in seeing the patients heal and mature and blossom into contributing citizens of our community." Dr. McConnell's personal ethics and sense of self are fully integrated with his vision for Volunteers in Medicine.

Dr. McConnell is very clear about the obstacles in the way of his goals for Volunteers in Medicine. "The problem that we face is that there are 48 million without access to health care in the United States. And there is no state, except Massachusetts, that is ever going to supply all of the care that is needed. It is not honest of us to spend our money on a war that is a disaster rather than spend that money on health care for the 48 million who have no access to health care and are being neglected."

Jack is equally clear on what he sees as the solution. "There are 250,000 retired physicians, and more than twice that many nurses. Using a portion of them, we could provide care to most of the uninsured without costing the government a dime, and create joy along the way." He sees no reason it could not be done and reiterates that it is achievable without the federal government being involved at all and at no cost to the nation.

Asked to detail the obstacles, Dr. McConnell elaborates. "We needed to get legislation passed in the House and Senate to provide malpractice protection for those who volunteer their time in free health clinics." He was excited when he received an invitation from the White House to meet with then-President George W. Bush in North Carolina, where he was to speak endorsing Elizabeth Dole for the Senate. Ten physicians were invited and two brought a patient along with them. The president brought with him Secretary of Health and Human Services Tommy Thompson.

During the discussion that followed, Jack had a chance to talk with Bush. "I told him I was a retired physician and not in practice but I developed free health clinics for the uninsured. I asked if he could help me get a law passed to provide protection from malpractice for the retired physicians and nurses who volunteered their time in the free health clinics. I quite obviously had thrown him a question he was not expecting and was unable to answer." Jack describes President Bush as fumbling with a response and then moving on to the next question and a short speech. The president later said to Jack, "'You were wrong about the 43 million not having access to health care. They do. They can go to the emergency rooms. The docs there are good docs and strong docs. So there!' And with that he got up abruptly, walked out of the room, and left."

At the end of the meeting as everyone was gathering their effects, Jack noticed that Secretary Thompson was the only one left in the room. Dr. McConnell asked if he could come to Washington to visit with him to explain what he did. "Without hesitating he reached into his bag and gave me his card and, while looking me in the eye said, 'Call me.' It was not an invitation but more like a command. I liked his straightforward manner very much." Clearly, this opportunity foreshadowed important progress to come.

About 3 weeks later, Jack received a call from Thompson's office asking him to come visit in Washington, D.C. Dr. McConnell went and was permitted to give a very brief pitch for his idea. About 4 months later, he got a call from a staff member who said, "here are the names of the four congressmen that you need to contact." Jack followed up and 8 months later received a call saying that the bill had been passed, and they hoped it was satisfactory for his needs. Jack noted that they had expanded and improved upon his request. Dr. McConnell hopes that our newly elected officials "will look favorably on our project, and see the value of using the retired medical professionals to provide care for the uninsured in our nation."

Jack believes wholeheartedly in the value of his initiative and is deeply invested in it. He notes that the clinics can unite a community in a way that many projects cannot. There were a total of 60 clinics from coast to coast at the time of our interview, with plans for 30 more in progress.

When I asked Dr. McConnell how he keeps from getting burnt out, he stated, "I don't get angry or frustrated. It is the wrong way to use your energy. Persuasion is what you want to be able to do, and if you're not calm and confident within yourself, you're not going to be able to convince anyone else of the merit of your project." Dr. McConnell has learned to center himself from within in order to be able to make the best and most effective use of his strengths to the benefit of his projects and for those who benefit from them.

Dr. McConnell used to play golf to maintain his balance from day to day but has learned that helping others who are in need is one of the most rewarding things anyone can do. "Nothing can compare to it. I learned that golf is fun but helping others is joy." Dr. McConnell has found a way to make his work be his way of maintaining balance, a trick many other professionals would love to be able to perform.

Dr. McConnell denies that he ever gets upset; he says, "I just don't get steamed up. I used to at times but learned that it did not help and often made matters worse." He actively pursues a habit that helps him maintain his sense of humor. "If I'm feeling fatigued, I have a set of joke books, and I will get one or two out and lean back in my chair and read a few of those, and it cleans the air in no time at all. A good laugh is therapeutic. There is nothing like it." Joy, laughter, and a sense of purpose keep Dr. McConnell going. His long marriage to wife Mary Ellen is a gift as well. "I could not have married anyone I would have loved more or who would have been more suitable for me."

> Burnout is the result of rushing to make money, and the way to solve it is to give yourself away free of charge. If you can't do it in the middle of the week, do it on the weekends or in the evening. It is therapeutic, relaxing, and good for your soul.

I comment that Dr. McConnell's wife helps him maintain balance in his life, and he wholeheartedly agrees. "Does she ever! She is extremely bright, valedictorian of her class. I met her when both of us were working for Lederle Laboratories."

Dr. McConnell recalls times of courage and of cowardice. "When we first tried to get the free health clinic under way, the chairman of the hospital pretty much tossed me out of the door. But I knew I was not going to allow him to prevent the poor from obtaining health care that they desperately needed. And then there was the time I went up to the state capital to get a special license for the physicians who were going to be practicing in our free health clinic." Jack is not sure what happened, but in spite of being there waiting his turn to speak, he got knocked off the agenda. He was treated in a patronizing fashion. "I found myself in a bit of a mess. We had about 20 physicians and 30 nurses revved up and raring to go, but they could not practice without being licensed in South

Carolina. The only thing I could do was get in my car and get out of there. That was the only time in my life that I ever remember being despondent. I was in the middle of the project, and I had just been undercut for reasons unknown to me."

Jack recalled an occasion when he gave a talk to a group in Columbia, the capital of South Carolina. One of the attendees was on the governor's staff. "I called and asked if he could help me. He said, 'I know what you want but I can't help. You need to go through a member of the legislature; call this congressman.'" Jack called and told him what he wanted. "I told him that I wanted him to get a one-sentence amendment attached to a bill going through the legislature that no one was going to read and everyone was going to vote for. He said, 'Jack we don't do anything like that around here.'" But Dr. McConnell countered that since the general assembly would be adjourning in a few weeks, the pressure on the legislature would be more frenetic and intense, so that maybe the strategy would work. "He called back the next day and his only words were, 'You keep your head down and your mouth shut.'" Toward the end of the month the congressman called to say, 'Jack, come up here day after tomorrow and bring your pen for a signing party.'" When Jack arrived he learned that the governor had been very much in favor of what his group was doing. This was a big step forward for Volunteers in Medicine and gave all of Jack's colleagues some hope.

Dr. McConnell continues to be creative whenever it is necessary. "Some of the volunteers did not have malpractice insurance, and they would have been at risk for a lawsuit. At the recommendation of the president of the South Carolina Medical Association, I contacted the head of the Joint Underwriters Association, which insures most of the physicians in the state. I received a letter from him saying he would do it for $50,000 per year. At the time the project had less than $15,000 in the bank. I wrote him back and said his secretary had made a mistake and misplaced the decimal point, but I had corrected it so that it read $5,000, and I was including my check for the amount. He called me back and with a chuckle said how surprised he was to see the amount, but he understood fully and would accept the money I had offered. We became very good friends and were until the day he died." This is yet another example of effective persuasion by Dr. McConnell.

Jack firmly believes that there is a spiritual component to what he does. He sees the manifestation of this in his clinics. "If you were to come into one of our clinics, you would see that it is one of the most happy and joy-filled places one can imagine. Everyone who works there is happy. When we first opened the clinic, the people would come in and sort of slide in quietly as if they were trying not to be seen or heard and did not belong there. Now we greet them, shake their hand and those we have known for a long time give a big hug. There is a place for the children to play while their mothers and fathers go into the examining rooms. This is the way medicine ought to be practiced. Nowadays, when you go to a doctor's office, you might get 15 minutes of his time and then you are ushered out. That is not the way medicine ought to be practiced." Dr. McConnell believes that if medicine is practiced in the way it is intended, patients and physicians will experience true connection and fulfillment.

Dr. McConnell also suggests that burnout is the result of "rushing to make money" and the way to solve it "to give yourself away free of charge. If you can't do it in the middle of the week, do it on the weekends or in the evening. It is therapeutic and enormously rewarding. It is enormously relaxing and good for your soul." He wishes his physician colleagues could be brought in to speak to groups of young students and share the joy of helping others.

Jack recognizes that giving one's self to one in need is the stuff life is made of. Work is the stuff a living is made of. Each is essential for a full life. Dr. McConnell would like to be remembered as someone who "treated everyone with equality, courtesy, and respect." He would like his legacy to be "that I helped those in need, even if my own schedule was disrupted. And I hope one can say that I lived a healthy, wholesome, and honest life and set a good example for my wife and children."

Dr. McConnell has no regrets about the way he's lived his life. He states, "I have had a good life. I have enjoyed every minute of it and the things I have done." Confident of his ability to make the most of life, he adds, "If I had taken a different road, I expect I would have had a good time doing that as well."

CHAPTER 6

A Voice for the Urban and Rural Poor

Dr. Bruce Gould

Dr. Bruce Gould is the associate dean for primary care at University of Connecticut Medical School, medical director of the Saint Francis/ University of Connecticut Primary Care Center at the Burgdorf/Bank of America Health Center in Hartford, Connecticut, and medical director of the Hartford Department of Health and Human Services. He also serves as director of the Connecticut Area Health Education Center Program, which is dedicated to providing better and accessible health care for marginalized populations. Long a champion of interdisciplinary care, Bruce thinks that differences between disciplines seem to dissolve when individuals from varied professions realize that they share a common vision of providing quality care to the underserved.

Dr. Gould has created innovative programs to provide medical assistance to migrant farm workers. Under his direction, the farm workers program has flourished and is now part of a larger collaboration of organizations. Staffed in part by University of Connecticut medical students, the program also enlists students from the dental, pharmacy, and nursing schools, as well as healthcare students from other colleges and universities. He is the faculty advisor for the University of Connecticut medical students' chapter of Habitat for Humanity. He helped to create the Connecticut Youth Health Services Corp to help inner-city youth pursue careers in medicine.

An Eagle Scout, Dr. Gould has served as a Cub Scout and Boy Scout leader, as well as an assistant soccer coach for his son's team. The family is also involved in his activities. He is known to bring his children to work at homeless shelters, migrant worker camps, or to read in clinic waiting rooms as part of the Reach Out and Read program.

Dr. Gould attended Cornell University in Ithaca, New York, and went on to study medicine at SUNY Upstate Medical Center in Syracuse. Following residency training in General Internal Medicine at the University of Massachusetts Medical Center in Worcester, Massachusetts, he became chief medical resident there and then completed a fellowship in general internal medicine and primary care.

Dr. Gould is the recipient of community service awards from Hartford County Medical Association and the 2006 Making a Difference Award from the National Health Service Corps Ambassadors Program in Washington, D.C. He has served as chairman of the National Advisory Council on Migrant Health, a program of the U.S. Department of Health and Human Services, Health Resources and Services Administration.

Bruce Gould knew he wanted to become a doctor when he was quite young. Childhood thoughts of becoming an archaeologist, paleontologist, or astronaut were left behind with the death of his uncle, a physician, when Bruce was 5 years old. The critical role of a pediatrician impressed him when he was 3 years old and was mauled by a dog that bit his eye out, leaving his lid hanging by a thread of skin. His pediatrician, familiar with the wounds of war from which he had just returned, was able to stitch the eye so that Bruce could see and had no visible scars. This skillful craftsmanship was very impressive to young Bruce.

By the time Bruce was in high school, he was still pretty sure he wanted to be a physician. He remembers that he confided his plans to his dying grandmother. Summer camp had helped his plans to jell. The camp doctor told him how wonderful it was to be a doctor, and that it was a way to help people. Bruce had been looking for something that would have some impact, and becoming a doctor certainly fit that criteria.

His intention was further solidified by spending his final high school semester doing medical research at Creedmoor State Hospital, a psychiatric institute, in Queens, New York. He was able to do this because he had completed enough credits to graduate by the end of the first semester of his senior year. The experience gave him insight into the plight of the elderly disabled and mentally ill who were warehoused at the sprawling asylum and reinforced his commitment to social and healthcare justice.

In college, he studied neurobiology and enjoyed it very much. He found an important early supporter in a biologist/endocrinologist professor at Cornell. Bruce recalled that Dr. Van Tienhoven (Dr. V.) "saw something in me and encouraged what he saw." The professor provided a home in his lab for Bruce. Dr. Gould thinks so highly of Dr. V that he keeps in touch and recently made the professor pay up on an old bet by buying Bruce dinner. Thirty years ago, Dr. V had bet Bruce that he would end up in an affluent suburb working with wealthy patients like so many of his other premed students.

Meeting his future wife in college meant that Bruce had another supportive companion. "Lisa has allowed me to do what I needed to do. When I had to go off to the National Advisory Council on Migrant Health meeting, or wherever, she didn't make me feel guilty or beholden—unlike some of my colleagues. She has been a partner in everything I've done."

Bruce was strongly influenced also by Rabbi Sokobin, his rabbi growing up, whom he describes as intensely bright, but humble and approachable. "He has great integrity and walks his talk." Dr. Gould remembers sitting in the congregation and watching the rabbi holding an article he had cut from the New York Times, "incensed at the injustice and the lack of action by all the rest of us." One of the effects of being influenced by the rabbi is Dr. Gould's strong sense that "we all have responsibility for the well-being of those around us." He lives this every day, even stopping at traffic accidents to see whether he can be of help.

Dr. Gould's personality does not let him give up with patients. "I go into a room and for the 30,000th time I say, 'you gotta quit smoking.' I never know when I might be the one who makes the difference." Affirming that change is possible, he is also a realist sensitive to different needs and personal styles among his patients. "There are certain patients where I don't even have to say anything. They say, yep, I know, I gotta quit smoking, but they're not ready and I understand that. So I don't harangue them and I don't embarrass them, but they know that I'm there for them when they're ready." Being there for his patients and for his close friends and family is of primary importance to Bruce.

> You never know when you are giving somebody a goal at an early age that keeps them on track.... There are so many ways that kids can get diverted and waste their lives. If you can just put out that little extra something, you may be saving someone's life.

A friend's health crisis had an intense impact on Dr. Gould. He still feels angry about some of the ways that the friend, who had chronic lymphocytic leukemia, was treated by the healthcare system, despite his efforts to intervene. Bruce recalls one incident. "I went over to see him and I was afraid he was going to go into respiratory arrest. I called the ICU and they said, 'well, he doesn't meet criteria.' I called his attending and said, 'I was just in seeing him, his respiratory rate is 25, he's in pending respiratory failure, and he's at the end of the hall where no one's watching him. I was going to lose sleep all night tonight worrying about him, but I can't do anything about it. You're the attending, you can do something, so guess what? You can lose sleep about it now.'" On that occasion, Dr. Gould was successful; the attending physician responded and his friend received more appropriate care.

But the last time he was in the hospital, Dr. Gould recalls, "he was quickly failing; his kidneys were shutting down, his lungs were filling up, and they wanted to intubate. I remember him turning to me and saying, 'Bruce, what should I do? Should I let them do this?' He needed it. But I couldn't get them to tap a collection of fluid in his lungs. The staff who normally does that had left for the day. I tried pulling strings, but it just wasn't going to happen." He died the next day and although it would not have changed anything, Bruce is still haunted by this failure of caring.

His friend's nurses and residents were "wonderful, but they were practicing at the very edge of their comfort zone. And the nurses knew it." Dr. Gould went to the administration to share his concerns and see if some positive change might come out of the tragedy of his friend's death. "When you take care of the poor, you figure out how to make the system work even if it doesn't want to."

Dr. Gould has used the knowledge and understanding he gained from his friend's experience to his patients' benefit. It was a reminder that, "The healthcare system is a very dangerous thing, and it's gotten more dangerous as the level of complexity has increased, and the number of things we might do to people has proliferated." When his own family members have had medical crises, Bruce has monitored their care very closely. For one family member, he "lived at the hospital for a week . . . hovering over her and protecting her from the healthcare system." Dr. Gould explains, "There are basic things you have to do, because the healthcare system is so incredibly chaotic. Unless the patient marches in step with the expectation for recovery for a particular illness or procedure, they may be doomed." Bruce notes it is extra work to pick up those patients who have fallen off the critical pathway to recovery. Dr. Gould seems to be especially attuned to helping those who have gotten left behind.

Bruce is a major proponent of the role of nutrition in medicine. He is very aware of the hugely underdiagnosed problem of malnutrition in the elderly. Having expressed an interest in the issue, Dr. Gould was assigned to direct the nutrition curriculum at the medical school. He does not consider himself an expert, but as having learned a lot, and knowing a lot more about the subject than most of his colleagues.

He has had difficulty expanding nutrition into the medical school curriculum, but, as with his patients, he has not given up. "Certainly it's about persistence," he explains, "If I look back over my life, what has served me best probably is persistence."

One of his first introductions to underserved communities came from attending the funeral of a colleague's brother who had died of AIDS. "It was the late 80s in inner-city Hartford and having moved from Worcester, it was a real cultural shock. But I liked the diversity, I liked the challenge. I wanted to work with people who really needed help . . . I went into a community where I was taking care of the poorest of the poor. Many are immigrants. We see dengue, we see leprosy."

Dr. Gould contrasts this with his previous practice at the University of Massachusetts, where he was taking care of the "White worried well, middle-class or above. Of course, you can have an impact with them." But Bruce feels his influence is much greater with his marginalized patient base. "A lot of my patients have such low expectations of what the healthcare system and life have to offer them, that just a kind word and caring has incredible repercussions for them and their families."

Bruce offers an example from his morning clinic, when he went in to do a physical with a young Black woman from Hartford who had completed community college and was going to Virginia to complete her undergraduate work. She had brought two nieces along, aged 4 and 10 years. Bruce took his stethoscope off and showed them how to use it.

They listened to his heart and their own. He asked if they wanted to be doctors, and they said yes. He recognizes that next week that idea may evaporate, but "you never know when you are giving somebody a goal at an early age that keeps them on track. . . . There are so many ways that kids can get diverted and waste their lives. If you can just put out that little extra something, you may be saving someone's life."

Listening and being in the moment with patients are central to Bruce's practice. "The patient needs to feel that you are really there for them." He recalled a patient who was an alcoholic, a former drug addict, and was dying of lung cancer. He sat down and asked what was on her mind. He asked if she believed in Jesus. "Yes," she said. Did she believe she was going to a better place? "Yes." He told her that, "this may be the best time in your life because you really don't have to worry anymore. You can't do anything after you're gone. You've done what you can do, and God will take care of the rest." She smiled. Reaching beyond his own personal beliefs, Bruce is able to be in the moment with his patients. "Cultural competence means understanding the beliefs of your patients, and reaching into those beliefs to better understand their perception of their illness or treatment, to give them comfort or to give them what they need, so that they can either make it through treatment or perhaps let go."

Dr. Gould has learned to set boundaries. He tells students they can help, advise, and coach, but their own self-esteem cannot depend on whether the patient follows their suggestions. "I've slowly realized that you can't do everything for everyone. You have to remind yourself that you've done what you can do." In a note Bruce sent me prior to our interview he spoke to this balancing act . . . "At times I'm tired and drained . . . but "I like what I do, I just sometimes do it more than I like!" I have my moments . . . they are fewer perhaps and farther between . . . of inspiration, of zest, of wanting to do battle with the world and fix it. But there are also mornings when I say . . . I don't want to do this anymore, at the top of my lungs through the steam in the shower. I don't really mean it . . . I just don't want to *have* to do this anymore . . . don't want to be paid, to have it be my job. I just want to heal and be healed in the process . . . the pure act . . . not adulterated by the economics and realities of the marketplace of medicine."

For Dr. Gould, however, that is counterbalanced by going the extra distance to overcome the barriers of what he describes as an anachronistic healthcare system. One frustration is getting specialists to waive their substantial fees to do a 20-minute procedure that could rule out cancer. Although Bruce is careful not to shame his patients, he feels he has no choice but to shame his colleagues, because, "by and large, unless I grovel, the patients don't necessarily get the care. Some specialties are more difficult to access than others. Time and time again, some colleagues will see the patient in the hospital, but not follow up on the outside unless they bring 200 bucks." Yet he does not expect them to sabotage their own practices. "If a doctor opens his practice to Medicaid or nonpaying patients, they will be bankrupt within a month. You have to open all the practices at once; you have to share the load. It is a systemic problem of our American healthcare system!"

Asked about his biggest failure to date, Dr. Gould strongly states, "There are always things that you did or missed, that you feel badly about. If doctors say they don't, they're lying." The case of John, an 88 year-old bricklayer who was still working, is one of those cases for Dr. Gould. John was found to have colon cancer on screening colonoscopy and had it removed. About a year after his colon cancer surgery, he became anemic, so I had him scoped again through the colostomy; they found some polyps and took them out. That's the good part of the story. He went home on Friday. On Monday morning, John and his granddaughter were waiting in the parking lot for Dr. Gould. In pain since Saturday night, he refused to see anyone else. Bruce examined him in the parking lot, suspected a bowel perforation and sent him to the emergency room. Calling the emergency department later, he was told that surgery had seen John and sent him for a computerized tomography (CT) scan. They would handle it from here. Bruce thought great, he's tucked in. Following his Boy Scout meeting that evening, he was driving by the hospital around 8:30 and decided to stop. He found John sitting in the corner of the emergency room. He was getting a bag of saline, but otherwise, "they forgot about him. No antibiotics. He kept getting bumped for the CT scan. The shifts had changed. And I had a tantrum. I don't usually have tantrums, but I was really upset."

> Cultural competence means understanding the beliefs of your patients, and reaching into those beliefs to better understand their perception of their illness or treatment, to give them comfort or to give them what they need, so that they can either make it through treatment, or perhaps let go.

Within an hour, John was in the operating room. He lived. But he never laid brick again. He wound up in a nursing home. "I don't know that anything would have turned out differently. You never do. But I feel badly. The healthcare system failed." Dr. Gould asks himself what part of this might have been his failure, and he is unsure. "Should I have been more suspicious? I thought I had handed off. In fact I had. But someone needed to turn the light on. And it didn't happen. He died about a year later."

Dr. Gould's failure is inseparable from the failure of the system as a whole. He believes it is necessary for each patient to have an advocate in order to do well in the healthcare system. Both his mother and his mother-in-law would be dead if they had not had the benefit of his advocacy.

In the face of his many challenges, Dr. Gould maintains a sense of humor. He has "always had the sense of the absurdity of life and of humanity" and attributes his ability to joke about serious things in part to his Jewish culture. He uses this type of humor with his patients, and claims that he can "usually make people laugh about almost anything." He also uses humor with his colleagues, saying funny things at meetings—not, he points out, hurtful zingers, but "just things that bring up the absurdity of what we're doing." Asked what led him to practice in the way he does, Bruce recalls again his own pediatrician. "Maybe the stories and my memory of him," Dr. Gould conjectures, "reinforced by the Marcus Welby mystique, led me to where I am and the way I practice medicine." A genuine liking of people also led him to medicine. "I value or accept as a gift the fact that people let me into their lives, the intimate nooks and crannies of their lives." This access also gives Bruce a perspective on his own life as he compares the level of chaos in their lives to his very rich and fulfilling life.

> I value or accept as a gift the fact that people let me into their lives, the intimate nooks and crannies of their lives.

Bruce also credits his parents for teaching him care and giving. Their activism also influenced him. "My mother's mother actually chained herself to the capitol in Albany on behalf of rights for elders. My mother did the same at the UN. The Goulds have a long history of chaining themselves to public buildings in protest of injustice." Having spent time in orphanages as a child, Bruce's father was "caring, giving, and appreciative of the blessings he had, and that transferred to me."

Every time a patient dies, Dr. Gould looks through the chart, asking himself whether there was something he did or something he missed. From time to time, he thinks about a patient he had as an intern. Bruce was tapering his high-dose steroids that were being given as treatment for rheumatologic disease. "The patient had a stroke and eventually he died. To this day I don't know if my tapering his medication so quickly had a hand in his death. I still remember his name and can see his face . . . If you take things to heart, how do you not let them drive you crazy?" he asks rhetorically.

Despite this, Dr. Gould says he does not have many regrets. Sometimes he looks at more successful friends and regrets that he did not pursue a similar path. "But most of the time," Bruce avers, "I don't regret a moment—I think I've had a lot of impact."

Dr. Gould hopes that his legacy will be the Area Health Education Center (AHEC) program. AHEC was started in the 1970s by an act of Congress to address quality of and access to health care for underserved populations, in large part through workforce interventions. Its goal was to get culturally appropriate health care to populations by getting kids from underserved communities and disadvantaged backgrounds into the healthcare professions across disciplines.

Dr. Gould denies ever having had a career plan. Instead, he explains, "in part because of the migrant program that I started 10 years ago . . . I have become, for better or worse, the go-to person for migrant health in the state of Connecticut. In part that's how I ended up as the chair of the National Advisory Council on Migrant Health in Washington in 2004. It's all serendipity . . ." He advises his students, "Just make sure you're putting your heart and soul into what you're doing at that moment, because otherwise you will go nowhere, or you will do great damage to those you are working for or with along the way." Dr. Gould has invested so much into migrant health care and has seen success in his career as a result.

Dr. Gould's familiarity with migrant needs is obvious. "Connecticut is a tobacco state; we grow a whole bunch of it for leaf wrappers for cigars. We have between 10 and 20,000 migrants who come into the state each summer and they don't have any access to health care." During the hot months, Dr. Gould has three students working with him, paid by the county medical association—"picking other people's pockets," Dr. Gould calls it—and the students organize, with all these different health professions schools, and we go out to the tobacco camps in the summer and we set up field clinics 3 nights a week to do primary care. We've got 30–40 community and university physicians with us and a lot of them have regained their souls. Some of them are specialists, nephrologists, and they've forgotten why they went to med school, they bemoan the fact that the healthcare system has devolved to its present state, and they come out one night to the fields, and they remember why they went to med school." I wondered if Bruce realized exactly how much he's helping his colleagues in addition to his patients.

Bruce has experienced epidemics at the camps. Three or four years ago, he recalls, he was in Philadelphia and "kept getting a call from the outreach worker, that there were a bunch of guys coughing up blood and having high fevers. These are young, otherwise healthy workers. He kept saying, what are we going to do? I said, I'm going to worry but you're going to call the Department of Public Health. And 2 hours later I got a call from the Department of Public Health, saying we got a bunch of guys coughing up blood, what are we going to do? It turns out if it's not TB or anthrax or smallpox, it's not their problem. These guys were incredibly ill, and I was put in the unenviable position of having to figure out how to get care out to them on short notice. It was graduation time. I called the medical students; they were studying for their finals, and I called the Infectious Disease (ID) department; they were having their dinner that night, and I wound up getting my residents at my clinic, probably about 20 of us, and we treated who needed to be treated. But what occurred to me, was that I really needed a group of people who were trained and willing to be called on short notice, and knew they could be called, and would come out for these types of episodes. I thought about having a Connecticut health service corps."

Dr. Gould developed a program in response to the need to deliver health care on short notice. "About a year later, I was on the advisory commission for health care for the homeless for the state. We were talking about how to get health care into homeless shelters. I said, why don't we have a student health service corps? Martha Okafor, director of the maternal and child division of the state health department, was there, and had access to pregnancy prevention grant money. Turns out, if you give a kid a goal, they don't get pregnant. They gave AHEC $50,000, and Tricia Harrity, one of my AHEC center directors, understood what I was trying to do, and the Connecticut Youth Health Service Corps was created."

Dr. Gould has continued to expand on his idea. "I've networked it into the National Health Services Corps; we now have a nine-module curriculum that students are taught. And if they do all nine modules and do 50 hours of service, they receive the AHEC/National Health Service Corps community service recognition award. And for an inner-city kid who may not be at the top of their class, we've arranged for them to get that award at their school's awards assembly. It's a big deal. We've now created the National Youth Health Service Corps, and we're developing the College Health Service Corps, which is a modification. That I'm very proud of, because it started from nothing and it's having a real impact, not only by virtue of affecting the kids that go through it, but also the communities it's serving." Obviously, serving the community is a driving force in Bruce's life.

> Make sure you're putting your heart and soul into what you're doing at that moment, because otherwise you will go nowhere, or you will do great damage to those you are working for or with along the way.

Dr. Gould believes there is a spiritual dimension to his work. He states, "Probably a large part of the motivation that one has to do the types of things that we in medicine should be doing, valuing and reveling in, and getting fulfillment from, are things that have to do with the greater good that one might say is being done for religious reasons." On an interpersonal level, Dr. Gould experiences God in "that interaction in helping another human being." He feels a sense of awe when he is able to connect with someone or fix something, and he attributes much of this sense of worth from his Jewish cultural heritage.

Dr. Gould is concerned about tying religious groups or organizations to health care, feeling that the caring relationship should be on a one-to-one level and that there should be no requirements of belief in order to receive care. He notes that the highest form of giving is giving anonymously, without concern for personal benefit or even acknowledgement. He is aware of the huge challenge in the medical professions of selecting students who are entering the field for the right reasons. To Dr. Gould, that means, "truly desiring to help other people; there's not a lot of selfish intent there." Bruce also recognizes the danger of beating the altruism and spirituality out of them in the process of acculturating them into the medical profession.

Dr. Gould recalls an occasion when this work and the care and caring of his students were recognized. Several years ago, Francisco Jimenez, PhD, was asked to be the commencement speaker at the University of Connecticut. Dr. Jimenez grew up as the son of migrant farm workers from Mexico who came to the United States to work and has written about his experience in a book entitled *The Circuit*. In his address, Dr. Jiminez thanked the medical students for caring for his people. "And it was such a poignant moment," Dr. Gould recalls. "It reminded me, of all the trials, tribulations, and challenges in developing just this one program, let alone, all the other programs; and that if you bang your head against the system and don't give up, some of these programs will become mainstream, become part of the culture, and will change the culture. For the students graduating that day and their parents to hear this was magical. Even if someone doesn't wind up being a primary care doctor caring for the underserved, one would hope that it reinforces their heart and their soul. So maybe they don't spend all their time working at an inner-city or rural underserved facility, but maybe they're the gastroenterologist that waives their thousand-dollar fee in caring for an uninsured patient." Dr. Gould credits the medical school for creating a requirement in community service for students in 1990, so that students could get official credit for what they were already doing—going to the farms and homeless shelters—and so that any doctor who has a University of Connecticut appointment that oversees the care the students provide would be insured by the state of Connecticut because of their involvement in the four-year medical school curriculum. Like other situations Bruce is part of, it's a win-win.

> My goals in my job, in my life are all wrapped up in ethical constructs. Tikun Olam . . . healing the world . . . making it a little bit better of a place for your having passed this way. Each of us has a responsibility to those around us and to all in our community.

Dr. Gould is very proud of what he does, and he's often taken his children with him to the farms when he does his work. "I remember being out at a camp with my daughter . . . and having a farm worker come up to us and say, I just want to thank you for caring. That was one of those moments—the sun was setting over the fields—it was a very bucolic setting out on one of the farms, and it was a magical moment with my child there sharing the moment with me." Bruce thinks that other doctors who join him in this work will be rewarded. He has even gone as far as to say, "They can regain their soul" by joining in this invaluable work. He thinks that other doctors like him can enjoy the interactions with patients, glory in the diversity, and come to deeply value as a gift the fact that their patients let their trusted physicians into their lives.

    Again, I return to the note that Bruce wrote me when I first contacted him about talking with him. "My goals in my job, in my life are all wrapped up in ethical constructs. Tikun Olam . . . healing the world . . . making it a little bit better of a place for your having passed this way. The responsibility of each of us to those around us and to all in our community. And our responsibility to care for and safeguard the earth. Perhaps my sense of Jewish guilt or my fear of shame is too strong and that drives me to do what in my moral world, is 'right' or 'just'. Part of that construct is the 'no backsies rule.' . . . It derives from the childhood game of tag . . . If you are tagged there's no backsies . . . You can't tag back the one who just tagged you. In a similar way, once I become aware of an injustice, or someone who is sick, it is my responsibility to the best of my ability to address that injustice or person's frailty. I say to the best of my ability because I know I'm not all powerful and many things are beyond my feeble abilities. But I should try to ease the pain of those around me." After he shares his philosophy, Dr. Gould adds that he still feels lucky to be paid for what he loves doing.

CHAPTER 7

Making Common Ground for Faith and Health

Dr. G. Scott Morris

Dr. Scott Morris, a family practice physician and ordained United Methodist minister, founded the Church Health Center in Memphis in 1987 to provide quality, affordable health care for uninsured working people and their families. Thanks to a broad base of financial support from the faith community and the volunteer help of doctors, nurses, dentists, and others, the Church Health Center Clinic has grown to be the largest faith-based clinic of its type in the country. Currently, the clinic cares for 50,000 patients of record without relying on government funding. Fees are charged on a sliding scale based on income. The average visit costs about $20.

Dr. Morris began to plan and raise the initial funding for the Church Health Center as soon as he was appointed as associate pastor in 1986 at St. John's United Methodist Church (a position he still maintains). St. John's purchased the center's first building, a run-down boarding house across the street from the church, and agreed to lease it to the center for $1 per year, a fee that remains the same to this day.

In addition to the medical services, a new wellness ministry and center offers everything from personalized plans and cooking classes to group exercise classes and activities for children and teens. The Church Health Center won the 2003 Innovations in Prevention Award from the U.S.

Department of Health and Human Services for its hope and healing wellness ministry. The program has been so successful that replication workshops are held quarterly at the Church Health Center, attracting participants from all over the country. Each workshop brings new people together with fresh ideas, questions, and enthusiasm.

Dr. Morris is the author of a number of articles on ethics and health ministries. He has written Relief for the Body, Renewal for the Soul, *a book about his experiences with patients who come to the clinic, and* I Am the Lord Who Heals You, *a collection of sermons by distinguished preachers on the nature of healing. Scott is a past winner of the Distinguished Physician Award from the state of Tennessee. Dr. Morris has an undergraduate degree from the University of Virginia, a Master of Divinity degree from Yale University, and an MD from Emory University. He completed his medical residency at the Medical College of Virginia.*

Scott Morris was only 7 or 8 years old and a member of the United Methodist Church when his pastor introduced him to the district supervisor and said, "This boy's going to be a fine preacher one of these days." Scott said that even at that early age, that the thought of "preaching 52 sermons a year sent shivers down my spine," but from then on, he never seriously considered any career other than being professionally involved in the church, "except for maybe pitching for the Atlanta Braves." He spent time thinking about what being professionally involved with the church would look like. He read the Bible and "saw the stuff in there about healing." When he looked around at his church, he realized that the scope of the church's healing ministry did not extend beyond the congregation's praying for people on Sunday mornings and the pastor's visiting the sick. "People have built large hospitals that have church names on them and do good work," Scott said, then added, "but the hospitals have very little to do with worshipping congregations. It seemed to me that there ought to be more than that." This line of thinking led him to envision what a healing ministry in today's world could look like.

Since high school, Scott had known that he would go to both seminary and medical school. He remained firm in the decision that he did not want to be a preacher, but wanted to be professionally involved with the church, and he had read the Bible and felt that fully a third of it has to do with healing the sick. "Every time Jesus called the disciples together," Scott notes, "every time, they were expected to do three things: preach, teach, and heal. We had the preach and the teach down, but it didn't seem like we had a clue about what it would mean to have a healing ministry in today's world." Scott's vision would change that. To develop it, he felt he needed to have medical skills.

Before he went to medical school, Scott attended seminary. He grew up in Atlanta, completed his undergraduate education at the University of Virginia, and then went to Yale Divinity School. It was at Yale that he spent most of his time looking at where the church had historically stood on the issue of healing. The medical school at Yale had a full-time chaplain who was very influential for Scott. In the chaplain's office one day, Scott happened to see a pamphlet entitled, *How to Start a Church-Based Health Clinic*, and he knew that was it; that was what he wanted to do.

> Fully a third of the Bible has to do with healing the sick. Every time Jesus called the disciples together, they were expected to do three things: preach, teach, and heal.

The pamphlet was written by a Lutheran pastor from Chicago named Granger Westberg. The next summer Scott went to Chicago and met the pastor and the people working with him. The connections in Chicago pointed him toward the Church of the Savior in Washington, D.C., a very unusual church that had also created a health clinic. What they had done resonated with Scott; it was what he himself wanted to do. From that point on, he worked with his peers to prepare himself for that goal, until he felt ready to start his own gig.

Scott recognized the disconnection between the church's traditional healing role and its current practice. In seminary, he had come to realize that "the way it is is not the way it has always been." He learned that prior to the Civil War, anyone who was sick and looking for health care would go first to his or her pastor. Ministers provided the majority of health care in this country. Also he discovered that the older hospitals in this country were started by churches, primarily for the purpose of providing health care for the poor. And as Scott learned all this, he came to believe that there would be a place in the world for him to do these things.

A hands-on type of person, Dr. Morris would not have been satisfied with merely being the administrator of a program. "Just sitting back and watching something unfold has never been what pulled my chain," he explains. It is still the idea of hands-on ministry that drives him. Even though he spends most of his time in the role of physician, he thinks of himself primarily as a pastor. The best parts of his day involve his hands-on work with "an amazing group of folks," older African Americans who have nothing, not even "social capital," because their families are extremely dysfunctional. Yet when Scott asks them how they are, their response invariably is, "I'm fine and blessed." "How can you be fine and blessed when you have nothing?" Scott asks, and he tries to find the answer. After checking their blood pressure and blood glucose, he spends their visits "trying to figure out how can I get to be fine and blessed." He wants to know what they have learned about life that he needs to know. He wants to understand how they have acquired their "spiritual capital," and how his health center can encourage them and others to spend some of their spiritual capital on their physical well-being. Being able to spend personal quality time with people who are in such a state of perpetual gratitude is one reason Scott has chosen not to be an administrator. His management staff, he points out, has to spend its time mostly with him.

Scott was encouraged in his life's work by a variety of people he met along the way. The youth minister in his church always told him that he could do whatever he wanted to do. But because everyone else seemed headed in other directions, Scott recalls having to be self-motivated. Although he "always had people who were inspirational" to him, he did not meet the person he considers his mentor, William Coffin, until he was an adult and his clinic was already open. Coffin was the chaplain at Yale, but ironically left before Scott got there. He was one of the leaders of the antiwar movement in the 1960s and was an original Freedom Rider. He was the pastor at Riverside Church in New York and then left to help found Sane/Freeze, an antinuclear group. "Coffin is an amazing force," Scott exalts, "He's known for 'Coffinisms,' these little pithy sayings. There's actually a book of them." But Scott's admiration of Coffin goes beyond his quotability.

Scott met Reverend Coffin soon after the Church Health Center opened. Coffin was in Memphis preaching, and he and Scott "just clicked." Soon after, Coffin asked Scott if he wanted to do a project with him. "When Coffin asks you to do a gig, you show up." After that, they were "sort of bound at the hip." Coffin performed Scott's wedding. He died 2 years ago, ending their conversations but not their relationship.

Scott considers Reverend Coffin's hallmark teaching to be the difference between charity and justice. Coffin would "endlessly rag on" him about this difference, telling Scott that he had "a nice little charity going there in Memphis," but that he should never forget that charity, in and of itself, does not bring about justice. He would tell Scott that the only thing he should focus on was whether what he was doing was leading to justice for the people for whom he was providing care. "I had that cute little story about people who are fine and blessed," Scott explains, "but if the Church Health Center isn't making their lives such that Jesus would smile and say, this is how it's supposed to be, then we haven't really done anything." Scott continues to question whether he is participating in the creation of justice.

Professionally, Dr. Morris has sailed his own ship. His father does not really understand what he does. He thinks his mother would have understood, but she died when he was a freshman in college. As an only child, his church youth group was very influential for him. The ministers there and the people in the youth group shaped him. Scott was encouraged toward his goal by a few people at the prep school he attended in Atlanta. More importantly, his schooling convinced him that he "had to do something that had a lot of quality to it" in order to be successful at the level he wanted. The many friends he has made along the way have wished him luck but have not really understood his mission.

> If you only are looking at the mechanistic aspect of the physiology of the human being, then you're going to miss half of who that human being is. You cannot MRI somebody's spirit.

In addition to having few people in his life who understand his goals, Scott has met obstructionists "all along and at every turn." He has not listened to them. His father thought he should go to medical school first, before divinity school, primarily out of a concern that if he did not go first he would not go at all, but Scott stayed his course. He continues to have naysayers, although not as many. One of his strengths is to be unaffected by either criticism or praise. "We have more awards than I can possibly count," he contends, "but I couldn't tell you what they are or where they are." When he accepts an award, he uses it as an opportunity to talk about the work he is doing, and the fact that the church is "exceedingly good about starting things, but terrible about sustaining things." He has been doing his work for 21 years and considers that a good start. He adds that he may feel more confident when he has been doing it for 30 years or so.

Scott recalls two courses he took in divinity school that made a difference in pushing him toward his life's work. One was a seminar on the chronically ill. The class was made up of small groups comprised of a medical student, a divinity student, a nursing student, a law student, and a public health student. Every team was assigned a patient-teacher, a person who had a chronic illness, and the weekly assignment was to spend an hour with that person, not using the discipline you were learning, but just sitting and talking with him or her about what it meant to have a chronic illness. Then the whole class would reconvene and talk collectively, using their respective disciplines to address how they might proceed. This was a particularly instructive experience for Dr. Morris considering he now spends most of his time caring for the chronically ill.

The other course that influenced Scott was called Body and Spirit. In the class, the students read a textbook of physiology in parallel with the work of major theologians such as Paul Tillich, asking, "what in the world do these two things have to say to each other?" They would read, for example, how the kidney cleans the blood, and then theology about the Holy Spirit, and attempt to answer what these have to do with the ways we live our lives. "That's sort of what I do these days," Scott explains. He brings together these two seemingly very disparate things, physiology and theology, in people's lives.

> Nobody has to be taught how to keep their distance from another human being. What you do have to be taught is how to get close to somebody else, and most doctors are unbelievably terrible at doing that.

It was classes like these that set Yale apart for Scott and lead him to describe Yale Divinity School as "the greatest thing I ever experienced." When he was applying to seminaries, he wrote to the schools and asked what they thought about combining medicine and ministry. Most of them either replied that it was an interesting idea but they did not offer anything, or that it was a nutty idea and he needed to choose one field or the other. Yale, on the other hand, sent him a 10-page statement, so he never applied anywhere else. The chaplain of the medical school encouraged him to go on to the medical school at Yale.

In contrast to the enlightened atmosphere he had found at the divinity school, the medical school was "the most archaic, Byzantine structure I had ever been in." He had barely matriculated before he felt he had to transfer. Scott notes that had he stayed at Yale, the class he would have graduated with was the only medical school class in America in which not a single person became a family practitioner. "Their feeling was that becoming a family practitioner was throwing your life away," Scott recalls. Not a big fan of traditional medical education, he completed his medical degree at Emory University, which he found "a little" better.

Dr. Morris learned his respect for humanity from his mother, a "very compassionate person." Scott describes her as "incredibly smart, a woman who would have flourished remarkably in a more egalitarian time." She spent most of her life as a housewife but, according to Scott, would have done much better as a high-powered executive. She was "always out trying to do good, to take care of people, through the church." She "had the mind of a CEO," and used it to do good and bring compassion to the process.

Too early in Dr. Morris's life, his mother died of ovarian cancer. At the time, he did not really understand what was going on. Now he has many regrets, having been in the confusing period of adolescence while she was sick. Neither does he remember anyone every talking to him about his mother's illness or death, and "shame on them," he says now. His emotional and spiritual needs were forgotten, and this experience may have contributed to his forming a mission, as an adult, in which emotional and spiritual needs never go unaddressed.

With regard to his own personal experience with a medical crisis, he has had both his hip and knee replaced, and needs to have his other hip and knee replaced as well. He regards this as his "cross to bear these days." During his surgeries and recoveries, "they treated me like I was the King of Siam," he recalls. He explains: "In Memphis, particularly in a place like that, I'm pretty well known, so people bent over backward to be nice to me, which was great, but still . . ." Scott wishes that everyone received the same level of care.

Dr. Morris believes that listening is critical in his work. He insists, "you can't practice medicine if you don't listen." Second-year medical students learn that patient history is key to making a diagnosis. Scott adds, "It's not just listening. It's equally important to ask the right questions." Further, he notes that human beings are both body and spirit, and that "if you only are looking at the mechanistic aspect of the physiology of the human being, then you're going to miss half of who that human being is. You cannot MRI somebody's spirit." He continues,

"Almost by definition in allopathic medicine, the spiritual dimension of life does not exist. And yet for most people, that's where they spend their life and their time. They don't spend much time thinking about how their body functions. And so if you as the physician go in there as a technician, like an auto mechanic, and you're only focused on how the body works, without understanding how the body lives, you're never going to make a connection with that patient."

Scott points out that the most common complaint people have about their physicians is that they do not talk to them. Yet doctors feel that they do everything they are supposed to do, everything they were taught about clinical methods. The problem is that doctors are not taught how to be spiritually connected to people; in fact, they are almost driven away from that when they are accused of being too close to their patients and told that it affects their objectivity. Scott argues that "nobody has to be taught how to keep their distance from another human being. What you do have to be taught is how to get close to somebody else, and most doctors are unbelievably terrible at doing that." A large part of Dr. Morris's mission is to work against this ubiquitous paradigm in medicine.

Scott gets up in the morning and perseveres because he likes what he does, and he is "driven by the mission." He knows that if he does not do what he is supposed to do, no one else will, and that will impact the Church Health Center. One thing he is supposed to do is raise $13 million every year. "That means you have to fund raise every day," Scott explains. The Church Health Center administration is trying to ensure that it is not dependent solely on Dr. Morris, but he is committed to doing his job as long as he is the head of the center. And yet, despite the requirements of development, he draws a firm line and remains determined to spend at least half his day seeing patients.

Scott's goals are linked to his sense of personal ethics. Ultimately, his motivation is to live out his life being faithful to God. He does not differentiate between his work life and his personal life. He clarifies that to raise as much money as he has to raise, he has to see the people he is raising it from as more than "targets." On some level, like his patients, they have to be friends. So Scott has a lot of friends.

Dr. Morris's personal credo strongly reflects his sense of self. For many years he recited to himself daily a passage from Colossians, "You are the children of God, therefore God's chosen people, wholly and dearly beloved. Clothe yourself with gentleness, kindness, compassion, humility, patience, and love. And above all put on love, the harmony which binds all." He tries to exhibit those virtues every day. In addition, those qualities have been incorporated into "everything that happens" at the Church Health Center. The focus for every patient is to enable them to live a life centered on these six virtues. The Center's employees are evaluated in part on how they manifest these virtues in their daily work. Scott acknowledges that even he messes up. But he always returns to upholding them and continues to see these virtues in his head every time he looks.

Scott's biggest obstacle to accomplishing his goals is the fact that there is not enough time in the day. He remembers that when he first started the Church Health Center he used to call the founder of the health clinic at the Church of the Savior often for guidance. "Finally," he admits, "she got on a plane from DC, came to Memphis, sat in my office and looked me in the eye, and said, stop calling me." The point was that she could not give him the answers no matter how badly he wanted them. The answers had to come from the "called people," the professionals who had given their lives to the work at Church Health and saw it as their ministry, too. The problem Scott has now is trying to determine who among the center's staff of 200 are truly the people who feel this deep vocation alongside of him. "The called person could be working in our facilities staff, in our wellness arm; they could be a nurse or doctor," he says. Once he locates them, he struggles to find ways to spend enough time with them.

> Half of the people who go to primary care doctors have no medical problem, but their life is falling apart. People come to doctors today for reasons that they use to go to their priest.

Scott thinks his biggest failure is a personal one, a past divorce. In terms of the center and his mission, he cannot recall any big failure, and does not remember the ideas that did not work. "I'm sure I had a million of them that didn't work, but I'm having a hard time remembering them," he states.

Scott has the following approach to resisting burnout: when he is away, he is away. "I can absolutely not think about the next thing that I have to do for the center," he asserts. When he goes to a dance lesson with his wife, he is not thinking about the center. "I'm thinking, where do I put my right foot?" He is able to compartmentalize so that his work does not interfere with other stuff, and he can enjoy other aspects of life without anxiety. He "sleeps great," he says, and his only issues are his joint problems. He thinks that if that is the biggest problem in his life, he will be fine.

Dr. Morris also maintains balance by managing his time well. When he is at work, he is working, but he makes sure he has plenty of time with his wife. "We don't have any children. The health center is our child, really," he explains. He also ensures that he spends enough time with friends. He used to play golf, but his joint problems no longer permit it. He does not miss it. Instead, he enjoys the variety in life, which he says is the most important thing. Scott is glad not to be doing the same thing over and over every day. He is currently involved in a clergy group that is trying to address the issues of violence in Memphis, and he is on the board of a small, historically Black college that has more problems than he can count. He sees all these things as linked together, but feels that the variety of them helps keep him from burning out. He also cultivates a sense of humor. His wife lives to laugh, and he has a medical assistant who is assigned the job of reminding him to smile whenever she sees he is not.

Scott's style is to make sure that his patients know that he understands the social pressures they have in addition to their physical complaints. None of his patients have health insurance, but all are working. The number one question they inevitably have is about when can they go back to work. Dr. Morris does not take any of that lightly. He conveys to his patients that, while he is not poor and never will be, primarily because of his education, he is fully with them, and the center is a safe place for them. He is not thinking of something else while he is in the room with them; his hand is not on the door. Scott also emphasizes partnership with his patients. He is going to do his part, but they have to do their part. If they have diabetes, they have to go to the center's diabetes class—it is not an option. If they do not go, they cannot return to the Church Health Center. Scott explains these hard lines. "The problem with being poor is often times nobody ever tells you the rules. Poor people are very good about living by the rules, but nobody ever tells them what they are. So we make very clear what the boundaries are. A lot of our patients are very concrete thinkers, so we make sure they understand the plan, and generally they appreciate that."

Scott has disappointed himself at times for not living up to his mentor Bill Coffin's standard of valuing justice over charity. He has been in situations in which he has been with someone wealthy, whom he was hoping would make significant financial gifts to the Church Health Center, and that person was telling "some outlandish racist joke," or saying something he absolutely did not agree with, and instead of interjecting and pointing out that it was wrong, he let it go. He has rationalized his inaction by telling himself it was for the greater good, but at the same time he knows that Bill Coffin would never have let it go. For the most part, however, Scott does not think about either acts of cowardice or acts of courage in his work; he does not let himself get too high or too low. He acknowledges that people both praise and criticize him, but "it just rolls off a duck's back."

Scott recalls a time when he felt he knew the best course of action to take on behalf of a patient, but it was not possible for him to follow through. A woman with breast cancer was convinced that it was God's will, and all she would allow the center to do was to treat her wounds, which had become a fungating mass on her chest. She would talk to Dr. Morris for hours about how she knew that God had a plan for her, and it was not for her to die, but she also knew that she was not supposed to have surgery to have the tumor removed. She bled out and died at 45 years old.

> There aren't any pills out there that can make a person's life better when it is an issue that is fundamentally of the spirit.

Scott has nothing "that even comes close to regret" about his life's work. Sometimes he thinks he might have done things differently to get one of the Memphis hospitals on board as it has been an endless struggle to get them to fully support the center's work. Then again, he realizes that "the bottom line is, they don't get it. All they see is the money, and I can't change that." Scott almost regretted having a big "tell it like it is" with the governor a few years ago. Then again, because the center does not ask for state money or pursue any government funding, he was able to speak his mind.

Scott's entire practice is spiritually informed. The Church Health Center is all about connecting body and spirit. Scott elaborates, "It's about calling people of faith together and saying that we have an obligation to care for the body that God has given us, but also about calling the medical community together and saying, there is a spiritual dimension in life. If you ignore it, then you are not really being a good physician." Dr. Morris points out that the work of the Church Health Center is not about a particular religious viewpoint; it is about the fact that half of the people who go to primary care doctors have no medical problem, but their life is falling apart. "People come to doctors today for reasons that they used to go to their priest," Scott contends, and adds, "It's all very complicated." Scott's bottom line is that doctors are not very good at dealing with what are fundamentally spiritual problems, but that spiritual problems require spiritual solutions. "There aren't any pills out there that make a person's life better when it is an issue that is fundamentally of the spirit," he states. He thinks that doctors are going to need to address the issues that bring patients in, and to do that, they are going to have to be able to communicate with people on a spiritual level.

Scott hopes that his lasting legacy is that the work of the Church Health Center provides a model that other communities can emulate. His long-term vision is an America in which it would be unusual to go into a church and not find some kind of health ministry. Dr. Morris would love it if people made their decision about whether to join a particular church based partly on whether the congregation has a health ministry that meets theirs and their family's needs. "We are in the middle of what we believe is a movement in America, if not beyond, around reclaiming a commitment to care for our bodies as well as our spirits. A faith and health movement is afoot, and we want to make sure that the city of Memphis is thought of as a center of that movement," Scott declares. He is not done yet. In fact, he is looking around for some more good souls who can dream a bigger dream with him.

CHAPTER 8

Listening to Many Truths

Dr. Coleen Kivlahan

Dr. Coleen Kivlahan is senior medical director for innovation at Aetna/ Medicaid. She is a leader in creating models and tools to improve medical cost containment, the integration of physical and behavioral health, reduction of disparities in access as well as quality improvement for complex, vulnerable populations.

Coleen is a family physician with more than 30 years of experience in medical settings and public health. She has held positions at the national, state, and local levels including serving as the first female director of the Missouri Department of Health and as chief medical officer for University Hospital in Columbia, Missouri. She founded and directed the Sexual Assault Forensic Examinations (SAFE) network, a statewide cooperative of physicians in Missouri who provide high-quality, sensitive examinations and protection to children who have been sexually or physically abused. She also was the medical director of Fantus Health Center, Cook County Bureau of Health Services, Chicago, Illinois. Additionally, Dr. Kivlahan served as the chief medical officer for the Health Resources and Services Administration of the Department of Health and Human Services in Washington, D.C.

Dr. Coleen Kivlahan has a long history of volunteering with the civilian relief agencies such as Project Hope and Operation Crossroads. She has participated in medical missions in Sierra Leone, Haiti, and Guatemala. Working with Doctors of the World, she joined the Florence Project Board of Directors in Arizona, where she focuses on immigrant and refugee rights. Currently living in Fairfax County, Virginia, Coleen is also a clinician at the Jeanie Schmit Free Clinic.

Coleen has been a recipient of the Association of American Medical Colleges' annual Humanism in Medicine Award. She has served as a reviewer of Family Practice Research Journal *and the* Journal of Family Practice. *She earned her undergraduate degree at St. Louis University. Her medical degree is from the Medical College of Ohio. Dr. Kivlahan earned a master's degree in public health from the University of Missouri-Columbia. She was on the faculty at the University of Missouri-Columbia School of Medicine where she also was the assistant to the dean for health policy and director of the Office of Clinical Effectiveness.*

Coleen Kivlahan's love for the outdoors and her interest in the order of the natural world were the earliest hints that her future might be in medicine. As a young Catholic observing the no meat on Fridays edict from her family, she hunted frogs for food at the end of the week. She spent time dissecting them and understanding their anatomy. Another indication of her future path came as the result of her father's having nine brothers and sisters, all of whom lived within a short distance and many of whom were elderly and sick. At a young age she had continuous exposure to people with significant illnesses and found herself in a nurturing role with them.

The moment at which her future course became clear occurred when she found books on Dr. Tom Dooley in the local public library. Coleen read Dooley's books in rapid succession. At the time the heroic missionary "Jungle Doctor of Laos" was a fascinating figure for our nation. She pulled that first book off the shelf and was captivated the second she opened it. *The Night They Burned the Mountain* was a title that intrigued her at a tender age. As she read and learned that an American had gone to another country at great personal risk and immersed himself there in order to help people in distress, she knew, "That's what I want to do in my life." In the third grade at the time, she never doubted that she could do it—despite her family's poverty; neither parent attended college, and one struggled to finish high school.

Coleen always remembers being "aware of and amazed by the miracle of human beings." Her parents taught her respect for hard work, but, like many working-class people in the 1950s, they held prejudices based on wealth, race, religion, culture, and class. Nonetheless, Coleen's awareness of the long hours her parents put in at work and their commitment to contributing to their family and neighborhood was fundamental for her. Observing her mom and dad provided her with a sense of who she was, where she came from, and what she needed to do in the world. Her broader mission of commitment to humanity came from reading about her childhood hero, Tom Dooley.

> Medicine is listening to the body, to the conversation, to the dialogue, to the metaconversation; it is listening to your own gut, your head; and every single medical interaction is consolidating all those forms of listening into the next action steps.

Coleen found an early supporter in a paternal uncle who had never finished the eighth grade. An Irish immigrant, he had gone to work for the railroad. "He just loved me deeply," Coleen recalls. "He said I could do whatever I wanted to do in life." He provided personal support rather than any kind of knowledge or guidance as to what lay ahead for Coleen. His support was invaluable in allowing her to remain "totally convinced" that she could do whatever she wanted to do. Coleen is grateful for that and finds it difficult to imagine not having had a sense that someone believed in her. She was also supported on a personal level by the family of a friend who nurtured her throughout elementary and high school. Her friend's family was "a loud, exuberant Italian family with limited religiosity," whereas Coleen's family was very Irish-Catholic. The time she spent with her friend's family, in which verbalizing feelings, hugging, and strong emotions were all normal events, provided Coleen with a different perspective than her family's more stoical approach.

When Coleen was growing up, her family could not afford to access physicians. She was well aware that other children saw doctors, and that it was the norm, and was not quite sure why her family went to the health department for their shots and care. The first time she saw a physician was when she was in her junior year of high school and fell on the ice while skating. A broken beer bottle, frozen in the ice, cut deeply into her knee.

She delayed telling her mother for a day because she knew they did not have the money to have it treated. Finally, when her whole leg became swollen, she went to the doctor for the first time. While she saved money for a year to have surgery, she had to get her knee drained monthly due to internal bleeding. Coleen recalls that it took her and her mother a long time to pay that bill.

Dr. Kivlahan had been familiar with medical crises from a young age. She changed colostomy bags for an uncle when she was only around 8 years old and cleaned up after another uncle who had tuberculosis. She was a caregiver for her father multiple times as he recovered from injuries due to his alcoholism and again at the time of his accidental death. She is still the doctor in the family now. "So it was then, and it is now," she reflects. She has witnessed up close the very serious personal challenge of a close family member with a history of childhood trauma. "This has profoundly affected my life in so many ways," she says. She was in a caregiver role in that situation, too, and even today continues to learn about the impact of trauma in the lives of children and political asylum seekers in her work with Doctors of the World and in her daily care of her patients. "The personal impact on me is hard to overstate," she asserts.

The only person Coleen can remember opposing her progress towards her goals in any significant way was the guidance counselor at her high school. The advisor told her, "You might be able to make it through nursing school, but you'll never make it through medical school. I can't believe that, as a woman, you'd even think about being a doctor. It's important for you to be married and have children, and you might be able to be a nurse." Coleen felt deflated, and was ready to quit school; she thought that if she could not be a doctor, there was really no reason for her to finish high school. She decided to go to the school principal to discuss the matter. It was a big high school and Coleen had no appointment, but she was able to meet with the principal. Coleen told her what the guidance counselor had said, and that, as a result, she was struggling with staying in the private high school she was attending. Tuition was $1000 a year, and Coleen was paying for it herself. If she was not going to be able to be a doctor, she said, she could go to the local public school and then become a nurse if she wanted to. Coleen remembers that the principal looked right at her and said, "You can do anything you want to do." This was the only time she had ever talked to the principal alone, yet the very strong message conveyed was, "I want you to stay; you're working really hard and you can do this. Just let me know if you ever need a reference." The timing of this was critical. The principal's encouragement created a tipping point for Coleen. She also modeled for Coleen the value of having the ability to connect with the people in front of her, and figure out what they need to hear. This moment taught her that the long-term impact of a few well-chosen words can be invaluable.

The other personal barrier that Coleen encountered came from an unexpected source: her mother. Her mother never really believed that she could go to college, let alone medical school. Even today, when Coleen receives an honor, her mother is very cautious about celebrating it. Coleen attributes this to her mother's having had a challenging life, serving as the primary support for six children. She was fearful about risk, and Coleen's goals just seemed out of reach for one of her children. Although she knows her mother is proud of her, she grew up feeling very aware of her mother's concerns about how realistic her dreams were. In response, however, a part of her said, "Well, I can show her and everyone else." Coleen did not let her mother's doubts slow her down.

> My clinical work isn't "volunteering." For me it's fundamental. Without access to clinical work, I'd be a terrible physician leader in administration."

The next major influence was her choice in medical schools. She attended a new medical school in Toledo, Ohio. The curriculum was a 3-year, year-round medical school with several distinctive components. One was the insistence that doctors should learn from each other and from other health professionals in a collaborative manner rather than in a competitive environment. This was in stark contrast to other medical schools where the message in the first semester is usually, "Look around the room and know that a percentage of you won't be here at the end of the year." The school used a problem-based curriculum, also a rarity at the time. To be in a medical school that was committed to having its students learn in teams was a great experience for Coleen. Also extraordinary for her was the Dean, Dr. Lane Gerber, a clinical psychologist. He created an environment in which collaborative learning, truth, honesty, and integrity were core principles. He also modeled balancing hard work with "having another life" by bringing his children to the office and by having his students over to his house for picnics. His humane perspective on the practice of medicine shaped Coleen's clinical style.

In medical school, Dr. Kivlahan came to appreciate the synthesis between physical and behavioral health. She understood that medicine is not just about the body, but that the mind is integrated in all aspects of medicine. This expands the concept of balance beyond the work–life duality to include the interactions between mind and body. Coleen believes that it is incumbent upon all doctors in training to develop a deep understanding of this integration.

Not surprisingly, Coleen's perspective on the role of listening in the practice of medicine is that "medicine *is* listening." She elaborates, "Medicine is listening to the body, to the conversation, to the dialogue, to the meta-conversation; it is listening to your own gut, your head; and every single medical interaction is consolidating all those forms of listening into the next action steps. Medicine is fundamentally listening, reflection, and then action. We learn to listen to ourselves, to the patient, and to the environment." Perhaps Coleen's understanding of the importance of listening goes right back to her conversation with her high school principal, and to her very early experiences of paying attention to the natural world.

> I believe there are many truths. There's your truth, there's my truth, and there's the patient's truth. All exist independently, simultaneously. And I can live with that ambiguity with no crisis in my heart. Who cares whether somebody did five days a week or six days a week of exercise?

Coleen explains that she does not feel the need to persevere because she loves life and making the time to do what she loves to do. She is motivated equally by her two important and fully integrated roles: a national medical policy role for Medicaid, and a local clinical role. Each informs the other, and she cannot imagine doing one without doing the other. In her clinical setting, she is continually influenced by what she knows are current health insurance policies (or lack thereof), medication policies, access policies, and mental health policies; and in her policy job, she is influenced by the patient she saw yesterday. She does not view her work in these two spheres as a dual career or even as two separate roles; although she realizes that others in her sphere do. For her, each is necessary for the other.

Currently Coleen's clinical work is being done at the Jeanne Schmit Free Clinic in Herndon, Virginia, where she does diabetes and hypertension management for immigrants and populations without insurance. When she won the Pride in the Professions award, she was doing similar work at the St. Vincent de Paul clinic in Phoenix, taking care of obese immigrant Latino children with diabetes risk and providing forensic evaluations for victims of torture who were applying for political asylum in the United States. Coleen objects to others referring to her clinical work as volunteering. "For me, it's fundamental," she protests. "Without access to clinical work, I'd be a terrible physician leader in administration." She believes that doctors in administrative roles who must recall practice from 20 or even 5 years ago rather than being influenced by current patients can be less impactful because their insights may not be grounded in today's patient needs.

Dr. Kivlahan's personal and professional goals are inextricably linked to the personal ethics that drive her work. First among them is a sense of honesty and personal integrity. She struggles in situations in which she is not comfortable with the rules being imposed. She is currently involved in just such a struggle. The clinic where she works has employed a three-strikes policy to improve compliance. Patients are issued a strike when they show up late, do not show at all, or do not adhere to recommendations. Thus Coleen frequently finds herself with patients who live in fear of getting a third strike and asked to not come back, because the clinic is their medical home of last resort. Rather than seeing this as an issue of morality or of science, several staff at the clinic have told Coleen she is "a kind doctor who just continuously believes in people who may not always tell the truth." The staff tell her she has the patience of a saint. But Coleen denies that her approach is related to tolerance; she insists it is "really about empathy." She explains, "We have to understand the impact of poverty on health in the struggle with just getting to the doctor—three buses, and bring all your meds, and oh my goodness, you forgot your glucometer? So first of all, our patients have all the tactical issues of getting to a doctor. Secondly, they get there, and for most of us, going to the doctor is not a positive experience, and if you're poor, obese, have poorly controlled hypertension and diabetes, it can be punitive." Dr. Kivlahan sees a need for everyone to "do a little reflection: 'I wonder how difficult it is to get something other than the sugary cereal from the food pantry to eat in the morning?'" She has been feeling torn by these contradictions. She loves the patients, but cannot sit with a policy that is not grounded in either science or humanism.

Dr. Kivlahan understands that the clinic staff's frustration with the patients is mostly due to burnout and is initiating strategies to help the staff deal with the challenges of caring for indigent, sick populations. She'd like to see staff have the opportunity to meet briefly at the end of every clinic session to reflect on what occurred during that day and how frustrating it is to see people not be adherent. She wants to work with the staff to develop methods of active listening and reflection that enable them to develop more personal objectivity about what is going with the patient, and to help staff learn how to depersonalize the fact that "in a 15-minute interaction once a month, our patients are not going to do everything you say." Dr. Kivlahan's goals include a commitment to this practice, but the "three-strikes policy" violates a principle of her ethics. She is also "noisy about things, not in the sense of volume, but in the sense of persistence." Thus she repeatedly asks, "Are we doing what we really need to be doing? Are we doing our best? Do we have staff who are learning how to separate this important work from the rest of their life?"

Coleen's beliefs and questioning about principles of ethical practice can have surprising effects. One staff member told her, "My worst days of the week are when you're in clinic," and went on to share that she felt badly about herself on the days Dr. Kivlahan was there. Coleen thought that was very revealing, and asked how she could improve herself. The staff member said "You believe these people when they lie to you about taking their medicines." Coleen explained, "I believe there are many truths. There's your truth, there's my truth, and there's the patient's truth. All exist independently, simultaneously. And I can live with that ambiguity with no crisis in my heart. Who cares whether somebody did 5 days a week or 6 days a week of exercise?" When Coleen's work goals conflict with her personal values, she has followed a pattern of the following two strategies: she either leaves or she confronts the issue and sees whether change can be made so that she feels more personally comfortable.

Dr. Kivlahan understands that overload, fear, and personalizing workplace dynamics are issues for everyone working in healthcare organizations. She believes, however, that reflection and awareness of bias, prejudice, and assumptions can counter these reactions, and she thinks that it is possible to simultaneously be both present and conscious of these influences. Coleen believes healthcare teams can develop responses that are respectful and sensible and hold both patients and staff accountable. At the same time, she acknowledges that she has her own fears about not doing a good enough job with this difficult, complex population. Yet she also knows that when she feels confident, she "shows up, listens carefully to the environment, and makes decisions about the next right thing." At clinics, she has held sessions where "we put everybody's burnout in a room, we start giggling, and then we start healing."

Coleen identifies her greatest personal success as parenting and her greatest personal failure as a divorce she went through. Professionally, she considers her greatest success to be setting up a network of 350 physicians in Missouri to educate each other on child sexual and physical abuse, and to use each other to resist despair and to enhance their collective knowledge. Setting up the network was innovative and met a tremendous need for those kids who were being seen by the local child protective services staff. It also created a sense of collegiality between urban and rural physicians that replaced a sense of the ivory tower vs. the real world in rural Missouri. It added to new research where there was very little on a national level at that time. In the process, Coleen found that having to organize across boundaries was something she loved, and she continues to do it.

In contrast to how she views establishing the network, Coleen considers her recent experience in Haiti to be both a success and a failure. "I'd put it in the 'challenge' category," she remarks. On a Project Hope trip that combined military presence with a medical mission, she walked into a third-world country to provide medical care with armed guards for the first time. She was not aware of the extent of the military mission, so it was a shock. Coleen explains, "all of a sudden I was in the middle of a mission with several purposes for the first time in my life, and I felt anxious that my medical care was compromised to the point that I wasn't sure I could deliver it effectively." In Haiti, there was a huge need, and so she chose to stay, although there were several healthcare professionals in the same situation who were unable to carry out the mission. Coleen believes that by staying engaged, she learned about the human beings who serve in the military. She listened to them and learned about their challenges. For the most part she feels that she met superb doctors and left with "considerable respect for my military peers." She learned to tolerate what was foreign to her, limited her judgment, and was able to integrate other peoples' beliefs, ethics, and attitudes in a high-stress work environment. The teams

> Every single time I see my patients, it requires courage for me to stay present with their pain, to not absorb it, and to do what I can to help them relieve it to some extent.

worked 12 to 15-hour days and saw thousands of people, one after another, in 100-degree heat with no air conditioning in a foul-smelling, burned-out university hospital building. In that situation, her success was in being able to reduce her personal biases about the military and engage in the bigger purpose of the mission.

Coleen resists burnout by engaging in exercise, meditation, knitting, and music. She has an awareness of the cues in her body—tense shoulders, gaining 5 pounds, a craving for chocolate—and when she experiences these changes she knows it is time to heal herself. Coleen keeps her sense of humor through a love for funny movies and of little kids who "laugh at anything." Interestingly, her partner for the last 2½ years has been "a military guy," a helicopter pilot whom Coleen describes as "fascinating" and "very funny." "He sees humor in simple things," she explains. "If there are birds singing a funny song, he'll say, 'Isn't that funny, Coleen? Listen to the song of that bird!'" According to Coleen, he is very present, so the balance and the good humor are a great combination.

Coleen believes that the challenges of her childhood led her to the type of practice that she maintains today. Growing up in poverty, with no insurance, an alcoholic parent, and a parent who overachieved in her job made her highly independent and gave her a love of problem solving. "I can work just about anywhere and medical complexity doesn't scare me or bother me," she proclaims. The people she sees in clinic now have many comorbidities, sometimes with 12–15 chronic health conditions, along with 2–3 behavioral conditions, and of course they require polypharmacy.

Dr. Kivlahan brings a type of everyday bravery when she sees patients who have so much disability. "Every single time I see my patients, it requires courage for me to stay present with their pain, to not absorb it, and to do what I can to help them relieve it to some extent," she elaborates. She adds that it would be easier to turn off empathy and kindness and even stop deeply listening because it is such a difficult task. To simply "sit and be present with patients whose lives have had tragic outcomes, significant trauma, and serious diseases, and to evaluate their physical signs, and then to walk out with a sense of inspiration and peace," and to do this without getting caught up in the "resentment and pessimism of, 'Gee, aren't human beings terrible?'" requires considerable emotional resources.

Most of the time, Dr. Kivlahan is able to prioritize with consideration for the patient's needs and desires and develop the best next action step. The type of patient who is the biggest challenge for her is the patient who has decided that it is too late or who chooses not to do anything that would be of benefit. She describes one patient who had chronic obstructive pulmonary disease, diabetes, arthritis, multiple other medical conditions, and was on home oxygen, yet continued to smoke two packs of cigarettes a day and sit in her recliner all day. No matter what behavioral strategies Coleen gave her to try to decrease her smoking or treat her depression, nothing reached her. Even invoking their patient–physician relationship, which was very close and full of humor and affection, was unsuccessful. Nothing in Coleen's toolbox had an impact on this patient's desire to live, and so she finally stopped trying. Instead, she said to her patient, "Every one of the things you're doing is killing you. So how can I be most helpful to you?" and the patient answered, "I can't afford it, but what I really want is a small waterfall that sits next to my oxygen tank, so if I close my eyes, I can listen to those little waterfalls. Like the ones you see at Wal-Mart for 30 or 40 dollars. I could see the water coming down, and I could imagine that I was someplace beautiful instead of in my apartment." Coleen bought her one that very day and went to her home and set it up next to her oxygen tank. Coleen believes this act created an implicit agreement that her patient's way of living was going to be their central focus, and that whatever Coleen did would support her decisions about that. Her patient died 6 months later.

Coleen's only regret is an anticipatory one. She would very much like to do at least a year with an organization such as Doctors Without Borders. She thinks their approach is highly consistent with her belief system, but she also knows that an extended commitment is critical to this kind of international intervention. Going on such an extended tour would require changes in her primary relationship as well as impact her ability to support her sons. Speaking in the hypothetical, she says that if for some reason it were to be the last year of her life, she would want to be there for her loved ones. So at this point she does not foresee being able to spend that amount of time with humanitarian missions overseas, and instead spends evenings providing forensic evaluations for victims of political torture from across the world.

Coleen does see a spiritual component in her work. As a practicing Buddhist, fundamental respect for every living being is a key principle for her. In addition, she tries to maintain a sense of a bigger purpose as to why she is meeting with her patients or engaging in other job tasks at this moment in her life. She admits to having much to learn from her patients, and it is typical for her to see every patient interaction as an opportunity for her to learn. This perspective also helps her reduce burnout.

Dr. Kivlahan does not know whether she will have a lasting legacy—she thinks it is a funny concept to think that any one of us could believe that we do things that last forever. But, she jokes that her epitaph will be, "Just give me 5 more minutes." She has been teased relentlessly for 30 years about always wanting just 5 more minutes to do one more thing or solve another complex problem. It is a sign of her dogged persistence, which always brings her back to this: "It is not so hard . . . there ought to be a way we can figure things out together." Coleen perpetually wants a bit more time to come up with just the right solution.

CHAPTER 9

Inheriting a Commitment to Service

Dr. Mark Asperilla

Dr. Mark Asperilla has been an advocate for the diseased, disabled, and destitute in America and other countries for more than 20 years. Throughout the 1980s, he headed numerous medical missions to his native Philippines. In 1994, Mark cofounded ACCESS Care Inc., a nonprofit organization that sends teams of doctors on medical missions to Central and South America. After the 2004 Pacific typhoon, he provided medical supplies, scholarships, and 30 new homes through the Gawad Kalinga homeless program for people suffering in the Philippines.

In his adopted home in United States, Dr. Asperilla started an organization in Charlotte County, Florida, to provide wheelchairs, computers, and social activities for the disabled. Mark has donated over 2500 hours to the organization. Also, he founded the Charlotte County HIV Clinic, which has rendered more than $2 million in free medical services. When that clinic was destroyed by Hurricane Charley in 2004, Mark opened a trailer to serve the patients until a permanent structure could be rebuilt.

Dr. Asperilla established the St. Vincent de Paul Charity Clinic and Pharmacy where he serves as medical director. Through a partnership with Volunteers in Medicine, the clinic is staffed by about 30 volunteer physicians. Dr. Asperilla also donated a 1,000-square-foot office facility for the clinic's use. Ever the entrepreneur, Mark develops new businesses—

from a grapefruit orchard to a hotel—to help finance his various community health projects.

In response to the terrorist attacks on September 11, 2001, Dr. Asperilla recognized the need for a unified team to deal with the threat of bioterrorism. He created a multicounty medical response group in Florida, for which he received the Presidential Service Volunteer Award and a personal visit from then-President George W. Bush. This was followed by former President George H. W. Bush, presenting Mark with one of two national Points of Light Awards for service to American society. Dr. Asperilla is the medical coordinator for the United States Medical Reserve Corps serving southwest Florida.

Mark attended medical school at the University of Santo Tomas in the Philippines. He completed his internship at Makati Medical Center in Manila before moving to the United States in the 1970s to complete residencies in internal medicine at Frankford Hospital, affiliated with the Medical College of Pennsylvania in Philadelphia, and at Atlantic City Medical Center in Atlantic City, New Jersey, where he was named associate chief resident. Dr. Asperilla completed fellowships in infectious disease at Chicago Medical School and at Albany Medical College of Union University in Albany, New York. He is a fellow of the American College of Physicians and the International College of Physicians. Dr. Asperilla sits on the board of directors of the Charlotte County Medical Society and is a member of the Health Care Committee of the National Small Business Association of America based in Washington, D.C. In 2007, Dr. Asperilla received the Charles Donnegan Award for Volunteerism from the American College of Physicians.

Dr. Marianito "Mark" Asperilla was born and raised in the Philippines, one of six children. Part of the reason he became a doctor was the experience of having an older sister contract meningitis as a child. "I was so close to her, and she almost died," he explains. As a result of the meningitis, she became hearing impaired. "I saw her transition from a person who could do everything to a person who was disabled," Dr. Asperilla recalls. "She learned sign language and I also had to learn signing to communicate with her."

One of Mark's sisters had a congenital heart defect and died at 11 years old from surgical complications, an event Mark found very traumatic. Only 2 years separated them, and he was close to her, too. Observing his sisters' conditions and experiencing the effects of those illnesses were galvanizing events in creating Mark's interest in medicine. He notes, "I wanted to do something to help people." From such a personal place in his immediate family, Dr. Mark Asperilla moved on to touch thousands of families with his efforts.

Dr. Asperilla's grandfather was a surgeon. When Mark was growing up, he used to go to his grandfather's office to see him and the people that he helped. "I could see the outcome, the warmth and thankfulness of people he helped. They didn't have money, but they would put food outside his door, lots of fruits and vegetables. We never went hungry." Being appreciated in this warm and generous way appealed to Dr. Asperilla, and it drew him further toward medicine.

> [My parents] were concerned about how well we did as community leaders, as humanitarians—they counted that more than anything else. How we carried ourselves, how we served our communities.

Mark's first support for his future role came from his parents. His mother was a pharmacist, his father, a lawyer. It was his parents' modeling of service that most affected Dr. Asperilla. They became involved in a cerebral palsy group because one of his sisters had cerebral palsy. They founded a local group in their town for people with disabilities and contributed a lot of community service.

This service extended even into their own home. Because one daughter was impaired and one had died early, Mark's parents decided to adopt another girl, an orphan who had been left behind in a convent. "We would invite the whole orphanage over every Christmas to our home. I would see sharing and giving, and my parents helping the orphans as much as they could. I saw them helping the disabled and the less fortunate."

Dr. Asperilla never felt any pressure to choose one of his parents' professions. They "felt good about my choice of careers." One of his brothers did follow in his father's footsteps and became a lawyer, the other became an engineer, and his adopted sister became a nurse. Mark believes that his sister, too, was affected by their mother's modeling. "I think she chose nursing because she saw how my mother was caring and helped out poor people who came through the pharmacy. It was a family business, but the pharmacy didn't really make much money because my mother kept giving away medicine to people who couldn't afford it. Same thing with my grandparents. My grandmother was an educator, and my grandfather was a surgeon. They served the community well, and when my grandfather passed away, the community felt a big loss. I didn't fully realize how much he was loved by the community until then." Caring for the community seems to have been an Asperilla family tradition, a legacy passed on from one generation to the next. In fact, following directly in his mother's footsteps, the pharmacy Mark founded has given away $4 million in free medication.

Mark also gained exposure to the medical environment through his mother because he helped her all the time in the pharmacy. "I was able to develop some acumen at an early age." Because of all the time spent with his grandfather at his medical office, "I kind of did my first internship when I was a kid."

Years later, during his formal medical residencies, Mark encountered some individuals whose attitudes were less than encouraging. "I had just started a residency where I was the only minority. Part of the problem was that the chief resident didn't like minorities. I also saw other examples of discrimination in this country when I came here." He was not thwarted or discouraged by such events. "I just put it behind me and moved forward. On my down days, I immersed myself in music and played the piano. If I got upset or angry, I played the piano. Instead of seeing a psychiatrist, I played music."

Growing up in the Philippines deepened Mark's commitment to serving the community through the practice of medicine. "I saw a lot of poverty. I saw how health care was being delivered in third-world countries. If you don't have any money, and you don't have any medicine, then you die." Dr. Asperilla was able to understand this early, perhaps precociously, and was therefore able also to recognize his parents' contributions. "That's why I saw the value of my parents' generosity. I saw my mom give medicine away from the pharmacy. She made a difference." Mark's parents clearly prioritized the care of others ahead of financial gain for themselves.

I inquired whether there was a special teacher or class that helped Dr. Asperilla. His answer was surprising. He had gone to Catholic school all his life, and his first school was run by Belgian nuns, one of whom was his music teacher. "When I started playing the piano, she told me that I wasn't going to be a good musician. She would hit my hand with the ruler when I made mistakes, and eventually I learned to play. I learned discipline—the same kind of rigor and discipline you need to do well in medical school. The way I was trained by the Belgian nuns, I got to be a little compulsive. I carried that compulsion and drive to perfection through school. That's why I was an excellent student, very detail oriented." It is striking that Dr. Asperilla was able to draw a useful lesson from what many would judge a harsh learning experience. Amazing, too, that he still enjoys playing the piano so much after such a punitive approach.

> Before you can make effective decisions, you have to listen. You might be the best and brightest doctor in the world, but if you don't know how to listen, or if you don't have the emotional IQ to bond with your patient and understand how they feel, you're not a good doctor.

Had there been any readings, perhaps the story of a physician, which had caught Dr. Asperilla's attention early on? He described a lesson learned as from this morality tale: "My early readings were mostly Hemingway books. *The Old Man and the Sea* teaching about persistence—he didn't give up. The way I view life is never to give up. If you're persistent, you reach your goal; you catch your big shark." I imagine Mark remaining undefeated in his struggle to do so much for so many.

Dr. Asperilla also learned his respect for humanity from an aunt, "an extremely wise lady." She became a nurse educator after receiving her master's degree at Ohio University and her PhD in education at Columbia. Then she went back to the Philippines and established one of the first nursing schools there. Mark looked up to her. "She was one of my supporters when I came to the United States and guided my career. She was extremely bright, and she wrote a lot of books. She was like my second parent." His aunt came back to the United States and became a dean of nursing at Beth Israel in New York. Like Dr. Asperilla's parents, she "did so much community service. She established the first nursing association for Philippine nurses here in the U.S. When Philippine nurses initially came here, they had to learn the language and culture, and many were taken advantage of at their work and treated unfairly. She started this group to get fair treatment. Now it's one of the biggest organizations in the U.S. for nurses from a third-world country."

I asked Dr. Asperilla how he had felt about the medical care of someone about whom he cared. He spoke of his mother. "We all immigrated here during the 1970s and got training, but my parents went back to the islands. That's where they knew people. That's where they grew up. They were going back and forth, 6 months here and 6 months there. Of course, as they got older, they got sick. My mom was visiting me in Atlantic City when I was a resident, and she had a heart attack. We had to put a pacemaker in. I had to help put that into my own mom. She survived, and I took care of her here. You know, human life is frail. When people get older, they have a lot more medical problems. At the two ends of life, you are very dependent on people to take care of you."

His mother did not speak English well. Difficulty in being understood along with cultural barriers were "part of the reason why the care was, although technically good, not more than adequate." When she went back to the island, hospital care had more warmth, but they "didn't have the technical abilities or medications." Dr. Asperilla acknowledges that his role influenced the level of care his mother received in the United States: "If they were looking after her well, it was only because they knew me and that I was watching out for her. She got better care and special treatment because people knew she was the chief resident's mom. If she had been from outside, not related to anyone, it might have been a different story."

> "There are two types of people who go to medical school: those who went for the wrong reason and those who went for the right reason. The wrong reason is to make money, and the right reason is to serve humanity and mankind. It's basically the Hippocratic Oath. It's like a vocation, like being a priest or nun. It's a calling.

Mark reflected on his parents, what they wanted for themselves at the end of their lives, and how they felt about the legacy they had passed on. "They knew that their life was limited, and they wanted DNRs. They didn't want to be a burden to their kids. They said early on, 'if the time comes, we had a good life, and we have good children who were productive in this world. We couldn't ask for more.' They were not concerned with how much money we made. They were concerned about how well we did as community leaders, as humanitarians—they counted that more than anything else. How we carried ourselves, how we served our communities; it's not the money." Mark returns again and again to the family theme of valuing service; it is a foundational belief for him, inseparable from his identity.

I asked Dr. Asperilla what he considered to be the role of listening in his medical practice. He stressed, "It's one of the most important things a doctor should learn. Before you can make effective decisions, you have to listen. You might be the best and brightest doctor in the world, but if you don't know how to listen, or if you don't have the emotional IQ to bond with your patient and understand how they feel, you're not a good doctor. You have to be sensitive to their needs." He went on to say, "I've seen the high-IQ, academic types in medical school and university. They're extremely bright, but they don't have the emotional IQ to be a good doctor. You have to know how to be empathetic with your patients. They don't teach that in medical school." I was pleased to report to him that the U.S. medical schools have made some progress in teaching empathy in recent years.

Dr. Asperilla considers how doctors could learn this skill. "Maybe offer a sensitivity course in third-world countries—like this group that goes to Central America. Part of the healing comes from understanding and listening to your *patients* and not just to the CT scans or MRIs. You're up in the mountains with just your stethoscope, and you treat people by learning how to listen to them and their needs." Mark's comments made me think about medical education and how many faculty are currently sounding the alarm that some students are actually becoming deskilled in basic human relations because of the new technical advances.

Dr. Asperilla's primary motivation is helping people, especially those who have very limited resources. He sees medicine as a helping profession, and he differentiates between those doctors who, like him, practice medicine in order to serve and those who practice for other reasons. Mark believes "there are two types of people who go to medical school: those who went for the wrong reason and those who went for the right reason. The wrong reason is to make money, and the right reason is to serve humanity and mankind. It's basically the Hippocratic oath. It's like a vocation, like being a priest or nun. It's a calling. There are doctors I know who went to medical school for the wrong reasons. They should have just gone to business school. I've seen many people with a lot of money in my life, and no matter how much money they have, they're not happy. Money doesn't make you happy." Certainly Mark's mother, in particular, modeled this perspective for him by giving away medicine rather than making a profit from her pharmacy.

There is a direct line between Dr. Asperilla's family history and his personal ethics, which clearly revolve around humanitarian efforts. He describes helping people as "basically my elixir; it gives me those endorphins. It gives me jubilation. The most satisfied doctors I see are the ones who put the money behind them and just serve." Dr. Asperilla's sense of self and identity are tied to his ability to provide access to health care in underserved communities. He sees himself as responding to a vocational mission.

Dr. Asperilla balances a private practice with outside community projects to help disenfranchised people who have no insurance. For this he uses not just his skills as a doctor, but what he refers to as his entrepreneurial mind. He explains, "There are people who use their minds to start businesses and banks. I use mine to start up charity franchises. I started a prescription pharmacy, the only free pharmacy in the state of Florida. Because of the hepatitis epidemic, he worked with the health department to open the first hepatitis C clinic in southwest Florida. It opened the week before our interview. This year, he is putting up a new clinic in his town, because it has the second highest uninsured rate in the state.

This is not the first clinic he has started in his town. At the height of the HIV epidemic in 1994, he opened the first HIV clinic in town. He enlisted four volunteer doctors. Initially they did not have funding, but later, because of Ryan White funding, they got money to take care of all of the uninsured HIV patients. "We have given $2 million of free care to those people. Those are the kind of challenges I like to take on." As Dr. Asperilla described these projects, I was struck by the fact that he is completely unafraid to think big.

In contrast to some other medical professionals, Dr. Asperilla seems to have made use of his personal initiative to find ways to achieve his goals in spite of the current chaotic state of the U.S. healthcare delivery system. He explains, "Instead of relying on politicians, I package resources within the community itself to solve our own problems." His community was devastated by Hurricane Charley, a level 4 hurricane. His office was destroyed, but after taking care of his own family, Mark opened up a pharmacy even before the Federal Emergency Management Agency (FEMA) came in. "We were on the front line to deliver medication to those people who didn't have prescriptions. We used emergency radio, and we served thousands of people."

Then FEMA started a clinic in a trailer. The agency did not agree with Mark's operating a pharmacy at the same time. "They didn't want to foster a feeling of community. I disagreed with them; I said, you need to use the local resources." Mark preferred to meet people in front of the FEMA clinic so they would not crowd the emergency room, the more expensive option. "We got help from then-U.S. Representative Mark Foley, who found a way through the umbrella of the health department to establish the first free FEMA clinic in the whole United States. He was instrumental in getting drug companies to give medication to the pharmacies, and he always visited our pharmacy."

Dr. Asperilla does admit that some obstacles still get in the way of what he wants to do. He has already put packages together for a new free clinic in Orlando, and has located a 3500-square-foot space. He partnered with Volunteers in Medicine (VIM), founded by Dr. Jack McConnell (see Chapter 4 on McConnell in this book) who established the first VIM clinic. Mark had met McConnell when he received the AMAF award, and Jack encouraged him to set up the clinic. Mark was able to use their template for a charity clinic and was able to get funding through the free hospital. His biggest obstacle is the county. "They're giving me a hard time. Because they're broke right now, they're giving excuses not to allocate money. I'm going to the commissioner's hearing this coming Tuesday. They told me, 'Don't come to us if you want to ask for money,' but what I'm trying to get from them is a piece of property for that clinic. I already have 22 volunteer doctors lined up to serve the clinic. This would be the fourth Jack B. McConnell VIM clinic here in Florida set up to serve the uninsured." I was struck by how one winner of the Pride in the Professions Award profiled in these pages was able to inspire another and create an exponential leap forward in health care for so many.

Dr. Asperilla clarifies that the obstacles are not all political, but it is the "structure of the government. When I established the hep-C clinic, it was the health department that gave me a hard time. They wanted to put up all the memorandas of agreement. We lost six volunteers because we had to go through so many hoops. The volunteers are taking the time out of their own private practice, but the government drove the volunteers away, because they made it so hard to volunteer. It's the bureaucracy that drives people away." Mark echoes a sentiment I hear all across the country.

Mark reports that it is his family that keeps him from getting burnt out. He elaborates, "I have a supportive family; I have three beautiful kids. My wife is great, she's a school nurse. I enjoy my kids. They're my elixir. They charge me up. We joke around and mimic." To maintain his balance, he offers this list: "I play music. I do sports, I swim. I play piano . . . . My house is right off the water, and I go fishing."

He also owns an orange grove in Arcata, which is about 20 miles away, so sometimes he farms and drives a big tractor on the weekend. One time he was mistaken to be an illegal immigrant on his 300-acre grove. A local man was delivering fertilizer. "I was sweating, not looking that good. He called out to me, 'Hey, boy!' and tried to tell me to unload the fertilizer. I said, 'No, I own this grove. You better unload that fertilizer or I'm not going to pay you.' Later he became my friend." This is typical of Mark's generosity of spirit.

I asked Dr. Asperilla what he considered his biggest failure to date. He immediately responded, "Not doing enough for poor people." He particularly regrets not having done more for poor people in the Philippines. "Since I came here, I have done a lot of community stuff that benefited my adopted country. I felt bad, though, because I hadn't contributed much to the Philippines because most of my success has been here in the United States." To redress this imbalance, Dr. Asperilla has begun to allocate resources for the Philippines. Through a nongovernment organization similar to Habitat for Humanity, he started a home-building project 3 years ago, and this year is finishing his 30th home. "I kind of adopted the families that occupy those homes. I established scholarships to help them out; I have one scholar now who's finishing medical school. They have a school there that didn't have money for books, so I gave money to establish a book scholarship for 100 kids." This sounds very much like what Mark's parents did with the orphanage. Yet he feels that he "didn't do much down there." The local people disagree. They named a village after him in Tower Ville, Bulacan.

Dr. Asperilla recalls what he considers a personal failure. "I had a patient, a young patient with severe meningitis. I tried to save her, but failed. She was also Asian and reminded me of my sister. It was traumatic for me when she passed away, despite all the things that we did." Pushed as to how *he* failed the patient, he explains, "The patient came in so late in the ballgame; the parents didn't really identify the signs and symptoms early." He is still unhappy with himself, but accepts that "she came in so late, there was nothing much we could do."

Mark believes it is the good basic training he had and the discipline he learned that led to the quality of clinical practice he has today. He expounds, "I already had the emotional training growing up with my grandfather and mother—like a musician who trains from being a young kid—and then I was polished by going to medical school." Born and raised Catholic, his approach to patients is also informed by his religion. "Going to church," he says, "I learned a lot about people. My faith taught me to give back."

Although Dr. Asperilla finds that he performs better in stressful situations, when asked to reflect on a time when he lacked courage, he expressed regret that when he was in residency he observed things being done in a way he believed was not right, yet took no action to right them. "There was a pecking order. When you're doing a residency program, you have to follow the senior resident, the chief resident, and if you're an intern you're at the bottom of the totem pole. Sometimes I saw an uninsured patient, and I didn't say strongly enough that this is what you should do. I didn't assert myself. I probably could have helped out a lot of patients by being more confrontational with my chief resident, and telling it the way it was. The culture that I was brought up with stressed being nonconfrontational. When I started here in the United States, I was still adjusting to the culture." In fact, I was reminded that more hospitals now run orientations to help newly hired healthcare professionals with this issue.

> We have such a dysfunctional medical system in the United States. We're the most affluent country in the whole world, but we can't find the solution to take care of everybody here in the United States. We're more concerned about war overseas, taking care of other people's problems overseas. Yet there are 48 million people who don't have access to care.

These days, Dr. Asperilla's courage comes in the form of saying things the way they are. "I don't know if it's courageous or not, but that's how I deal with life," he observes.

I wanted to know if there was ever a time when Dr. Asperilla felt that he knew the best course of action to take on behalf of a patient, but for some reason could not get it done. He recalled, "I had a young woman, a Jehovah's Witness, who needed a blood transfusion. The religion prohibited her from getting blood, and she died. I tried to tell her that she needed blood, and she refused. I felt badly that I couldn't talk her into it. That brought me nightmares. She was so young; I could easily have saved her, but she wouldn't permit me. I couldn't convince her. I pleaded with her; I told her you're going to die if you don't get this blood. She was only in her 30s!"

Mark also remembered a different situation in which the best course of action could not be taken, for other reasons. One of the four clinics he founded was in the mountains of Peru. "We did the best we could to save a 21-year-old kid who had appendicitis. I had a doctor there who could do the surgery, but because of the limited access that we had, the appendicitis perforated. We had given the last dose of antibiotics to the patient before him, and the nearest place to get more was probably about half a day by horse. He died. I felt bad that I had given the antibiotic to the patient before him who was in less serious condition. If I had known we would need it that night, I would have held it." I feel Mark's desire to take on the powers of a prophet if it would mean that fewer patients would suffer.

Another regret Dr. Asperilla expressed was "that we have such a dysfunctional medical system in the United States. We're the most affluent country in the whole world, but we can't find the solution to take care of everybody here in the United States. We're more concerned about war overseas, taking care of other people's problems overseas. Yet there are 48 million people who don't have access to care. It's a very expensive system that doesn't deliver very good dividends. There are a lot of countries less affluent than ours, but have a better delivery system. Look at our neighbors in Canada; they have universal health care, everybody has access." Mark echoes a frustration I hear from so many providers.

Dr. Asperilla affirms a strong spiritual component in his work, especially at the end of life. He explains, "I feel strongly that there's life after death and there's a spiritual component to life. There's always a spiritual component to working with humanity. When my patients are getting ready to go to the next level, I always ask their family, is he or she prepared spiritually, or whether they would like to call a rabbi or minister or whatever. I want them better prepared for the next life, to make peace with themselves here on earth."

One of the most difficult things Mark has seen here in his career as a physician is people dying alone. "It's very difficult to die alone. When I started the HIV clinic, people were dying like flies. I found a group of ministers who would go with the patients into their rooms so they wouldn't die alone. I think dying is much easier if you die with loved ones, or someone praying with you." I thought about how Dr. Asperilla was ahead of his time in terms of the AIDS hospice movement that grew later in the 1990s.

Although he says it depends on the case, Mark brings the component of spirituality to his daily practice. He offers to pray for his patients. "I see a lot of patients and they heal quicker if they pray. There's been some studies that show if you pray for your patient, they heal quicker. We can't figure out what's causing it. So I do pray for my patients. I say to them, I will pray for you because of my faith."

Dr. Asperilla thinks there's validity to prayer in medicine and is not afraid to talk about it. "I think the best doctors are not only physical doctors, but also spiritual doctors. If you do both, that's a more holistic approach to medicine. I don't see this quality in many of my colleagues here; it's all go, go, go. I think I'm one of the few doctors in our hospital who prays for their patients." Mark's comments made me think about how the practice of medicine as purely secular might be changing. In the past few years, several journals, including the *Archives of Internal Medicine,* have been including research articles on the value of prayer. Some of Dr. Asperilla's colleagues might step forward within their traditions as the integration of prayer becomes more commonplace in medicine.

Dr. Asperilla's legacy extends the legacy of his parents. His hope is simple. "When I came to this world, I made it better." He elaborates, "That's not a matter of giving money, but helping people out." His chosen community, Charlotte County, Florida, has the oldest population in America, where the average age is 64 years. It has the highest rate of wheelchair use, one of the highest drug use rates, and one of the highest uninsured rates. Because of the age distribution, the school system is not well funded. "So basically the county I adopted is a special-needs county. My legacy would be, I came to this county and made it better. Not by getting involved in politics, but by doing it quietly and getting it done. I've founded about eight nonprofits here; I did it because I was on the front line being sensitive to the need. All the bureaucrats didn't help; I went to the community resources to do it. I think if all communities are like Charlotte County, instead of relying on federal or state agencies, they could find solutions to their own problems."

I thought about how Dr. Asperilla broadened and enlarged the legacy of his parents. He has done their work on a much grander scale, bringing help to countless numbers of people. He sees medicine as a service profession, and believes he was called to it. His first inkling that his service to others would be through the practice of medicine came when he helped his grandfather in his surgery and his mother at her pharmacy and experienced the gratitude of the people for whom they provided care and intervention. In addition to providing another model of service, Dr. Asperilla's

Catholic upbringing prepared him to affirm the role of spirituality in health care and to actively ensure that this need of his patients is met. Unlike some other medical professionals, Mark has avoided being discouraged by the state of healthcare delivery, instead using his entrepreneurial mind to find ways to circumvent it. Still he decries the problems caused by unnecessary bureaucracy and by the dysfunction of the delivery system that prevents so many people, most particularly the uninsured, from getting their medical needs met.

CHAPTER 10

What Is Harder Than Brain Surgery? Mobilizing the Healthcare Community

Dr. Gary VanderArk

Dr. Gary VanderArk is known for his devotion to the underinsured and uninsured patient. In 1988, he founded the Doctors Care program by successfully signing up his peer physicians of the Arapahoe Medical Society and persuading them that if they all did something to help the plight of the uninsured, then it would not be too burdensome on any of their practices. The nonprofit program has grown and provided access to quality, affordable medical care to over a million children and adults. In addition to his work with Doctors Care, Dr. VanderArk's leadership with the Colorado Coalition for the Medically Underserved (CCMU) has brought together the best and brightest thinkers, legislators, policy makers, providers, consumers, and business leaders to address the growing crisis of health care. CCMU is now an all-inclusive bipartisan effort, composed of over 150 individuals and organizations representing healthcare providers, consumers, business, government agencies, philanthropic organizations, and others. By initiating these access-to-health-care programs, Gary's efforts have impacted so many people who otherwise would have not been able to get the treatments they desperately needed.

In 1988, his vision and commitment led him to found a premier regional neuroscience center at the Colorado Neurological Institute (CNI). Gary believed that a doctor-driven rather than hospital-driven multidisciplinary program based on research, education, and patient care would also more effectively meet the business needs of physicians. After guiding the organization through 14 years of milestones, Dr. VanderArk stepped down in 2003 as president of CNI to accept a position as director of the neurosurgery residency at the University of Colorado Health Sciences Center, where he successfully led the program to full accreditation. He remains on faculty as a consultant.

Dr. VanderArk was honored by the American Association of Neurosurgeons with its Humanitarian of the Year Award for a lifetime of community work. Gary graduated from Calvin College and the University of Michigan Medical School, where he also completed his residency in neurosurgery.

Gary VanderArk made his commitment to neurosurgery in the third grade when his teacher asked him what he wanted to be when he grew up. Striving to outdo his peers even at that age, he named the most difficult occupation he could think of: brain surgeon. "I never ever wanted to in any way go back on my word to Ms. Katz, who was the most loveable person in the whole world," he explains, "There wasn't any way I could ever change my mind." Although Gary's mother encouraged him, his father, a minister, was disappointed that his son chose medicine instead of ministry.

Gary has never regretted his promise to Ms. Katz, but there were times when he worried that he wasn't going to be able to stay on his chosen path, given the difficulty of getting into medical school and into a neurosurgery residency. Gary says it "requires divine providence." Gary must have been the recipient of some luck and grace, then, because he made it through in record time. By spurring him on, the competitiveness may have benefited rather than hindered him.

Gary realizes that he made the commitment to being a brain surgeon before he really understood what that meant. As he continued in his studies, however, he became fascinated with the nervous system. "What a beautiful thing—to spend your life dealing with something that is so profound and so beautiful, so wonderfully arranged and such a challenge." He became even more enthralled as he continued to learn neuroanatomy, until, "There was no question, there was no turning back, there was no settling for second best, there was never a possibility then that I could do something 'simple' like heart surgery. The nervous system was just absolutely the ultimate," Gary contends. No one in Dr. VanderArk's immediately family thought he couldn't become whatever he wanted, but it was his mother who was his first cheerleader. She joined with him in always thinking that he could do anything and affirmed his inherent belief in his own abilities. When he talked about medical school, she simply said, "Well of course you can do that."

His father was his main role model in learning respect for other people. When Gary was young, his dad owned a hardware store, yet spent his free time starting missions and doing other religious work. Later in life, his father became a minister. "My father was the epitome of walking the walk of what it meant to be a Christian," Gary states. His father never passed a car sitting on the side of the road. He was a lifelong model of "you can't just talk about being a Christian; you've got to live that out every minute of your life." As far back as Gary can remember, "It was always about acting justly, loving mercy, and walking humbly with your God." Service was a driving force in his family, and Dr. VanderArk has striven to follow his father's example. Despite not going to seminary as his father wished, Gary sees his work as a doctor as being his ministry, and religion has been the primary influence on his life and his work.

> My father was the epitome of walking the walk of what it meant to be a Christian. . . . You can't just talk about being a Christian; you've got to live that out every minute of your life.

Gary would later meet another important influence in his mentor, Eddie Kahn, the chairman of neurosurgery at the University of Michigan. Dr. Kahn is rumored to be the neurosurgeon about whom the book *Magnificent Obsession* was written. In the *American Association of Neurology Bulletin*, Dr. VanderArk shares his thoughts through a book review he wrote.

> *Magnificent Obsession* was written by the Rev. Lloyd C. Douglas . . . [who] was the minister at the Congregation Church in Ann Arbor, Mich., which is only a few blocks from the University Hospital. It has always been a poorly kept secret in Michigan that Edgar A. Kahn, MD, was the inspiration for *Magnificent Obsession*. The novel tells the story of Bobby Merrick, a neurosurgeon who is given the secret journal of his mentor that contains the magic formula for success. The journal is written in code, which is miraculously

solved by the young neurosurgeon. He learns of a "particular investment of himself as a high altruism." Dr. Merrick finds that fulfillment is best achieved by providing secret service for others. He experiences the joy of doing wonderful things for people in need. He requires secrecy, and suggests, if possible, the good deed be passed on to someone else in need . . .

Dr. Kahn was my hero and he made me a neurosurgeon. It has always been my goal to emulate Dr. Kahn in my practice of neurosurgery. He certainly passed on his magnificent obsession to all of his residents. We were amazed at his ability to give of himself to his patients. Even when Dr. Kahn reached retirement age, he lost none of his passion for his patients. Dr. Kahn spent his entire career at the University Hospital in Ann Arbor and always worked for $1 per year. (VanderArk, 2001, p. 36)

Eddie Kahn grew up in Detroit, the son of a financially successful architect who designed not only all the assembly lines of the Michigan automakers, but also the university hospital in Ann Arbor. "Eddie was the embodiment of the principal of doing wonderful things for people in need," Gary recalls, "So I really had the perfect mentor that I had been striving for and looking for." What Gary particularly noticed about Eddie was how intent he was on overcoming whatever obstacles got in the way of doing things for people. "He would never, ever take no for an answer," Gary recalls, "He always attempted to do what other people said was not possible."

As a hard-working champion of excellence in medicine, Gary was not impressed with one aspect of the care he received during the 3 months spent in bed with a serious illness in 2007. He found himself very angry at his insurance carrier because they gave him the least expensive medication available to treat his infection. It was not until he had gone through a series of six different antibiotics that they finally gave him a more expensive one that worked. He cannot help but think that they should have treated him with the more expensive medication at the beginning, so that he would not have suffered 3 months of bed rest and a lot of unnecessary treatments and complications. Gary did find his day-to-day care to be wonderful, but attributes its quality to that fact that he has made waves in the community for a long time. Profoundly meaningful to him, though, was the incredible outpouring of love and support he received from his community while he was ill.

Gary learned a lot about the role of listening during his prolonged illness. His wife kept asking him what he was supposed to be learning from the experience, as did a friend one day. The friend, a thoracic surgeon, was part of a small doctors' Bible study group that Gary had been participating in for 20 years. He said, "Of course we all know what you're learning from this." Gary was shocked, and asked him to explain. His friend pointed out, "Everybody who knows you thinks you've always lacked two things, and that's what you're supposed to be learning from this." Gary asked what those two things were, and his friend replied, "patience and humility."

Dr. VanderArk might be saving up most of his forbearance for his patients. Gary encourages healthcare practitioners to pay attention to the details in the clinical encounter. With regard to his own consultations, Gary has "always been a firm believer that the patient knows better than we do what the appropriate treatment is." He clarifies, "I've had many patients tell me 'enough already.' When it gets to the point of 'enough already,' it often means we haven't been listening to the patient. They often know much better than we do."

Gary has no trouble getting out of bed every morning and persevering. "I greet each day with enthusiasm. I think life is wonderful and that while I've been given an exciting mission, every day I'm presented with just phenomenal opportunities," Gary declares. Attempting to retire in 2003, he found himself back at the medical school, and reports that it has been an incredibly rejuvenating process for him to discover that "the medical students are absolutely wonderful." Gary finds the new crop of students to be idealistic and committed to service. He notes that when they finish school with an average debt of $193,000, they understandably want to get a paying job; but as new providers in the making, they are looking forward to a lifetime of service.

> The patient knows better than we do what the appropriate treatment is. I've had many patients tell me 'enough already.' When it gets to the point of 'enough already,' it often means we haven't been listening to the patient.

Gary's goals are 100% tied to his sense of personal ethics. During a recent seminar on health policy for junior medical students, he was asked what inspires him. His students were flabbergasted by his answer: his religion. They took exception to his disclosure that he has practiced for 35 years, and every patient who has ever seen him knows that he is a Christian. The students responded by lecturing Dr. VanderArk on the separation of church and state and proffering the opinion that one's faith should not filter into clinical practice. Gary disagreed, saying, "We're not talking about the state here; we're talking about me and my patients, and it would be a mistake if my patients didn't understand my faith." He hopes he set them straight. There is no question as to what fuels Gary; he is not at all hesitant to share his source of motivation, and is in fact quite proud of it.

Gary's personal credo reflects his sense of self. It is "absolutely the most important thing," he asserts, quoting, "Only one life, 'twill soon be past, only what's done for Christ will last." He acknowledges that he wears his religion on his sleeve, almost literally in that he almost always wears a cross or some other symbol that allows people to identify him as a Christian. He has an open Bible on his desk and the physician's prayer in his examining room. He believes that because of the presence of these symbols, people feel free to talk to him about their faith.

Dr. VanderArk's primary goal in life is to help the medically underserved. What gets in his way is the bottom line. For example, the University of Colorado Health Sciences Center is in the process of moving its campus 5 miles east to a new $2 billion campus. To build the new hospital, it has been necessary to sell bonds, and "it's terribly important that these bonds be given at a favorable rate. Whether you get the right kind of bond rating depends on your bottom line. As a result, for the last 10 years since this decision was made, the university hospital has done everything within its power to keep people without insurance and without money away from the university hospital, and they have built this Taj Mahal which looks like it's built only for Warren Buffet and Bill Gates and their ilk. In light of that, I have a constant battle with the hospital, the dean, the chancellor, and just about everybody else. I think the role of the hospital here ought to be to serve everybody regardless of their financial situation. As a result of that, I'm constantly at war with the powers that be." The biggest obstacle, as Gary sees it, is a type of elitism that keeps people away from quality care.

> My students have taken exception to my religion inspiring me. They lectured me about the separation of church and state, and that one's faith should not filter into clinical practice. But we're not talking about the state here; we're talking about me and my patients, and it would be a mistake if my patients didn't understand my faith.

In addition to his work at the medical school, Dr. VanderArk continues to run the Doctors Care program for indigent residents on the south side of town. Ironically, the leading source of referrals to Doctors Care is the university hospital. "Wow, what an incredible embarrassment," he admits. The mission of the hospital, as described in its founding documents, is to take anyone who is sick, "not just rich people or people who have insurance," he notes. This ongoing point of contention with the university hospital is most frustrating to him.

Gary denies that he ever faces the challenge of burnout. "I'm one of these people who never gets discouraged. I guess it's just my personality," he explains. He also feels an obligation to maintain a certain level of optimism, believing that others depend on him for it. "If I were to be pessimistic," he explains, "it would really affect a lot of people. So, if I have those feelings, I have to keep them extremely quiet." He gets his motor recharged every morning with prayer and meditation. "And when I finish laying all my concerns on somebody else's shoulders, then I'm ready to continue the fight. If I don't fight, who will?" he asks. He strongly believes that the world needs him to carry on this struggle toward justice.

Gary identifies being unable to replicate Doctors Care on a much larger scale as his biggest regret to date as a "terrible, terrible failure." His founding of Doctors Care grew out of his realization (gained when he went into private practice) that it made a difference whether or not someone was insured. "That's why I got involved with organized medicine," he explains. By the late 1980s, he was president-elect of the Arapahoe Medical Society, and they had a crisis. The university hospital announced in July of 1987 that because the state funds for the medically indigent were exhausted for the year, they would no longer see any patients from the city and county of Denver. This was not an immediate concern because most people from Denver went to Denver General Hospital; However, Denver General was beginning to turn away more patients as well. That was concerning because Denver General had always been the one place that any poor person could go to receive care. As a result, the emergency rooms in the metropolitan areas surrounding the city filled up with uninsured patients, and those hospitals asked the medical society to do something about it. As president-elect, Gary felt responsible for resolving the problem. He reasoned that if everyone did a little bit, no one would have to do too much, so he sent out a letter to the entire medical society saying that they were all going to see the poor, and to contact him if they did not want to participate. He then went to the two hospitals in his area and told them that there was a plan to keep the uninsured out of the emergency rooms, and they both agreed to participate by providing not only inpatient care but imaging and lab services as well. Dr. VanderArk admits that the hospitals might have agreed to be part of the program because they feared that they would make their doctors angry if they did not participate.

The doctor with the big heart got the Doctors Care program started on Valentine's Day, 1988. Patients were expected to pay on a sliding scale. By the end of the first year the program had 1000 patients. The hospital foundations paid for prescriptions, all of which were filled at the hospital pharmacies. It soon became apparent that half of the patients were children. Because the segments of the profession least able to afford to deliver free care are the pediatricians and the family practice doctors, a clinic for sick children was started and staffed by physician assistants who were supervised by a group of pediatric internists. Medicaid patients were not seen initially because it was assumed that they would be seen in the doctor's offices; when it became apparent that they were not being seen because no one was accepting Medicaid, the program agreed to see those patients as well.

Doctors Care has always managed to stay flexible. When a need arises, the organization adapts. Over the first 20 years, it has provided more than $50 million in free care. Gary now truly believes that these doctors are meeting the needs of the medically underserved in the Denver area.

Gary describes Doctors Care as "a community solution to a community problem." Everyone is involved. All the service clubs in the area are invited to be part of the program and volunteers have made themselves available to do the necessary financial screens. All the government entities in the area participate to some degree. The state liability insurer, Colorado Physician Insurance Company, provides free insurance for everyone working at the clinic. More and more retired physicians are working at the clinic, and a local hospital has been a resource. One of the unique things that Gary has insisted on is that each board meeting includes sharing a story about a patient in whose life Doctors Care has made a difference. In this way, knowledge of the good that the program does is spread.

Dr. VanderArk states that if he has a talent, it is boldness in asking for help. He believes that "doctors become doctors to do good, not to do well," and he also believes that "you always get more than you give."

Perhaps this is why he is able to ask for so much from others. He explains by saying, "When we started Doctors Care, it was so easy because I happened to practice in a setting where there was not only a combined medical staff, but also two competing hospitals. In order for Doctors Care to work, we had to have both hospitals participating; attempts to replicate it have failed because the hospitals wouldn't go along with it. The way that we started Doctors Care was to tell one hospital that we were going to do this with the other hospital. Then I went to the other hospital and told them that the other hospital is going to participate, 'wouldn't you like to participate, too?' So we had a unique setting in which to make this work." In addition to having two hospitals, the center of Doctors Care's catchment area is where "all the rich people live," so the region as a whole has fewer medically underserved. "So," Gary explains, "because the hospitals agreed, and because it's the area with the fewest medically underserved, the program has succeeded." But Gary is not satisfied with having established such a successful program in Denver; he wants to be able to do as much for the poor and uninsured in other areas as well.

Gary feels he has had limited success. He notes that when it has been possible to replicate Doctors Care, it has been in situations in which the hospital can see the benefit of everyone having a medical home. Until recently, "This business of saving money with a medical home has been one of those intuitive things," that Gary always believed in but that was not supported by hard data. He has been following the emerging data on how medical homes can save money over time. Now that the Medicaid program in places like North Carolina has proven that expenses are cut when people have a medical home, Gary can be more persuasive. Although every community has some response to the medically underserved, not many places have the community involvement that supports Doctors Care. So Gary's biggest failure to date is that the momentum of the movement begun by his program has not picked up yet.

In addition to prayer and meditation, Gary maintains his balance through exercise. He runs or does something active for an hour every day. At 6′4″ and 175 pounds, he has "always been one of these people who is high energy. I can't stand still." Gary keeps his sense of humor by following in his father's footsteps. His father was a notorious joke teller, and now Gary, too, is expected to have a new joke whenever he sees people. He gets 20 to 30 jokes via email a day, from people all over the country.

Gary isn't sure exactly what has led him to the style of practice he maintains with his patients, but he is sure he is doing something right. Before he retired and began working at the medical school, he was in a practice with eight other neurosurgeons. From the beginning, he insisted on evidence-based practice, and so theirs was one of the first practices in neurosurgery that did patient satisfaction surveys. Gary always did better than the other eight surgeons on those surveys. The other surgeons joked that his patients reported higher satisfaction because Gary would not *stand* for their not doing well. Gary acknowledges that that probably does say something about his relationships with his patients. "The beautiful thing about practicing in one community for 30 years," he notes, "is that I never ever go to any meeting anywhere in the metropolitan area that I don't have someone in the audience or the group that I've operated on." Regardless of whether he has gotten good results because his patients do not want to disappoint him or due to other reasons, he is pleased he has a lot of happy customers.

Gary admits to times when he has shown cowardice in his dealings with a patient. He lived through the golden era of neurosurgery, which went from having to visualize the operatory field and positions, to being able to operate with the use of a navigational system. Dr. VanderArk thinks that his failures along the way were the times he said "there isn't anything we can't do," because he did not always recognize the limits of his craft. On the most difficult skull-base cases that no one else would do, he would convince a skull-base head-and-neck surgeon to work with him. They often took 20 hours to do a case, and over time it became apparent that "all of this was unnecessarily heroic," as those tumors were found to be better treated with radiation. Over the course of his career, Dr. VanderArk has performed surgery on patients who, as a result, had facial paralysis or double vision or were blinded in one eye, because he "attempted to do what most people had said was not possible to do." Gary acknowledges that at times he went too far, and people were hurt because he was not willing to acknowledge that. He admits that this was partly arrogance, but was also partly his desire to help people who came to him from all over the country and the world, desperate for a miracle.

There were also times of courage in Gary's career. He recalls when he operated on one of his best friends, who had a ruptured aneurysm in his brain. "Basically I did it because I didn't think anybody could do a better job than I could." His friend was one of Colorado's most famous people. In the course of operating, his friend had an uncontrollable hemorrhage, and there was no way that Gary could suck the blood fast enough to see where to fix the problem, so he just blindly put a clip beneath the blood without knowing where it was going. It turned out to be "absolutely the perfect place, it could not have been a fraction of a millimeter in either direction and had any possibility of success," he recalls. His friend not only survived, but also recovered such that he had no neurological dysfunction of any kind and was able to resume his public career.

"Those kinds of things happen in neurosurgery all the time," Gary clarifies, adding, "You have no explanation as to why it turned out the way it turned out." His courage, then, has sometimes been based on hoping to be lucky.

In neurosurgery, Gary explains, it happens quite often that as a doctor, he believes he knows the best course for a patient, but is unable to follow through. This usually happens because the patient says no. "Brain surgery still has a sense of fear and awe for people," Gary points out. Because of this, when patients are told what could be done and what he recommends be done, they often refuse. Gary attributes some of this problem to the relatively new need for informed consent. "The fact that you have to disclose so many things now that in previous generations you would never think about disclosing . . . Thirty years ago we put patients at terrible risk without giving them the choice about that. It was the paternalistic model. Nowadays it's the patient's choice." But perhaps the pendulum has swung so far in the other direction that this mandatory autonomy may not always be in the best interests of many patients who are not in a position to make the kind of decision required.

> I recharge my motor every morning with prayer and medication. And when I finish laying all my concerns on somebody else's shoulders, then I'm ready to continue the fight. If I don't fight, who will?

Dr. VanderArk has made addressing the needs of the uninsured his mission, and after 31 years of working on that mission, there are still 785,000 people in the state of Colorado without health insurance. Gary jokes, "I pointed that fact out to a church I spoke at last month, and someone raised their hand and said, 'Maybe it's time for you to quit!'" Joking aside, he greatly regrets that even with all his efforts, the problem has expanded rather than been reduced.

He is not done yet. To do more about the medically underserved, he joined the Colorado Medical Society and was put on the Medically

Indigent Committee. After a few years he was made chairman of that committee. Then the president of the Colorado Medical Society called and told him that the committee had been terminated. Gary protested, but was told the decision was final. He decided to run for president, and ran on a one-plank platform that the medical society must make the medically underserved their highest priority. To his surprise, he won, and started the Colorado Coalition for the Medically Underserved. "That's the new organization that will see to it that everyone in Colorado has coverage and access to quality health care," Gary proclaims.

Gary hopes that his lasting legacy will be that he lived and taught the biblical line quoted so often by his dad that advises working for justice, spreading kindness, and doing so with humility. It seems that he has already achieved this. At a talk he gave at a Denver seminary recently, the president introduced him as, "Dr. VanderArk, the personification of Micah 6:8. *He has told you, O man, what is good; And what does the lord require of you but to do justice, to love kindness, And to walk humbly with your God?*" When Gary heard this, he could not speak because he had tears in his eyes.

Dr. VanderArk has learned the lesson of perseverance well and will continue to push forward on behalf of others. In fact, the saying he uses often in the written description of his CCMU project is: "We Can, We Must, We Will." His friends and colleagues certainly noticed his attachment to his motto and in 2008, when Doctors Care celebrated its 20th anniversary, more than 400 people came out for the party. Somehow the staff of Doctors Care was able to maintain secrecy about a new award that was given out that day—it turned out to be the Gary VanderArk "We can! We Must! We Will!" award. The Arapahoe-Douglas-Elbert Medical Society announced that it had raised enough money so that the award could be given annually.

Dr. VanderArk is also fond of quoting this ancient Japanese proverb: "Vision without action is a daydream. Action without vision is a nightmare." Like his mentor, Dr. Kahn, Gary still thinks the secret is to do good things for other people, because by doing so, you receive even greater blessings.

CHAPTER 11

His Rx: Spiritual Healing

Dr. Gerald G. "Jerry" Jampolsky

Dr. Jerry Jampolsky is an internationally recognized authority in the fields of psychiatry, health, and education. In 1975, when there were virtually no emotional support systems for people affected by catastrophic illness, Jerry and some friends established the original International Center for Attitudinal Healing in Tiburon, California. The center helps children, adolescents, and adults facing life-threatening illness, grief, and loss find support that can be transforming for them and their families.

Many years ago, while making the rounds on a University of California Medical Center's pediatric oncology ward, Jampolsky overheard a child ask his doctor what it was like to die. The doctor hurriedly changed the subject. Dr. Jampolsky was to discover that physicians and parents alike avoided answering questions about death. Instead, it was the hospital's compassionate cleaning lady who answered the children's questions by sitting on the edge of their beds, speaking from her own experience, and as an equal. Jerry founded the center to create a safe place where kids with cancer could talk and share their feelings.

Through his work at the International Center for Attitudinal Healing (which is currently undergoing a name change to CorStone), Dr. Jampolsky created the first support group model now used extensively worldwide. In 1987, he and his wife, psychologist Diane Cirincione,

PhD, cofounded the AIDS Hotline for Kids based at the center. Jerry's work has been featured on many media outlets including 60 Minutes, CNN, The Today Show, *and* PBS. *Since its inception, the center has served more than 40,000 people free of charge. Support is now offered not only to children, but to people of all ages. Services are still provided by trained volunteers, just as in the very first group with children. Inspired by the original center, there are now well over a hundred independent Centers for Attitudinal Healing located in 27 countries on 5 continents that offer free support services to their communities.*

Dr. Jampolsky has published extensively and is the author of Love is Letting Go of Fear *and over a dozen books on attitudes and healing that have sold close to 7 million copies worldwide. He has been invited to lecture in over 50 countries. Jerry studied at the University of California at Berkeley as an undergraduate and earned an MD at Stanford Medical School. Jerry is a former faculty member of the University of California School of Medicine in San Francisco, where he has held fellowships in child psychiatry at Langley Porter Neuropsychiatric Institute. Dr. Jampolsky is a fellow of the American Psychiatric Association. Past his 80th birthday, he continues to give workshops and to write with his wife, Dr. Cirincione.*

Dr. Jampolsky opened our dialogue with this prayer: "We are only here to be truly helpful. We are here to represent you who sent us. We do not have to worry about what we are going to do or say, because you who sent us will direct us. We're content to be wherever you wish, knowing that you go there with us. We will be healed if you teach us to heal." He explains that for him and his wife, these words "set the ego aside and opens us up to a whole different way of talking."

Jerry believes there was a moment in his childhood that pushed him toward his life's work. His mother was born in England, but her parents moved the family to Russia. Hard-working people, they were very fearful about the future. Jerry summarizes their defining attitude as, "If today was awful, tomorrow's going to be even worse." The family was isolated, and there were no visitors to the home other than family members who occasionally came by. At Christmastime, however, his parents gave gifts to "the ice man, the mailman, anyone who gave service to the house." Jerry took note of this and developed a desire to "do something that would be helpful to the universe." His desire to make a difference continued to develop through grammar school and high school.

Dr. Jampolsky may have been influenced in regard to a career in medicine by his two older brothers. One was a biochemist, and the other became an optometrist and ophthalmologist. In medical school, however, Jerry set out on his own path by being the only person he knew who was interested in psychiatry. At the time, there was no department of psychiatry at Stanford; it was a little division under the department of medicine. "Everyone did everything they could to talk me out of becoming a psychiatrist," recalls Dr. Jampolsky. He was not persuaded.

Dr. Jampolsky's parents were not supportive of his goal. "My parents dubbed my behavior crazy; they called me "meshuggana." I thought that was my real name," he jokes. His mother told him not to go into psychiatry, because "all psychiatrists do is tell their patients to blame their mothers." But Jerry was drawn to psychiatry early on. He wanted to help people by "finding out what makes them tick." He liked listening to people and being supportive of people, and recognized that he was good at it. He was not a good student, however. He had dyslexia and was at the bottom of his class. Nonetheless, he knew he had a talent "of inspiring people by my ability to understand them." Knowing he had something to offer others motivated him to keep on moving forward.

Dr. Jampolsky does not recall receiving support from anybody as he continued on his path toward psychiatry. "In 1946, it wasn't a very popular thing to go into," he explains. During his rotations in Boston, despite the clumsiness that resulted from his dyslexia, a surgeon took a real liking to him, and among the interns, permitted only Jerry to do surgery. "He very much wanted me to go into surgery. He saw something in me that I didn't see, because I was just a clumsy clod," Dr. Jampolsky reflects. Although the surgeon was not a supporter of Dr. Jampolsky's pursuit of psychiatry, he supported him in the field of medicine.

During his 3rd year of medical school, he attended a conference in Norway, the International Association for Interns and Medical Students. It was an organization that was working to raise the salaries of interns, to discontinue the old boy's club, and to have more reasonable workdays. Because he attended the conference, "My dean wanted to kick me out of medical school," but Jerry reminded him that he went there as an unofficial delegate, and that if the threats continued, he would get a lawyer.

From this experience, Dr. Jampolsky learned "how important it was to stick my neck out."

Always a bit of a renegade, one way in which Dr. Jampolsky demonstrated courage was his early opposition to the Vietnam War. Jerry's opposition almost got him kicked out of his medical society. Being against the war was a very unpopular position, and his society "felt that anyone who was against the war was a Communist." Dr. Jampolsky remembers that period as a very difficult time.

Near the bottom of his class academically, Dr. Jampolsky learned to trust his intuition early in medical school. During his internship, he did not realize he was being graded, then discovered that he was, and that he was at the top of his class. He explains, "I had been very intuitive in medical school. I could give the right diagnosis for the wrong reason, not in an analytical tidy way." Interacting directly with patients brought his gifts to light, as he clarifies, "I knew I had a talent in that area and a way with working with patients that gave me confidence that what I was doing was helpful, and that I should trust in my intuition." Still, this realization did not come without a struggle. Despite his inner knowing, he also "had a lot of self-doubts along the way." Referring to the book his wife is currently writing entitled, *I Don't Know If I'm Good Enough*, Jerry makes his point, "I never asked myself that question. I *knew* I wasn't good enough." Dr. Jampolsky's view of himself changed along with the evolution of his work.

> Listening is unconditional love, not making judgments, not interpreting people wrongly. It changes things. . . . When you attune to the spiritual, your heart will open up with compassion.

Diane Cirincione arrived in his life about 5 years after he had founded the International Center for Attitudinal Healing and had become truly involved in the work of healing. She became his colleague, life partner, second wife, coauthor, and companion collaborator. None of his previous relationships had been successful. "I was an alcoholic and an atheist," Jerry acknowledges. "I had a spiritual awakening in 1975. And then Diane came; she helped me shift further."

He describes a big change that happened during their first lecture together: "We got down there, and her name was not on the program. She was really pissed. She said, 'I don't think I want to be here anyway, I'm not going to go in there; they only want to hear you.' I said, 'Diane, that's okay with me, even if you were on the program, you could choose not to go in.

But why did you come here?' She thought for a minute, and said, 'I came here to give love.' Jerry responded 'Well, do you think you're capable of doing that? I know I'm capable of doing that.' And out of my mouth came the words: 'that's all that you'll ever be required to do.' " This idea about showing up simply to give love became a core idea for Jerry and Diane.

Diane helped shape Jerry's work. Unlike Dr. Jampolsky, Diane had always been close to God. Both partners were students in *A Course in Miracles*. "We knew that we were soul mates. Our minds joined as one as we went on this course of healing ourselves rather than trying to change other people." Together they developed a concept they coined *practical spirituality*. "It's not about being rigid or using religious terminology," Dr. Jampolsky clarifies. When he first started the work, other doctors questioned what he was doing, using the word *God*, but Jerry was not concerned. "I knew I wasn't there to win a popularity contest; I knew that somehow, this was my direction."

Early on, Jerry found through his work with children that they were "like wise spirits in young bodies." From the kids, he and the other volunteers learned "other ways of looking at life and death and healing." As he began his new work, Jerry experienced an epiphany, in which he "felt an inner voice saying, this is your way home." He also had a new vision of God as "an energy of unconditional love that's in me and moves through me and directs my life." Dr. Jampolsky made the decision to follow his new vision. About the same time, he was able to resolve some long-term struggles with alcoholism and fear-based thinking.

Jerry did not know what direction his work with children would take, but he realized it was a whole different way. When the AIDS epidemic began, he worked with children who had AIDS and those whose parents were dying with AIDS. Later he began a person-to-person program for people who are not ill but who want to change their lives by "creating passion in their own lives, their own relationships and marriages, their own workplaces." Dr. Jampolsky's programs have expanded to offer help to so many.

Dr. Jampolsky experienced another epiphany when he realized he could write a book. He had failed English at UC Berkeley when he first went there in 1943, and he had to take a "dumbbell English course" in which he got a C−. He recalls that his instructor said to him, "I don't know what you're going to do in life, but for God's sake, don't ever try to write a book!" Jerry believed his instructor, because his grammar and spelling were awful. He did go on to write a book (*Love Is Letting Go of Fear*), and one day, he got a telephone call from actor and frequent

Tonight Show guest Orson Bean, telling him to watch the *Tonight Show* that night. On the show, Orson pulled out Jerry's book, saying, "this book changed my life; I want to talk about this book." Dr. Jampolsky recalls that he then spent 10 minutes talking about his book, and "all of a sudden I was invited to give trainings and talks, and interest started to build." His ideas spread onto national and international stages and now that book has been read by millions.

Still, Jerry had guidance that he should not charge people money for his support programs. He believed that "somehow we would be taken care of." After 2 years, however, his secretary informed him that they had bills to pay and no funds to pay them. At that time, Dr. Jampolsky had been in contact with book publishers about another book, but had not yet signed a contract; in fact, he had made a commitment to himself that if he couldn't get a publisher, he would publish the book himself. So, faced with financial difficulties, he thought he had "better go down to the bank and borrow the money," but that same day, in the afternoon mail, "we got a check for $10,000, just the amount of money that we needed." Such synchronistic events helped keep the center going in its early years.

A major learning experience for Dr. Jampolsky occurred when he had glaucoma in both eyes. His right eye developed an infection, and he had to have a needle put into it, which meant that he would not be able to use the eye for weeks. As a very giving person, Jerry found it difficult to open himself to being taken care of by someone else. The woman who came to help him arrived on her birthday. When he asked her why she was there on her birthday when she should be out celebrating, she said that when she had cancer, she did not know she would be there to celebrate her birthday. So he was the person she wanted to be with. "And she really taught me how important it was to accept giving from other people; it really opened my heart. I could see that I was giving her and other people a gift by allowing them to take care of me," Jerry explains. He learned that being resistant to accepting giving was "a part of my ego that really needed to be let go."

Realizing this has opened a door for Dr. Jampolsky to a whole different way of practicing medicine, in which "you aren't acting like you know what's going on and they don't." This new way results in a different kind of relationship between doctor and patient. Jerry is more open to being changed by his interactions rather than just providing a service in a unilateral fashion.

For Dr. Jampolsky, listening quite clearly has a very important role in the practice of medicine. He defines listening as "unconditional love, not making judgments, not interpreting people wrongly." He comments that listening has been very helpful to a lot of physicians because listening changes things. "When you attune to the spiritual, your heart will open up with compassion," he teaches. For Jerry, listening is about openness and empathy.

Jerry feels his purpose is to be of service and to "be a messenger of love and of God, and to celebrate." He recalls another experience that made things clear to him. In Denver for a speaking engagement, he met a teenager who had been in a bad car accident and was shining shoes. He was so engrossed in shining Dr. Jampolsky's shoes that it took him 30 minutes. Jerry asked him what was going on in his mind while he was doing it. "People have churches. Well, this is my ministry; I shine shoes with as much love and attention as I can." Dr. Jampolsky said to himself, "I want to be like this man." And like the teenager, he has given all his love and attention to his ministry, the work of the center.

> Everyone has an inner physician, and when people empower themselves around that, they go to their physicians in a collaborative way, rather than passively sitting there and taking threats around compliance.

In *A Course in Miracles*, Jerry learned that "integrity is having harmony in what you think, say, and do." From his own experience he has learned that "that's what authenticity and honesty is about. It's noticing people and sharing love, and going into relationships with a high tolerance." He describes himself as a work in progress and admits that he is challenged every day about making judgments, but he believes it is the intention that is the most important element.

Dr. Jampolsky elaborates on his philosophy in his bestselling book:

> Each instant of our lives can be regarded as a present opportunity for a new awakening or rebirth, free from the irrelevant intrusion of memories from the past and anticipations of the future. In the freedom of this present moment, we can extend our natural loving nature.
>
> When we find ourselves irritated, depressed, angry or ill, we can be sure we have chosen the wrong goal and are responding to fear. When we are not experiencing joy we have forgotten to make peace of mind our single goal, and have become concerned about getting rather than giving.
>
> By consistently choosing love rather than fear, we can experience a personal transformation that enables us to be more naturally loving to ourselves and others. In this way we can begin to recognize and experience the love and joy that unites us. (Jampolsky, 2004, p. 42)

Even though Dr. Jampolsky knows that our attitudes can cause us distress, he says he does not have a method for totally avoiding burnout or despair; he is challenged by it every day, and believes that no one escapes it. He does his best to notice it and not get stuck in it. His goal is to stay in the present. He resists beating himself up about it, instead trying to learn from it and move forward.

Another antidote for Jerry is to go to the center and attend a group for people with cancer. "Just being a participant in the group and getting so focused on being there and giving my love—all of a sudden I lose myself and I'm in another consciousness." Another thing Dr. Jampolsky does to deal with the inevitable feelings of burnout and despair is to ask for help. "Early in my life I was afraid to ask for help," he recalls, "and today I'm quite willing to ask for help."

Asking for help is something he and his wife do to maintain their relationship. They have an agreement that, when their egos get in the way and they get upset with each other, they will say three words, "I need help." When that is said, they will listen to each other and take care of everything before they go to bed. The idea behind this is that the person who is having problems takes responsibility for his or her emotions. "That's been very helpful, for us, and for other couples," according to Dr. Jampolsky.

When Jerry was a resident in psychiatry in San Francisco, he had a patient who jumped off the Golden Gate Bridge and killed himself. He blamed himself, thinking that he should have known more, and that it was his fault. He says that he was obsessed with it. Years later, he had a patient who had been very depressed who told him that she was going to jump off the Golden Gate Bridge. Dr. Jampolsky treated her for about 6 months, and then she moved to another city. In 2003, he was walking across the Golden Gate Bridge, and his former patient happened to be there, too, and came up to him and said, "Oh, Doctor, do you remember me? I was the one who was going to jump off the bridge." This was a big lesson for Jerry, that "it's possible to conquer your own biggest fear." He experienced "some sort of karmic balance."

Jerry thinks that the most important thing that led him to the kind of practice he maintained with his patients was working on himself to "let go of the obstacles that I put in the way of my being loving, compassionate, and kind, and to know that those things that I see in another person are a reflection of things I see in myself." He articulates a philosophy about owning his own projections.

When Dr. Jampolsky started his work with the center, he wasn't concerned about being popular; instead, he "just wanted to push the envelope," to expand what was being offered to patients. He was prepared for the inevitable criticism that comes when one does something different, and he wasn't fearful. In fact, in the beginning, the American Medical Association and others weren't really very interested in what Jerry was doing. Then its journal published a paper about his work that was very positive, and many medical professionals around the country began to come to the center to get training. Subsequently, these professionals began to change the atmosphere in the places they worked.

Jerry believes that "everyone has an inner physician" and that when people "empower themselves around that," they go to their physicians "in a collaborative way rather than passively sitting there and taking threats around compliance." This is an important aspect of healing. "And then there are so many unhealed healers among new physicians," he worries, "addicted to drugs, addicted to sex; high suicide rate, high divorce rate." Somehow, this shift in thinking about roles helped Dr. Jampolsky find "the space to be vulnerable," to share his own story without worrying that people would see that he had problems in his own life.

Jerry recalls the moral dilemma he faced years ago—before he got involved in attitude and healing—when he had patients who wanted his help in dying. He was able to put himself in their positions and feel empathic, recognizing that if he were the one who was dying, that is what he would want. Despite his understanding, Dr. Jampolsky was unable to assist them in dying, because it was illegal. "I had great conflict about that," he recalls. "My heart wanted to help them, but my ego was critical, about the price I would pay. I was thinking about myself and not the patient. That was my conflict; I imagine it's a conflict for a lot of doctors."

> It's not that I like everything that's been put on my plate, but I think it's possible to have a different attitude about what's on my plate.

When Jerry looks back, he has no regrets because he is clear that he needed to have the experiences he had. "It's not that I like everything that's been put on my plate," he clarifies, "but I think it's possible to have a different attitude about what's on my plate. I don't see them as regrets anymore. I stay in the present. I've learned a lot from the past, and I'm thankful for the experiences I've had, even though they seemed at the time very negative." He also expresses thanks for his many blessings.

Dr. Jampolsky maintains his personal balance by taking long walks with his wife and enjoying music with her. When they are in Hawaii, they walk 5 miles three times a week. He and Diane wake up at 4:30 in the morning, listen to meditations in bed, and say a little prayer. "That's an anchor, our rudder, our ship for the direction that we're going that day," Dr. Jampolsky explains. They then get up and do yoga. "Starting the day in the right kind of way helps with leading a spiritual life," Dr. Jampolsky avers.

Although clearly there is a spiritual component to Dr. Jampolsky's work, he contends that he does not try to change people, does not try to get them to become more spiritual. His work does include sharing the practical principles that he has found to be helpful in opening the door so that a person can "see that there's a doorway and they can choose to go through that door or not." For example, evidence is growing that not forgiving actually has negative physical effects, and Jerry's approach is to make it clear that it is a choice whether to forgive and to make choices available to people. "A lot of people are on automatic pilot, and there isn't a choice," Dr. Jampolsky observes, "but when they realize that their own thoughts and attitudes can hurt them, and that your attitude is everything, it's a whole new way of living."

> I believe that when you die, that's not the end of life. I think life is eternal, and that the work will go on whether or not I'm in a body. So I don't look at trying to leave a legacy, in the way that people will remember. I want to live in a way that helps people experience me today, and I can experience them today.

Dr. Jampolsky is not concerned about leaving a legacy. He is concerned about living authentically in the moment. "I don't need a legacy," he insists, "I do my best to walk a pathway in the present of loving and forgiving and helping others. I happen to believe that when you die, that's not the end of life. I think life is eternal, and that the work will go on whether or not I'm in a body. So I don't look at trying to leave a legacy, in the way that people will remember. I want to live in a way that helps people experience me today, and I can experience them today."

Again, from his writing:

> Let us recognize that we are united as one Self and illuminate the world with the light of love that shines through us. Let us awaken to the knowledge that the essence of our being is love, and, as such, we are the light of the world. (Jampolsky, 2004, p. 131)

In spite of his dedication to spreading the message, Jerry does not think that people even remember much of what is said in his lectures. What he believes is that they remember the experience of love and being inspired by what was said. He hopes that they continue to carry with them the idea that there is "another way of looking at the world and themselves," and that they feel hope rather than the illusion of hopelessness.

CHAPTER 12

Living from Mission to Mission

Dr. Jeannette South-Paul

Jeannette E. South-Paul, MD, is the chair of the department of family medicine in the School of Medicine at the University of Pittsburgh. A fellow of the American Academy of Family Physicians and a diplomate of the American Board of Family Practice, she is the first woman and the first African American, to serve as the permanent chair of a department at the School of Medicine, and she is one of a small number of African American chairs in medical schools nationwide.

Before joining the faculty at Pittsburgh, Dr. South-Paul spent 22 years practicing and teaching family medicine in the U.S. Army. As the Uniformed Services University's first vice president for minority affairs, she created mentoring programs that matched students with residents, faculty, and practicing physicians. In 2001, Colonel South-Paul retired as chair of the department of family medicine at USUHS. Her military career had begun 28 years earlier when she joined the ROTC army reserve in order to pay for her medical school expenses.

Dr. South-Paul is widely recognized for her research on the biological, social, and behavioral factors associated with premenstrual syndrome; treatment strategies for osteoporosis; exercise and aerobic capacity during pregnancy; infant nutrition; and exercise-dependent physiologic function in obesity. She has also developed training modules to create cultural com-

petence among healthcare professionals. Dr. South-Paul has been the recipient of many awards, including the Uniformed Services University of the Health Sciences Distinguished Service Medal and the American Academy of Family Physicians Exemplary Teaching award. She was recently honored in a special National Library of Medicine exhibition, "Changing the Face of Medicine: Celebrating America's Women Physicians." Dr. South-Paul also received the prestigious Joy McCann Foundation award for her accomplished work in mentoring.

Beyond her focus on family medicine, she also has an interest in sociocultural issues in health care and health care in special populations. Dr. South-Paul is a widely recognized presenter and researcher on cultural competence in medical education; the impact of race, ethnicity and culture on health; cultural diversity and academic medicine; and the development of minority faculty.

A graduate of the University of Pennsylvania and the University of Pittsburgh School of Medicine, Dr. South-Paul is a former chair of the minority affairs section of the Northeast region of the Association of American Medical Colleges. Dr. South-Paul has devoted her career to improving health care for the underserved. In the process, she has served as a role model to attract the next generation of clinicians to this essential service.*

Jeannette South-Paul was born into a family already committed to making a difference in its corner of the world. Her parents were immigrants from Jamaica who ran a rescue mission in downtown Philadelphia for almost 35 years. She lived at the mission with her parents, her two sisters, and three brothers. Without higher education or special training, her father, who "just wanted to do God's work," had become a minister devoted to helping people, many of whom had hit bottom. She recalled, "people would come in and they needed everything—not one thing, but everything." Her father spent a lot of time on the phone trying to find resources to help them.

Jeannette considered a ministerial role for herself, but ruled it out because her community did not believe in women clergy. She thought about social work, but decided that she could not accomplish enough that way. Much of her father's work was similar to that of the social workers that he contacted for help: facilitating assistance. "I wanted to do something more," she said. Observing that many of the problems they saw at the mission were health- or disease-related, she decided at the age of 12 years that she wanted to be a physician.

One of medicine's attractions to Jeannette's adolescent self was that it appeared that doctors did not have to work through others to get results. By contrast, she admired her schoolteachers but recognized they were constrained by the bureaucracy. It also seemed to her that as a physician she could do special things irrespective of being Black or poor. Yet she had no exposure to professionals or even college graduates. She had never met a scientist and had never heard of the allied health professions such as physical or respiratory therapy.

Both of her parents believed passionately in education, however. Their primary motivation in coming to America was to give their kids an education. "They said, 'when you go someplace, you have absolutely nothing else you can rely on besides your faith and your education. It's worth more than money, because it gives you skills to negotiate this world.'"

Jeannette applied to an academic, all-girls, public high school into which, even with her parents' prayers, admittance was difficult to gain. It had no frills, no SAT prep classes, but overall, was better than average. Strong in history, English, and languages, it was weak in science and math—because it was thought that girls don't do those fields. This deficiency did not faze Jeannette, however, as she was determined to go into medicine, and solidified that commitment by becoming president of the future physicians' club.

Dr. South-Paul identifies her first supporter as her absolutely special mother, whom she considered her best friend and earliest role model. When her mother's youngest child was 6 years old, her mother began working outside the home. She sought work with higher educational institutions because she had discovered they offered benefits for employees' kids. She went to work for the University of Pennsylvania, which offered tuition to her children.

Dr. South-Paul's mother began going to school herself while juggling her job and children—six of them born within an 8½-year period. The sweetest moment was when mother and daughter walked down the aisle together as Jeannette received her bachelor's degree from Penn and her mother received her associate's degree.

It was her mother's initiative that led to Jeannette's very first job during the summer after she graduated from high school. Jeannette knew she was going to Penn and that her tuition would be paid for, but she would need money for books. Her parents reassured her, as they always had, that although they "didn't have two nickels to rub together," she did not need to work. "You just study," they said, "that's your job." Nonetheless, she felt the need to work. Babysitting was not a possibility because "we lived in a pretty bad neighborhood, and I wasn't allowed outside after 6 at night." Her mother suggested that they write letters to people asking them to give her a job. When Jeannette asked who they were going to write to, her mother replied, "We'll write to the dean of the medical school."

Dr. South-Paul remembers laughing at this idea, but her mother insisted, and wrote to the dean saying that her daughter needed a job to help pay for expenses. At first it appeared that nothing would come of it. Weeks went by. One day, "We get a phone call from a Dr. Kefalides who asked if I would like to come and apply for a job."

On her way to the interview, she recalls, "I remember going past my regular stop, with my book bag. I went into the lab, and I'm like, 'wow.' We didn't have real science at my school, so I had never seen a beaker or test tube or anything. His chief tech walked me around and asked me if I knew how to do this and that. My answer to everything she asked me was, 'no, I don't know what that is.' At the end of the interview, she said, 'You have the job.' " Unlike others who might have attributed getting the job to having made a connection with someone who had power and influence, Dr. South-Paul attributes it to God having a hand in her life. "That's why I say that I've already had a lot of divine intervention in my life."

And so it was that young Jeannette went to work in a research lab at Philadelphia General Hospital for MD/PhD biochemist/internist Nicholas Kefalides. She admired how hard he worked and the long hours he put in, but notes that, as a lab technician not directly involved in his research, she did not understand much of the research he was doing. What impressed her most about Dr. Kefalides was that he had faith in her. He told her she could work as many hours as she wanted. If she wanted to come in on her day off or a vacation day, he would pay her for whatever hours she worked. She described this as, "He gave me no limits."

Dr. Kefalides gave Jeannette opportunities to learn, believing in her ability to succeed. She recalls, "I still remember the first week when I mixed everything wrong! Something happened with the experiment. They sat down and said, 'well, tell us how you did it,' and they didn't fire me!" Instead, "He said, 'look, we've got to teach you better how to do this.' And I worked there for 4 years." What Jeannette took from this that she would pass on was that "you've got to be forgiving."

Despite her positive experiences with Dr. Kefalides, Jeannette questioned whether he was truly aware of her. She "sometimes wondered whether he even realized I was in his world." Jeannette finally discovered that she had made an impression on Dr. Kefalides, however, and knew her 4 years working in the lab had not gone unnoticed when she got into medical school. He and the staff threw her a party and gave her a watch. This recognition from one of her first positive role models was, as Dr. South-Paul describes it, "really special."

Although Jeannette was unaware of it at the time, it was while she was working in Dr. Kefalides' lab that she first became a significant figure for someone else. An African American couple, Jenny and George Justice, worked in the lab, he washing dishes and she doing housekeeping. Thirty years later, this couple exchanged Christmas cards with Jeannette. Because they had a daughter living not far away, they visited with her. As Dr. South-Paul describes, "They talked about how proud they were to see this African American teenager working in this lab . . . they were so encouraged to think that I was going to be successful." She continues, "I remember how comforting it was to know they were there as well—cheering me on. It's funny how you get the opportunity to revisit these experiences. It helped me to realize that you never know who you're influencing. You just don't know."

Not everyone in her undergraduate years was so supportive. One of her biology professors was exceedingly patronizing. Jeanette recalls that "he patted me on the hand when I went to see him. He'd say, 'You don't have to worry about this because you're Black.' He wouldn't answer my questions and was absolutely disrespectful. I was totally disgusted. I don't remember his name, and I don't want to . . . It was bad."

Her first 2 years of med school were "a very negative experience, worse than in undergraduate school." Some people discouraged her from considering herself an equal competitor for high achievement. She encountered lowered expectations due to racial prejudice and misunderstandings and resentment regarding affirmative action policies. Jeannette explains, "I got stuff like, 'They only let you in the door because of what you look like. We don't have to work hard with you—it doesn't matter whether you're qualified or not.' Again, I was horrified. I thought, I'm low person on the totem pole; what can I do?"

Dr. South-Paul responded by increasing her determination to succeed. She thought, "well, what I'm going to do is be the best darn you-know-what I can be. I'll show them that just because I look like I do and I'm not particularly sophisticated doesn't mean I can't be good at what I do."

Lacking models of physicians in her family and social network, Jeannette borrowed models from books. One of them was by Dr. Paul Brand and his work with people suffering from leprosy. "When you were a leper, people didn't hug you anymore. The real pathology of the disease was not known then. Here was someone who chose to work with that segment of the population that nobody else even wanted to be around, and could make a significant difference. I often thought about that book." Dr. Brand's parents, like her own, had been missionaries, and Dr. Brand himself was a person of strong faith.

Immersing herself in reading was already a longstanding habit by the time Jeannette was in high school. She was reading everything she could about the Holocaust. This further shaped the humanitarian ethos she had inherited from her parents. "I was appalled at how so many people could suffer, and so many could ignore it. And that just recycled in my mind for years; there are going to be folks in society that are suffering right in front of your face. You won't have to go hunting for them, it's not a secret, but you can rationalize why you should ignore them. And I said, I don't want to ever be in that situation. I think it was Satayana who said, 'Those who ignore history are doomed to repeat it.' And I thought . . . we can't do that! How can you call yourself a cultured society if you allow that to happen?" This is a question she appears to still be asking of herself and the others around her today.

> There are going to be folks in society that are suffering right in front of your face. You won't have to go hunting for them, it's not a secret, but you can rationalize why you should ignore them. . . . "How can you call yourself a cultured society if you allow that to happen?"

Throughout her life, Dr. South-Paul's Bible has been her encouragement book. Her parents and her experience at the mission instilled in her a basic respect for humanity. "At the rescue mission where we lived, we took care of mostly alcoholics . . . Society called them 'skid row,' 'bums,' and other disparaging terms. They couldn't get health care, and there weren't a lot of shelters. Most shelters were provided by faith-based organizations. It became clear that it wasn't just men who were drunks who were on the street, but whole families. I used to run the thrift shop for our mission. On Saturday mornings we'd open it and sell things for a nickel. And I'd think, some of these people are really nice if you get to know them. Some of them, yeah, they drink too much, but they're not mean people.

They weren't mean drunks. A lot of them were mentally ill. Studies came out later on the fact that 30–40% of the people on the street are there as a result of us helping them by getting them out of the state institutions."

When she was in college, Jeannette suggested to her father that someone should open a clinic for these people. The only public hospital, Philadelphia General, was across the river on the other side of the city—a long ways to walk. People could sit for hours all day in the waiting room. If they were not seen, they were told, "Come back tomorrow."

Her father tried to interest a university in setting up a clinic. The authorities responded that if they wanted their students to have an "underserved experience, we'll send them overseas. We're not going to have them spend time with folks who want to be on the streets." Jeannette was shocked and disgusted, and vowed never to behave that way. She decided that if she could get to medical school, she wanted to take care of people irrespective of why they were there or who they were. "It was my parents. They really had this desire to take care of the least and the lowest. All comers."

Her own high standards have not always been reflected in the care her loved ones have received when they were seriously ill. During her father's final illness, his primary care physician and his colleagues had, in her view, been caring and attentive, although like Jeannette, they could not be there as much as she or they would have liked. Her father had not been a good patient, and she had concerns about his caregivers and the allied health team. Her sister, who was often with their father, would "get so furious, she'd say, 'you know, they treat him like this unimportant, inconsequential, old Black man.' And she'd be so angry . . ." As a physician, Dr. South-Paul would mediate, but her experience was that, "If I wasn't there; they weren't providing him the best care."

Jeannette had mixed reviews about the care her brother was receiving at the time of this interview. One of his surgeons had been very attentive, answering her questions and her brother's. But the physician orchestrating the rest of his care was inattentive, unavailable, did not answer questions, or return phone calls. "I just go nuts. I say call me up and tell me you don't know anything, have your assistant call us up and say you don't know anything, *but don't ignore us!* It's totally disrespectful. The experience is hard enough; you should at least feel like you're being cared for."

Dr. South-Paul thinks that burnout is part of the reason for disengagement of healthcare professionals from families and patients. Her own resistance to burnout and the biggest reason she gets up in the morning comes from the knowledge that "there's a lot to do and there aren't a lot of people doing it" coupled with her commitment to others. "It's not about me, it's about the people who have real needs."

Dr. South-Paul has a mission, and she is able to retain a sense of effectiveness even in the face of having limited power. She used to teach her military students that they can always help someone and do more than they think they can. "Don't ever think you're powerless. You're only as powerless as you allow yourself to be. You may think you're low person on the totem pole, but remember there are always people with less power than you whose lives you can possibly influence. If you don't speak for those one or two people, or 10 or 20 or 100, that you can positively impact, you have done all those people a disservice." Her philosophy echoes her experience in Dr. Kefalides's lab as well as her years living and serving in her parents' mission, where she was able to help others long before she acquired medical expertise and a position of authority.

> Don't ever think you're powerless. You're only as powerless as you allow yourself to be. You may think you're the low person on the totem pole, but remember there are always people with less power than you, whose lives you can possibly influence. If you don't speak for those one or two people, or 10 or 20 or 100, that you can positively impact, you have done all those people a disservice.

What keeps Jeannette going is not only knowing she makes a difference, but also her having decided in advance that the "little difference that I make is worth it." Rather than succumbing to burnout, as so many of her colleagues do when their efforts to push back the tide overwhelm them, she has already made the decision to accept that the small waves she can make are sufficient. "If you don't believe that, you won't keep doing what you do. And so I really do believe that what little I can do is better than not doing anything at all."

Dr. South-Paul is also motivated by her concerns for the future. She feels a responsibility to keep reinventing herself and is constantly looking for other people to do what she does. Many years removed from Dr. Kefalides's lab, she understands now that she is a model for others, and that the way in which she does her work matters. "I am not so arrogant as to think that I'm the only one who can do this," she explains, "but I do believe that I have a responsibility as an educator to educate others to do this. So I have to live it every day so that they see it's doable. If I get discouraged, they will not want to do this." Dr. South-Paul leaves the distinct impression that she does not want to miss out on any opportunity to recruit another companion in the work.

Jeannette's goals and personal ethics are intricately intertwined. A person of faith, she believes that she is here for a reason and that "everything I end up doing is because of a higher purpose." She sorts and prioritizes her goals and choices from that perspective. She draws her sense of self less from deeds that bear her name than from what will benefit others. She believes her time is well spent if a program benefits a large number of people, but nobody at the top knows about it.

Nonetheless, in academic medicine she has learned to market what she is doing and demonstrate her value. She is well aware of achieving a balance between doing work in accord with her mission and ethos and ensuring that she can continue to do that work. "A lot of what I do won't ever get NIH funding, though I'm working on that. You have to keep applying."

But there is another kind of value and validation that Dr. South-Paul believes is as important as grant funding. She asserts, "I've said it again and again to the institution; you not only need currency at the national level validated through a body like NIH, but you need currency in the community in which you sit."

According to Dr. South-Paul, this is a new concept for academic health centers. She contends, "For so long, academic health centers have not paid attention to their geographic partners. I tell them, I'm here to help maintain that trust. They look at the jobs they bring into the community, the taxes they pay, and the businesses that flourish because we're here. I say, yeah, but we need to do more than bring in national and international people for their expertise. Let's make sure we're taking care of the people who live across the street." It is in her ability to help these people that Dr. South-Paul identifies her core self. She is unequivocal. "That represents who I am. I can't separate that from me."

One of the challenges Jeannette faces with her outreach projects and solutions-focused research is the difficulty adhering to the strict schedules that conventional research funders expect. "When you work in the community, there is so little that you can control. You have to do all of these other things because you're building partnerships with people who aren't following your schedule. And they're not necessarily close to your office.

So you've got to go out and meet with them—sometimes it's evenings; sometimes it's weekends. And you have to do a lot of things that you can't document. It's not like you can set up a set of petri dishes and things, and then say I'm going to start at 8 this morning and by the end of the week all of the data will be collected. I can't draw a tight timeline on how to get things done."

Dr. South-Paul continued with an example. She has received some foundation money to develop a community-based intervention to see if her team can keep teen mothers from getting pregnant again in the next 2 or 3 years. Having delivered too many unplanned teen pregnancies, she knows their consequences—most likely they will not finish their education, and that will keep them poverty-stricken and in communities that do not have the resources to help them achieve their dreams. Cutting into that cycle is close to her heart.

Her pilot study explored barriers to receiving care. Most of the teenagers did not get in early enough for prenatal care. To find out why not, she offered $25 gift certificates if they would come in and answer her questions. Half did not show up. She had to find out why. That meant getting some money and a student with interviewing skills. The teen mothers could not find a babysitter, or this and that happened, or it was cold outside and the trip required waiting for two buses. "So that means that my timelines for my projects are often out of whack. I have to ask for no-cost extensions and all that. So I can't come out with the papers and the results in the same rhythm as someone with more control over their research material. Those things don't make you look good from an academic perspective."

Dr. South-Paul admits that at times she questions whether she should leave academia and become a community doctor. "It's much harder work being here, but how else do I recruit the next generation?"

From a professional perspective, Dr. South-Paul considers her greatest success to have been staying and surviving at an academic health center and being considered of value. "Women and minorities," she points out, "don't stay in academia. We don't." Ever mindful of her role as a model and a mentor, she speaks of her students. "I have a lot of young students who will say, 'I can't do this lifestyle.' They're part-timers. It's good for them, but they don't make the same impact as if they were full-time. I try to encourage them, and keep them going, because some do come back when their kids are a little older."

From a personal perspective, Dr. South-Paul identifies "staying married and having two good kids" to be her greatest achievements. She hastens to add, "And let me flip that. Family helps me to be who I am. Long after this institution kicks me out the door, my family will still be there to value and appreciate me." She speaks of the need to prioritize her children, her two really special boys who are ". . . the only people I try not to put on hold." She recalls a time when she did do that, and her son called her on it, asking her whether he wasn't as important as the other person. To be available when they have their days—that's really important."

> Continuing my practice helps me remember why I'm doing this. If you don't remember why you're doing it, then the days when you get really angry, you're ready to walk. But if I'm seeing patients every day, in my face, all the time, then I remember why I need to be here.

In her mind, her biggest failure is that she has not been able to bring more young doctors into caring for the underserved. She treasures the ones she has around her, but she thought there would be dozens lining up wanting to be a part of her team—not because it was hers, but because it meant doing wonderful things. It is almost as if she lives by the "build it and they will come" adage. She is waiting for more talented collaborators who have not yet appeared.

Jeannette agrees with me that she unfairly blames herself for not being able to recruit and retain at the levels she had hoped for. She acknowledges that she is trying to do this in a tough system, one that does not value all that she values. As successful as Dr. South-Paul has been, she has not met her own criteria of success. This is evident in her lament, "I was hoping that I could make a sea change in how academic medicine thinks. But we're not there yet."

How, then, does she prevent herself from becoming despairing and cynical when confronted with obstacles? Jeannette admits that she has been burnt out at times. She responds to these lows by "praying a lot, sharing with folks of like mind, and exercising. Every morning I go to the gym. I could probably use the extra hour of sleep a whole lot, but I really believe that staying fit, both spiritually and physically, helps me stay focused." She retains a sense of humor—and not of the dark and cynical variety common among clinicians. In addition, Dr. South-Paul maintains her balance by thinking about what will have the longest lasting value. "When I'm gone, have I made the impact that I need to make?"

Dr. South-Paul also keeps her balance and her focus by continuing her practice. While well-intended colleagues suggest her life would be less stressful and less busy if she were not delivering babies, she feels strongly that "it helps me remember why I'm doing this. If you don't remember why you're doing it, then the days when you get really angry, you're ready to walk. But if I'm seeing patients every day, in my face, all the time, then I remember why I need to be here."

She freely acknowledges that her style with patients breaks all the rules. "I hug patients, I cry with patients. I tell them I'll pray for them. I scream at them. 'What do you mean, you started smoking again? We had a deal here.' 'What do you mean you don't have time to get your mammogram? Do you want to die?' Patients need to know I care." Her comment made me recall this saying that has made the rounds in medical education circles: "Patients don't care what you know, until they know that you care."

Another way that Dr. South-Paul lets her patients know that she cares about them is by listening. She evaluates the role of listening in her medical practice as "really, really important," and elaborates, "We have the electronic medical record, and you have to fill in the boxes, but sometimes I just turn around and listen. Sometimes it's emotional pain that they need to talk about. We all need to be listened to."

> We have the electronic medical record, and you have to fill in the boxes, but sometimes I just turn around and listen. Sometimes it's emotional pain that they need to talk about. We all need to be listened to.

When asked if she could recall a time that she surprised herself with courage or with cowardice, she recalled her days as an intern in the army when "we were just getting battered and disparaged. It was really emotional abuse." One of the attending physicians, a colonel, called the interns "trolls." When he directed his questions to Jeannette, she, in uniform, raised in a strict environment, and now part of the military, ignored him. He asked, "Didn't you hear me?" She answered, "Yeah, but I am not a troll." From then on, he called the interns Troll number 1, Troll number 2, and Jeannette.

Recalling this self-advocacy from earlier in her life, Dr. South-Paul reflects, "Sometimes you have to say something. Am I doing it as effectively now as I did it then? I don't know. I try to be a quiet, persistent activist, but maybe I should be louder. That's where I'm not sure that I've demonstrated the courage that I should. I think it's because I feel like I should be inside the schoolhouse, not outside the schoolhouse, and I hope I'm not rationalizing too much, but I worry about that."

Never satisfied with herself, it seems that Dr. South-Paul fears that she has become less outspoken in order to be part of the academic system. Yet she was unable to think of a single time when she knew the best course of action but did not get it done. Still, the possibility weighs on her mind because she is so busy now that "I may be missing things, and that scares me."

Jeannette's biggest regret is that she has not done more, that she has not been able to change the system—a monumental task, and one requiring perhaps a different role than the one she is currently in. Even as she expresses her regret, she adds, "And yet I haven't been in politics. And you know something? I don't want to be. People keep asking me, don't you want to move up, and I say, but will I wake up every morning with a smile on my face? And the answer is no. Yet the things I want to do—I'd have to move up to make them happen. And then again, I don't know if politicians can get us where we want to be. I really think that we have to do it at the local level."

When asked about her hopes for her lasting legacy, Dr. South-Paul answered with, "I would love to change the health system so that every person, whether they have insurance or not, has a medical home. If that could be accomplished, and I could have a part in it, I would consider that a real achievement. The literature is clear; people who have medical homes do better. Their chronic diseases are managed better, they have fewer diseases, and they live longer. It's not a mystery!"

The word *mission* comes from a Latin derivative and is defined as an act of sending, sometimes accompanied by a strong inner impulse toward a particular course of action, especially when accompanied by conviction of divine influence. Certainly, divine intervention is a force by which Dr. South-Paul has felt continuously graced. The subdefinition of the word mission refers to a designated permanent embassy, which made me think of the mission house where she lived as a young girl. Dr. Jeannette South-Paul took on a specific mandate to help others at a much younger age than her peers. The patients and people whose lives she has touched have been blessed that she answered that strong summons.

CHAPTER 13

Having an Impact on Health in the Small City and Leaving a Bigger Legacy

Dr. Leonard Morse

Dr. Leonard J. Morse's roots in the state of Massachusetts run deep. Well past an age at which most people retire, he continues to serve his community as the City of Worcester's commissioner of public health. He maintained a private practice in Worcester for 36 years and then for 4 years focused his attention on the needs of inner-city residents by serving as medical director of the Greater New Bedford Community Health Center. He served as president of the Massachusetts Medical Society and as chairman of the American Medical Association Council on Ethical and Judicial Affairs. He is on the board of directors of the FAIR Foundation (Fair Allocations in Research), which was formed because of the inequities in disease research spending by Congress and the National Institutes of Health. A lifelong learner, Dr. Morse served as the president of Boston Medical Library for many years. He has authored more than 200 publications, editorials, and essays.

Dr. Morse is widely known as an accomplished epidemiologist, successful practitioner, and respected teacher and mentor. He serves as professor of clinical medicine and family medicine and community health at the

University of Massachusetts Medical School. He received a lifetime achievement award from the Massachusetts Medical Society and an Internist of the Year honor from the American College of Physicians—Massachusetts chapter. He has been active with the AIDS Project in Worcester. In his capacity as commissioner of public health, he led a successful campaign in 2008 to convince the city to place several yellow drop boxes around the town where injection drug users can safely discard their hypodermic needles and syringes. Throughout his distinguished career, the needs of his patients have always come first. His primary professional concern is caring for patients in a relationship of trust.

Leonard earned his undergraduate degree at American International College in Springfield, Massachusetts. His medical degree is from the University of Maryland, where he was a fellow in infectious disease and later chief resident in medicine at the university hospital. Dr. Morse also served as a captain in the Army Medical Corps, assigned to the Walter Reed Army Institute of Research in Maryland.

As a child during the Great Depression of the 1930s, young Leonard Morse was very uncertain as to his professional goals. Neither of his parents had finished high school. His brother, 8 years older, had attended college but left as a result of military service. Leonard vividly recalls the impact of the Depression. By the time he was 9 years old, things were very difficult. His father had lost his job, and on his 9th birthday, his family was just sitting down to eat when a man arrived at the door to repossess his father's vehicle. The man saw the birthday cake on the table, and told his father he would return the next day. During Leonard's school years, his family moved from Worcester, where their extended family was centered, to Athol, Massachusetts, for Leonard's father's employment opportunities.

In Athol, Leonard met many who would influence him in the development of his career goals. The most notable was Alexander P. "Johnnie" Johnstone, a dentist by training, who went into youth work and became the secretary of the Athol YMCA. Dr. Morse remembers him as a "splendid person and a wonderful role model." Dr. Johnstone also operated the YMCA camp in southern New Hampshire that young Leonard attended every year. Leonard felt very loyal to the camp and to Johnnie Johnstone and his wife, and progressed from camper to camp counselor to waterfront director. Dr. Morse explains, "he was one of the people who recognized in me the potential of seeking an education beyond college and in the health sciences." Leonard was also inspired by an uncle who was a dentist—and in fact began college with the goal of practicing dentistry. However, once he enrolled in college, a few of his professors in the bench sciences influenced him to apply to medical school by convincing him that more opportunities would be available to him if he studied medicine.

Of the eight or nine medical schools to which Leonard applied, the University of Maryland was the first to respond. He consulted a cousin who was a second-year medical student at Johns Hopkins. His cousin was enthusiastic about Maryland and about a young professor there, Theodore Woodward, an infectious diseases specialist. Leonard accepted the University of Maryland's offer of admission and withdrew his applications from the other schools. He discovered that a neighbor was also going to Maryland, and they drove together and were roommates.

> Medicine is about human relations. It's people, interacting with people. It's unhurried, it's unselfish, and you're really trying to energize yourself to help a person, in whatever your area of expertise is. . . .

Although Baltimore was farther from Worcester than Dr. Morse had ever been, his parents never discouraged him. He believes they were proud of his accomplishments and fully supportive of his going to Maryland. Leonard has kept all the correspondence from his father, letters sent to him during his years of college, medical school, and military service, and he encourages others to do so, pointing out that they do not take a lot of room in the attic and will provide a wonderful experience when reread later in life. Although his parents did not have a lot at that time, they had somehow climbed out of the Depression, and his father sent him a check for $25 every week.

One of the first people Leonard met at Maryland was Merrill Snyder, an instructor in microbiology, a "terrific man, brilliant," Leonard said, who became a lifelong friend. He worked for Professor Woodward, of whom his cousin had spoken so highly. In his 3rd year of medical school, Leonard was assigned by an alphabetical chance system to study directly with Dr. Woodward. He recalls the professor as being "very inspiring, a highly educated clinician, and a great scientist." Dr. Woodward and

Leonard also developed a friendship that would prove to be strongly influential in terms of pointing him toward the study of infectious disease, global epidemiology, and world health. After graduating from medical school, Dr. Morse stayed with Dr. Woodward for an internship in internal medicine. At that point, although he knew that he was going to disappoint Dr. Woodward by not continuing, he felt he needed to return to Massachusetts, so he took a 2nd-year residency at New England Medical Center in Boston.

But Dr. Woodward had transmitted his enthusiasm about infectious disease to Dr. Morse by being a real humanist. "He was never hurried in his conversations with people . . . As soon as you met him, you knew that he was excellent," Leonard recalls. "He came to the bedside and made eye contact and emotional contact with the patient in a very unhurried way." He was "a hero, just in his mannerisms and dealing with people." Dr. Morse still keeps his photo on his desk in his office, to remind him that "that's what medicine is about, that's what human relations are about. It's people, interacting with people. It's unhurried, it's unselfish, and you're really trying to energize yourself to help a person, in whatever your area of expertise is . . . . This is the model on which Dr. Morse has based his own practice. In fact, Leonard thinks that his time with a great mentor allowed him to recognize outstanding ability wherever it surfaces.

Following his second year of medical training, Dr. Morse was drafted into the army. Dr. Woodward, who was very involved in the Walter Reed Army Institute of Research and was a member of the armed forces epidemiologic board, again exerted his personal influence by asking Leonard whether he would like an assignment in communicable diseases at the Walter Reed Army Institute of Research. Dr. Morse had just met his future wife, a third-year student at Simmons College, so they had a quick wedding and moved to Maryland where Maxine finished her last year of college. Leonard's experience at Walter Reed was "a great expansion into the realm of global epidemiology." He became an expert in arthropod-borne viral infections, such as West Nile fever, Japanese B encephalitis, and viruses transmitted by the bites of ticks and mosquitoes.

Shortly after his marriage and work at Walter Reed, Dr. Morse was assigned to work with a team to prepare a vaccine to protect against Kyasanur Forest disease for the Indian government. The methodology for preparing the vaccine included growing the virus, harvesting it by hand, and emulsifying infected tissue with a mortar and pestle. Leonard was the most junior person in the group, and the more senior people had prior immunization. He and his colleagues were taking all the proper precautions—wearing face masks, gowns, and face shields, and using hooded work chambers and ultraviolet light. But the virus, transmitted in nature by the bite of a tick, was demonstrated in Dr. Morse's group to be transmittable by inhalation as well. Dr. Morse came down with Kyasanur Forest disease and was hospitalized at Walter Reed. He recovered, and in his usual style of capitalizing on every moment, his own case study was the first paper he wrote for a peer-reviewed journal.

Dr. Morse's experience with Kyasanur Forest disease occurred in 1957 or early 1958. That same virus is included among the types that might be used for a bioterrorism attack because it can be dried and aerosolized. When this became an issue after the September 11, 2001 terrorist attacks, Dr. Morse wrote a letter to the *Journal of the American Medical Association*, reflecting on the enormous shift from years earlier, when his group was simply trying to develop a vaccine that would prevent people from becoming ill in rural India. It is distressing to Dr. Morse "what's in people's minds now," that someone could take that life-saving information and use it to infect people in large numbers.

While Dr. Morse was in the military, he was assigned for 3 months to a study of hemorrhagic fever in children in Thailand. The head of the investigation was a great public health doctor, William McD. Hammond of the University of Pittsburgh. It was during that outbreak that a virus was first isolated (Dengue virus type 3 and 4) as the cause. "It was really terrific," Dr. Morse remembers. "It was in Thailand, in the rainy season, so there were abundant mosquitoes." The team was very proud of its work. Recently, when he was in Cambodia with his wife, Dr. Morse saw a sign at a children's hospital warning the public about the dengue virus alert, to watch out for mosquitoes, and he realized that this was the result of his work there 50 years ago. "It was nice to see that." Even Dr. Morse's prideful moments are understated.

After returning from his assignment in Thailand, Dr. Morse finished his military service, and then received an infectious disease fellowship at the University of Maryland. Once again, he was working with his main mentor, this time as Dr. Woodward's chief resident. Dr. Morse was invited to stay on as faculty at the medical school, but his parents were still living in Worcester, and his wife's parents were in Springfield, so he decided to go home.

Although Dr. Morse is clear that "I met my Marcus Welby in Theodore Woodward," he read and was influenced by the books of Rene Debos, a microbiologist at the Rockefeller Institute, and the work of Paul de Kruif. Leonard loves books and has an enormous library. He reads continuously in the fields of medicine, science, and epidemiology. "I can't keep up with those fields, let alone so many other fields," he laments. "I know what my limitations are, and I'm really excited reading in my field of special interest." He notes that his career has been unframed and that everything he sees ignites his interest. "So I'm always playing catch-up." To his students, PGY 1s and PGY 2s, he introduces himself as a "PGY 53," 53 years postgrad.

I wondered how great doctors would themselves be cared for if ever the need arose. In 2007, while exercising early in the morning, Dr. Morse got a very significant chest pain and knew that he was experiencing something very acute. He had nitroglycerin at home and slipped it under his tongue, along with aspirin. The pain decreased somewhat, but he woke his wife and asked her to take him to the hospital. They went to St. Vincent Hospital in Worcester, where he had been on staff since 1961. He arrived at the emergency room at 6:40 and had an immediate diagnosis: a coronary artery was blocked. The staff in the emergency room put in a dilating balloon, relieved the obstruction, and inserted a stent. By 8:15 in the morning, Dr. Morse was out of the cardiac catheterization lab and in the recovery room, and he has been fine ever since. "I have full confidence in the hospital, the emergency room, the cardiologist, and the postcardiac care," Dr. Morse reports. "I was just fully confident, and did not doubt anything that was being done, because I had a trusting relationship." He believes that the trusting relationship is what medicine is all about.

> We have to reach out to those people who are homeless, those who are imporverished, those who, as a consequence of risky behavior, have acquired illnesses—and without judgment, take care of them all, focusing on their medical needs first.

Dr. Morse considers the role of listening in medicine to be vitally important. He recalls how his primary model, Dr. Woodward, would "pull up a chair and sit by the side of the bed, and begin to talk with people, and he'd be listening." He notes that today on average a doctor begins talking 18 seconds into an interview with a patient. He advises that "you've got to listen. You listen with your ears, but you also listen with your eyes. You need to make eye contact with people, and you need sincerity on your face, in your handshake." Recognizing that everyone is different has served him well. "Our skin color is different, our accents are different, our fingerprints are different, and our DNA is different. But what's most different is each individual's personal history. Everybody's history is unique. That's why kindness is essential. You don't know how heavy another person's shoulders are. It's not just in the practice of medicine; it has to be in human relationships." When Leonard brought his father to one of the major teaching hospitals in Boston in 1962, this kind of care was not apparent. People were too busy and the environment was intimidating.

Dr. Morse continues to persevere. As soon as he retired, he was drafted back to work by the chief executive officer of the Greater New Bedford Community Health Center. He enjoyed his 4 years there, working with an impoverished, needy immigrant population. Returning to Worcester after September 11, 2001, he was contacted by the city manager and asked if he would be interested in returning to work, focusing on bioterrorism preparedness. He began working at the city's health department. The commissioner of public health in Worcester subsequently had to retire due to illness, and Leonard was asked to be commissioner, a position he has held now for 6 years. What keeps him going is his love of his work and its purpose, and his love for the people with whom he works. He is also very motivated by teaching young people.

> Our skin color is different, our accents are different, our fingerprints are different, and our DNA is different. But what's most different is each individual's personal history. Everybody's history is unique. That's why kindness is essential. You don't know how heavy another person's shoulders are.

Dr. Morse believes that preventing an illness from happening is more important than treating it once it happens. To reduce the costs of health care requires educating people on what they must do to stay healthy, and that education can be done through marketing, as in industry. He is enthused about this approach and excited about the purpose of the Department of Public Health, which, as Dr. Morse sees it, is to recognize that every member of our population is important. "There are 177,000 people in Worcester, and they're all important to me," he asserts. "We have to reach out to those people who are homeless, those who are impoverished, those who as a consequence of risky behavior have acquired illnesses—and without judgment, take care of them all, focusing on their medical needs first. I really believe in that," Dr. Morse states. He has made public health his mission.

Leonard's goals live in a tight union with his personal ethics. Dr. Morse's firm conviction is that ethics and professionalism are the "two most important bonding features of the medical profession." If the medical profession is to survive, he maintains that every doctor must uphold these principles; doing so puts the patient first. In the late 1990s, Leonard had the honor of being appointed to the American Medical Association's (AMA's) Council on Ethical and Judicial Affairs. The council is responsible for the code of medical ethics for the AMA. The code of ethics is updated every 2 years and, in his opinion, "should be on every doctor's desk in America, so that patients can see it." Even if patients do not read it, seeing it and knowing that there is an ethical code, a "bible" for the practice of medicine, is important.

Some of the obstacles that Dr. Morse faces in his work are political. In trying to reach out to the less fortunate members of our society, he has come up against political resistance. Leonard respects those who resist, but feels that they must appreciate public health decisions' being made on medical criteria, not on political persuasion. There is one project in particular that he has been pushing forward for years.

Dr. Morse has been persistent in his efforts to deregulate syringes and needles in Massachusetts. It has taken over 12 years, and he has attended every hearing at the State House. He wants to address the issue of the careless discard of used syringes and needles into the environment. "I don't think our children should have to witness discarded needles and syringes in their schoolyards, and parks, and streets, as part of their habitat," he insists. To this end, a project for the placement of impenetrable disposal equipment in areas where drug use is high was funded by grants. His hope is that the drug-using population will recognize that they have a responsibility to others, and that others are reaching out to them. The project is called Operation Yellow Box, "because yellow is the color of hope." The eight locations Dr. Morse has selected for the yellow standard-size mailboxes all wanted them, yet there were some political activists who did not want them in their neighborhoods. Dr. Morse went ahead and ordered the boxes, and the project is being implemented.

Despite his many concerns, Dr. Morse is able to get a good night's sleep these days, and this is what keeps him from burning out. When he was in practice, he had many sleepless nights worrying about people and their illnesses. But now, nearing 80 and no longer in clinical practice, he finds it much easier to "package these concerns and not let them interfere with what is appropriate."

Dr. Morse attributes his lack of regrets at least in part to having practiced in the same community for so long. Many of his patients knew him as a kid, as a young doctor, and stayed with him throughout their lives. "It's a wonderful experience to be in the community that I was raised in and find people with such strong affection and appreciation," Dr. Morse affirms, "I know this community like the back of my hand." His only regrets are for the things not done. He has often wished he could have stayed at the University of Maryland, and matured as a doctor under the tutelage of Theodore Woodward. Yet he recognizes that many of those in academic medicine "become peripatetic," moving from place to place, and do not have the rewarding community experiences that he has had.

Dr. Morse recalls only one occasion on which he was not able to follow through with what he considered to be the best course for a patient. On that occasion, he and the family disagreed on what should be done, and Leonard asked the family if he could select another doctor for them. The patient was a friend of the family, and he felt very bad that they disagreed, but he also felt that he could not ethically do what they wanted him to do. The patient was experiencing progressive dementia, and in Dr. Morse's opinion, it was "not at a level that one would want to hasten his demise." Leonard believes that the goal is to "make people comfortable, not to hasten their deaths." The patient was not in pain, and he could recognize his family. Leonard did not think it was this patient's time to die. The physician Dr. Morse recommended to the family took over management of the patient's care.

Leonard cannot think of any decisions he has made that he has regretted. He points out that his work in infectious diseases was not global epidemiology; it was treating people who got infections following surgery or injuries. Over time, the infectious disease consultation became a subspecialty of surgery. Dr. Morse does recall that there were instances when he felt that, desperate as the situation was, there was still hope. In these cases he would "really roll up my sleeves in the ICU and try to be creative with appropriate antibiotic use," which he believes made a difference. "There was survival," he says, "it may have been slow survival, but it was survival, and we didn't give up. I think you want that in a doctor." However, he draws attention to the line between learning from experience and going beyond what is reasonable in terms of evidence-based medicine.

One reason Dr. Morse retired from clinical practice was that he found himself having to increasingly defend his decisions. In his experience, for example, two antibiotics should be used for initial treatment of serious illnesses such as peritonitis or infections of the abdomen. New, younger doctors, on the other hand, were suggesting treatments that involved four antibiotics. He would expound and defend his decisions, and he sensed he would be labeled by the younger doctors: "He's an old man who only uses two antibiotics, instead of four."

"That's when I thought it was time to retire," Dr. Morse explains. He knows that it was the right decision for him. He followed that career with a wonderful career in a community health center, and is now in his third career as commissioner of public health.

Leonard maintains balance through his love of nature. When he and his wife bought their house in 1964, he bought the house lot behind them as well. Thinking that he should stay close to home while he had a young family, he transformed the house lot into a magnificent garden. One section was a play area for their three sons (Andrew, Jonathan, and H. Michael) and daughter (Elizabeth) and friends; when the children outgrew it, he planted dwarf apple trees; later, to avoid having to spray the trees every week, he took them down and created an English garden.

> When critical things happen to people—like a bolt of lightning, or young people dying, or people dying suddenly—how do they deal with it? Spirituality is really a collection of life experience that's different from individual to individual.

Dr. Morse keeps his sense of fun by reading old-style comedians like Henny Youngman, whom he finds both proper and clever. He thinks humor is very important in relationships and in "being able to deal with all the things we have to deal with." He emphasizes his like of clean stuff, however, and wants parents to be fully informed about the contents of movies so that they can prohibit their children from seeing what is inappropriate. He does not think those movies are suitable for adults, either, and asserts, "Just because you're 18 years old doesn't mean you can interpret all this violence and terror and drug use and profanity and sex." This is not a political position, he insists; rather, it "has impacts on the health and well-being and the mental judgment of all the people." There are

30,000 college students in Worcester, and he feels strongly that they are his responsibility.

Leonard does feel that there is a spiritual component in his life, and that it is based on respect for everybody's beliefs. He separates spirituality "into something even deeper than the motivation of trying to accomplish a goal." He associates spirituality with the chemistry of one's religion and what was inculcated as a child. His formative religious and spiritual images came not only from his parents but also from his very heterogeneous group of peers, among whom multiple religions were represented. "It was the combination of my religion, and my parents' religion, and that of my friends—it had an osmotic effect on me. When I dealt with sick people, I extracted the depths of their religious feelings, and then I asked them if they wanted me to call someone in from their religion. I really respected instances where critical things are happening to people—like a bolt of lightning, or young people dying or people dying suddenly—and how do you deal with it? It's more than emotion, it's—I'm using the word spirituality as a collection of life experience that's different from individual to individual."

With regard to his professional legacy in epidemiology, Dr. Morse notes that among his most interesting experiences in Worcester was an outbreak of hepatitis in 1969 that involved the College of the Holy Cross football team. A waterborne outbreak, it resulted in public health laws being changed to require that portable water at outdoor facilities be brought above ground with the faucet 3 feet above ground, so that there could be no back siphonage in that water supply. Leonard also described the first case of type 2 polio virus transmitted from an immunized infant to his mother who had never been immunized. That led to recommending the immunization of parents and caregivers for polio before giving live oral polio virus vaccine to the infant, "because the infant is one bundle of diapers after another, excreting the polio virus, and as it passes through it can occasionally regain its virulence," Dr. Morse explains. Most of this work he did in Worcester. "Louis Pasteur said chance favors the prepared mind, and I think I was prepared."

Most of Dr. Morse's experiences were published in refereed medical journals, and he believes they have lasting value. His hope is that what he has published remains information that can be referred to and used in new research, and, even more importantly, in teaching new physicians and nurses and the public health community how diseases can spread.

Leonard would consider that a great legacy. He quotes William Osler, who said, "The young doctor knows all the rules. The old doctor knows the exceptions to the rules." Dr. Morse would like his legacy to be teaching the new doctors the exceptions so that they will be ready when their moment comes.

Another legacy in which Dr. Morse takes pride is a medical student scholarship fund he helped establish for the Worcester District Medical Society. In 1963, the medical society conducted a large-scale polio immunization project. "We gave thousands and thousands of doses," he recalled, "but nobody did a business plan. So we bought the vaccine and charged 25 cents a dose, because it would be the easiest way to make change. When the dust settled, after 3 weekends of vaccinating, we had a $14,000 profit." It had not been their intention to make any money, so it was used to establish a medical student scholarship fund that Leonard estimates now has $600,000–$700,000 in it. "So," Dr. Morse concludes, "the scholarship has become an enduring legacy."

Having grown up during the Great Depression of the 1930s, Dr. Leonard Morse might have been expected to harbor a bit of self-doubt and uneasiness about the future. But his story is one of steady persistence and realistic optimism.

Dr. Morse continues to encourage the students he meets. He passes on the support he received as a young student. "It's not economics but human interaction" that motivates people to become doctors. He recognizes that the medical students who rotate through his service are very idealistic, and he is supportive of their zeal, even while knowing that it may be tarnished a little through life experience, as everything is. He hopes they will be lucky enough to live a life as fulfilling as his. And I am left to think about how the world could benefit from a new crop of humanist physicians as skilled and compassionate as Dr. Leonard Morse.

CHAPTER 14

Have Compassionate Care, Will Travel

Dr. Wendy Ring

Dr. Wendy Ring says that the idea of a mobile medical clinic simply just came to her one day. Yet she wondered if she went to underserved areas and provided medical care, would communities want the services enough to provide the resources to make it work? For starters, she would need permission to pull into locations like school, church, or soup kitchen parking lots.

With $5,000 dollars borrowed from her parents, she bought an old truck and a 24-foot travel trailer and filled a room in her house with medical supplies. She offered her services "as a kind of spiritual experiment— or perhaps a medical stone soup—to see if one person's intention could bring about something larger than herself." So the seeds for the Mobile Medical Office (MMO) were planted.

In the almost 20 years since the first roll out of services, her clinic on wheels has grown to include a staff of 14, 10 of whom provide direct patient services, and an annual budget of almost $1 million dollars. The Mobile Medical Office was designated as a rural health clinic in 1993 and turned over to a community board of directors in 1997. In 2002, MMO became a federally qualified health center.

Mobile Medical Office provides health care (including mental health, dental, and pharmacy services) for the poor, uninsured, and underinsured. As a mission-driven organization committed to health care for all,

Chapter 14 Have Compassionate Care, Will Travel

> *Mobile Medical Office reflects Dr. Ring's original vision to become an integral part of what rural providers refer to as the healthcare safety net. People who would otherwise never get to a doctor in the forgotten communities of rural northern California are able to access care because of MMO. Only about one third of MMO expenses are covered through Medicaid and Medicare reimbursement. Many essential program components depend on private donations and grants.*
>
> *"Dr. Wendy," as most of her patients call her, also had something else in mind when deciding to keep the clinics on wheels. She wanted to be able to respond quickly to local health emergencies such as fires, floods, and earthquakes. In early September 2005, Dr. Ring led a team of health professionals to Houston, Texas, to care for survivors of Hurricane Katrina. Staff from the Mobile Medical Office followed, driving an outfitted unit to Texas to bring health care directly to the people.*
>
> *Dr. Ring attended Yale University as an undergraduate and received her master's degree in public health and her MD from Columbia University.*

Dr. Wendy Ring describes herself as "not a very introspective person. I'm used to getting up in the morning and going mindlessly to work just like everyone else." Although she would rather do her work than explain why she does what she does, she is very engaged with what it means to be a healer in these times. On the occasion of winning the Plessner Award for being Rural Physician of the Year in California, she said:

> Society has invested in each of us so that we can be its healers, and the role of healer carries responsibilities and challenges that we strive all our professional lives to fulfill. In the old days, the obligations of a village healer were simple. Care for the people of your village and train someone to take over when you are old and can't do it anymore. Today I struggle to understand my obligations as a healer in a global village where violence is epidemic, infections travel on airplanes, radioactive fallout rides the wind, and children in one country die of malnutrition, infection, and trauma due to economic policies in another. In a global village, death respects no border and all the smallpox vaccine and duct tape in the world can't keep us from experiencing the consequences of our actions. As doctors, we know this better than most people, and we must speak out and teach as if the survival of the species and the planet depended on it.

Wendy has been someone who was for the underdog since she was really young. She recalls becoming involved in an organization that sponsored a walk for hunger as having sparked her first realization that people could organize to work on issues. She dropped out of high school after meeting some people involved with the United Farm Workers, and she became a UFW organizer. She also founded the American Friends Committee Peace Center in the town where she lived. "I got involved with a whole group of people who were older and had been doing this kind of work for a long time, and they mentored me. That was what really got me started with my activism."

Although no one else in her family works as ferociously on cause-based issues, she says she was brought up with a "very progressive outlook and a good set of values. I was raised to feel that everyone should have their basic needs met, and there should not be violence or discrimination." She realized the world was not the way she would like it to be, but there were actually things that could be done about it.

Like many of the other doctors profiled in this book, Dr. Ring attributes her respect for humanity to her parents. "If you're raised with a certain set of values and have a certain kind of personality, you end up being the type of person who doesn't compromise."

Born with a congenital abnormality, Wendy underwent numerous surgeries at a very young age. "I remember them tying me down when I was 3 because I'd just had surgery and I was getting all the kids in the ward to jump up and down on the bed." Rather than these hospital experiences pointing her towards a medical career, they revealed early signs of her being a rabble-rouser gifted with inordinately high energy.

Neither did her having a father who was a physician point young Wendy in the direction of medicine. He kept his practice and family life separate, and Wendy did not have opportunities to see her father interacting with patients. It was not until much later when she had some training that he began to share his love of medicine with her.

Her father's influence came through another route. "When I was little, my dad used to read me Dr. Dolittle books, and I have always wanted to be Dr. Dolittle." The main character, John Dolittle, became discouraged with big city medicine and decided to live the life of a naturalist in the country and learn to speak the language of his new patient population with four legs instead of two. Dr. Doolittle is portrayed as disdainful of hypocrisy, having a deep concern for humanity, and as a quintessential absent-minded professor who is a bit hapless. The parallels with Wendy's self-descriptions are striking.

It was a summer job as an electrocardiogram (EKG) technician at the local hospital at age 16 years that first piqued her interest in medicine. A woman cardiologist from India taught Wendy how to read EKGs. "I could actually look at it and tell what was going on with the person's heart." When she later began to think about going into medicine, she would think back on this experience and say, "Yeah, I could do this. It isn't out of my reach."

Still, when she entered college, Wendy intended to become an urban planner, and she chose Yale for its great program. "But when I arrived there, I discovered that they had abandoned the whole thing. There was no more major!" She began casting around in other directions, taking various classes, and ended up in a remedial biology class. Yale gave her no credit for a year of community college, and placed her in remedial classes because she had not completed high school.

"The regular classes were in a giant lecture hall, but we had this wonderful woman instructor, an MD/PhD, and there were maybe 15 students. We each had a teaching assistant [TA] that we were to meet with once a week. My TA was very inspiring and supportive, so it was a really great way to start thinking about science." The TA was a Puerto Rican woman, and Wendy admired how far she had come considering the discrimination and barriers at the time. The TA took the time to introduce Wendy to her lab and showed her all the research she was doing.

These two women were inspirational in showing Wendy what could be done, and, like the cardiologist, that women could find meaning and success in the biomedical field. Wendy remembers inspiring and helpful people all along the way. "Neighbors in the ghetto looked after me when I was at college and far from home. A young union organizer drove me halfway across the country to interview for medical school. The federal government gave me a National Health Service Corps scholarship, nurses and orderlies dispensed cocoa and encouragement in the middle of the night, attending physicians patiently taught me, and patients graciously let me practice skills and knowledge accumulated and passed down over centuries." As Wendy remarked in her Plessner address, "When I sit down with a patient in my mobile clinic, all of these people are there with us."

Among Dr. Ring's early supporters was a peer group in medical school. "When I was in medical school, it was very conservative. There were five of us who were more politically progressive, and I was grateful to find like-minded peers. We supported each other and validated that certain things were crazy or out of line. I remember a gynecology professor who stood up in front of a whole lecture hall asserting that women got toxic shock syndrome [TSS] because they picked their nose and then touched themselves! So a group of us got together and got the information about what TSS really is. We made a leaflet and passed it out to everybody." It is simply not part of Wendy's character to accept harmful ignorance.

Dr. Ring believes that the role of listening in medical practice is of major importance. She elaborates, "I think my patients sometimes feel that they don't want to answer all those questions. They'll keep trying to steer the conversation back to repeating their symptoms over and over. They don't realize that's how I figure out what's wrong," she says. "They don't know that there's this branching diagnostic tree going on in my head, and I'm sorting through all these things to tease out a differential diagnosis. They're like, why don't you just do a blood test? I can't just run a bunch of tests; most of my patients don't have health insurance. I'm listening to figure out which tests, if any, we need to run."

Wendy finds that if she persists in her question asking with people who have been patients for a while, they eventually appreciate it. "I've had a lot of people say, oh, you're the first doctor to really take the time to listen to me and explain to me." Dr. Ring makes the point that communication is comprised of not just listening, but also "the other side to listening, which is explaining." Like one of her very first models, Dr. Dolittle, Wendy sees the value of talking to her patients. "If people don't understand why they're being asked to do certain things, they're not likely to do them." She notes, "I think it's mostly about listening and talking." Her patients certainly do notice. I found a copy of a newsletter published for senior citizens in the area where Dr. Ring practices, and it included testimony that Wendy spends wonderful quality time with patients.

Asked about the biggest reason that she continues to persevere, Dr. Ring observes that practicing medicine without activism "wouldn't have any meaning for me." She also avows a need to give back. "I feel that a lot of people helped get me where I am, and that was a huge investment. I'm not just talking about the med school teachers. I'm talking about all the people who helped me along the way, and that has been considerable. I can't throw that investment away. Even if I won the lottery, I wouldn't

> I feel that a lot of people helped get me where I am, and that was a huge investment. I can't throw that investment away. Even if I won the lottery, I wouldn't stop working—because a huge investment has been made in me. I feel some obligation.

leave medicine. I wouldn't stop working—because a huge investment has been made in me. I feel some obligation."

Dr. Ring gives credit where credit is due and remarks on her amazing staff. "My job is to help all those people do what they do, so it's kind of like a family. We all really care about each other and look after each other. We all are trying to do this thing together, supporting each other. So even on the days when I'm not feeling the enthusiasm about what I might want to do, I'm still feeling connected to that family."

Asked about her goals for her practice over time, Dr. Ring reflected, "Our mission is to provide health care to the underserved. As the medical director of the clinic, part of what I do is monitor what's going on with the health of the community. I look at lots of stats and I talk with lots of people. When there's a need that's not being met with our population, I get to design a program to meet those needs," she says. We have a drug treatment program that we started here because our patients have a lot of problems with drugs. We have a Latino health outreach program that we just started because we were getting more and more Spanish-speaking patients. So our goals evolve in relation to needs."

Making such decisions is guided by her belief that "you do things because they are right, and not because of the outcome. If I think something should be, even if there may be no reasonable expectation of payoff or success, I just do it because you have to stay right with yourself, and with what you believe every moment of every day." Indeed, I got the sense that not living in this state of integrity would be deeply painful for Wendy.

That integrity is coupled with an empathic ability to put herself in the other person's shoes. "I'm always thinking about what it's like to be on the other side. If I were the patient, how would I feel? I'm genuinely very interested in other people. I'm curious; I like to know about people's lives and what's important to them."

The ease with which she feels and expresses emotion helps Dr. Ring establish real connections with her patients, but she believes that it also means that "sometimes I'm not very effective. It's hard for me not to show it if I'm angry or impatient. I cry too easily. I'm the medical director here, but I am also the problem child." Yet there is another upside "because it's good to have some sort of obvious weaknesses. Then people don't look at you and feel like you're unapproachable. I think the creativity that's the flip side of my emotions has served me very well."

Dr. Ring is trying to improve her administrative abilities and is working on them. "I'm kind of scattered. My son was formally diagnosed with [attention deficit disorder] ADD, and I have a few of those characteristics; I'm disorganized and in the moment. I can't multitask well. I have a problem with working memory." Although she is reasonably capable, she knows she comes across as being kind of hapless. Her experience has been that people take her under their wing and try to help. She loses things so often that her colleagues gave her as a birthday present a statue with wires coming off it and things on the end of each wire—things that she can't find. "My cell phone, my car keys, sometimes the car itself." Wendy communicates the image of the beloved, gifted, but truly disorganized professor.

> You do things because they are right, and not because of the outcome. If I think something should be, even if there may be no reasonable expectation of payoff or success, I just do it because you have to stay right with yourself and with what you believe every moment of every day.

Nonetheless, Dr. Ring views "the weakness of how my brain works" as an obstacle to achieving her goals. She is trying to recruit another doctor who could do some of the administrative work. She has learned to manage the problem of being interrupted all the time—which goes with territory in administration. When she is interrupted, she completely forgets what she had been doing. She still wants to snap at people when they interrupt her, but has been able to stop herself from doing it. She has negotiated a change in timing in the interruption process. "I've gently asked my coworkers to please wait until I've finished what I'm doing and then I will find them."

Wendy sees herself at the point in her career where she should be teaching and mentoring other people, and she is starting to do that. At the same time, she "still feels like a kid masquerading as an adult. My friends and I are saying good-bye to some of the elders and the people that we looked up to. They're retiring or some have passed away, and then you look around and you say, 'Oh, my God, we're in charge?' "

Yet not having all the answers is part of why medicine holds her attention. "In medicine, you can never know it all; you can never get perfect at it. There's constant learning and trying to improve the way that you do things, so you never feel that you've arrived. And that's good for me, because I have to be kept busy and interested. I hate being bored," Wendy says. "My husband once told me, if someone were going to design a personal hell for you, it would be sitting in some kind of lecture, where they've handed out written materials that already explain everything, and the person up there is saying the same thing as on the materials, and showing the PowerPoint of exactly what they're saying. That would be the worst torture for me of anything I could think of."

Wendy thrives on the constant novelty in medicine. "Even if I'm telling someone with diabetes information that I've told hundreds of other people, I'm still looking at this person and asking myself what's the best way of doing this for this person. Maybe I could explain this in a better way. Or maybe it isn't that they don't understand, but that they haven't accepted having a chronic disease." I am struck by how Wendy's personality has a built-in safeguard against becoming burnt out on the overly rote aspects of patient care.

> It's good to have some sort of obvious weaknesses. Then people don't look at you and feel like you're unapproachable. I think the creativity that's the flip side of my emotions has served me very well.

Dr. Ring differentiates between burnout and despair. "Burnout's one thing; despair is another. I have crashed and burned many times, and I've learned enough from it that when I see the first signs coming up, I start to really pay attention and do whatever I can to lighten my workload and take time to rejuvenate and do all the self-care things that I can do for myself." On an ongoing basis, when Wendy is not at work, she is finding ways to play. "I always have projects going on. Where I live, I have a beautiful place with a garden and I have animals and a husband. Any time I say, 'Let's go do this,' he's right there. We do a lot of physically active stuff—hiking, bike touring . . ."

Dr. Ring understands that burnout is "basically when you're putting out more than you're getting back" and tries to maintain a balance, although, "It's hard, because you know I can't just take off. Any time I take off, the other doctor here is burned and vice versa." Still, when she can get some time to herself she has hobby projects like papier mâché or silk painting going on. She says she never perfects anything, but it is fun. She thinks that it is "so neat to learn how to do something that I've never done before; there's always something I'm excited about in my life." Clearly, her passion extends to everything she takes on. I cannot even imagine her having a moment of her dreaded boredom.

Dr. Ring is able to practice the style that she maintains with her patients in part because she is able to be authentic at work. She explains, "What I really like about my work is that I can be myself. I don't have to pretend. If I don't know something, I say I don't know and I go look it up. I don't have to dress up; I just get to be myself with people." When I asked whether there was ever a time when she felt that she knew the best course of action to take, but for some reason could not take it, she answered, "All the time. It's about resources. Most of the time we are successful. If I really think that someone needs something, I can often get it for them. I can call the other doctors in the community and say, 'Would you please see this person for free?' Not 100%, but for the most part." Talking with Wendy, I get the distinct impression that she tries to do whatever it takes on a daily basis.

The issue of resources and what it means to practice in a rural community arose in her husband's care during a heart attack a couple of years ago. He did not know he was having one. He had been playing handball and started not feeling well, but finished the game anyway. At home he lay down, and Wendy, who just happened to be home, realized what was going on and took him to the ER. Because he is so fit and his lab work came back looking so normal, it took a while to figure out that he was having a heart attack. It took time to get him on the catheter table, because somebody else was on there first. As a result, he lost some of his heart function, but he is still real active, still plays handball, and he is doing fine. "If we lived in the city, that wouldn't have happened. Because he wouldn't have to wait his turn for the catheter table, and there would be more than one cardiologist available," Wendy says. Nonetheless, Dr. Ring describes the medical care her husband received as "Good. I know and like the cardiologist who took care of him. It's a small community; we all know each other. The guy who took care of him in the ER was very good, he decided to wait for another round of tests before he said, 'Oh, you're okay, go home.' I know they don't always do that, so I'm very grateful to him."

Asked if there was ever someone she could not inspire to do the right thing, Dr. Ring recalls a patient "who had endometrial cancer, diagnosed early, but she refused to get treatment. I took care of her until she died. She never had any regrets about it. Things went the way she wanted them to go, but I always felt bad that I couldn't convince [her] to have a hysterectomy, because she wouldn't have died from her cancer, but she just wouldn't hear of it."

Asked about other regrets, Dr. Ring concedes, "I'd like all my drug-addicted patients to stop using drugs. Some of them didn't, and they died from it. Probably because I do outpatient medicine—it's not like people are desperately ill and if I don't do something they're going to die. I do think about some of the people who have come through our drug treatment program who relapse and die. But you know, I don't run the world."

Dr. Ring notes that if she were to err, it would most likely be not on the side of cowardice but rather on the side of having too much courage. "If I do anything, it's more in the direction of not keeping my mouth shut when perhaps I should have. I'm not the person to sit there and let something happen." At this stage in her life, however, Wendy is able to prioritize and make choices about in what way her activism is best expressed and put to best use. She confesses, "I feel badly that I don't throw my whole life over and do something to stop the war in Iraq. Where is the point where you say, 'It's not business as usual! Everyone into the streets!' Every time I hear the news, part of me thinks I should just drop everything and go to Washington and not rest until it stops. In a way we should all drop everything and go to the streets, but I also know that if I'm the only one who does it, it's not going to do anything, and my patients will go without." That sense of being there for her patients seems to be the only thing that keeps her boarding the Mobile Medical Office instead of the next plane to Washington or wherever her voice might be most beneficial.

> The Quakers believe that god is in everybody . . . and that has always resonated with me, because that's how I really feel. When I'm taking care of somebody, I'm trying to give them the best possible care, because that's God you're taking care of there.

The self-described "loudmouth" balances her tendencies as a longtime attendee at Quaker meetings. Dr. Ring sees a spiritual component in her work. "The Quaker belief is that God is in everybody, and I think that's the way that I treat people," she affirms. "That always resonated with me, because that's how I really feel. When I'm taking care of somebody, I'm trying to give them the best possible care, because that's God you're taking care of there. In practical terms, that means trying to find people's strengths and pulling them out so that *they* can see them, and treating people with respect and deep care. I think a lot of what I say about doing things because they're right—that's a spiritual issue," she says. "There's something about trying to stay on the right path and not compromising yourself. As I get older, I'm learning to do it sometimes in quieter ways. But I think, at the core, those things are all spiritual. I don't believe in the stuff about doing it because you'll go to heaven later. Do it now because it's right, and to be in a good spiritual state myself."

Dr. Ring hopes that she will touch lives indirectly through her influence on patients. "I like to think that the people I take care of are going to turn around and do something good for someone in their lives. I'm very excited about the young people who have come to the clinic to volunteer and have decided to go into medicine, so I think I'm making a contribution that way." She adds, "It's cool to think that a year later some people will be out doing the kind of work that I'm doing because of the contact that they had with me. I like that. It makes me feel really good. I don't know, these are dark times right now. You're just trying to keep the flames lit, and hopefully better times are coming."

The dark times Dr. Ring alludes to involve the state of the healthcare system. "I feel a lot like what we do is Band-Aid work." But she balanced this thought by adding, "Well, a lot of the things that we pilot and perfect at Mobile Medical Clinic end up going on to provoke policy changes and be reproduced in larger organizations, so it does have some wider effect. But a lot of what we do is because the whole health care system is broken and we're slapping bandages on that," she laments. "I don't like that, because that's not the kind of person that I am, but that's what we do. I try to think that some things have larger benefits, but then that's how change really happens. I think it is kind of one person at a time, so if people who come in contact with the clinic get something from it, maybe that's the best you can do."

Wendy believes that what inspires premed and medical students is watching patient interactions because "it looks so much more doable on that small up-close scale. That's how it worked for me."

What she would like to pass along is her earned wisdom that, "when we treat people as if their lives are valuable, they respond by valuing their lives and the lives of other people. If we treat people as if their lives have

> When we treat people as if their lives are valuable, they respond by valuing their lives and the lives of other people. If we treat people as if their lives have no worth, it is not surprising that they end up feeling that all human life is cheap.

no worth, it is not surprising that they end up feeling that all human life is cheap. Sometimes this seems like a huge undertaking beyond what any of us can muster—but surprisingly, often all it takes is the willingness to see past the problems and differences to the essential humanity of another person. I have learned from my patients that even when the problems seem insurmountable, one person following his or her heart can make a great deal of difference in the world. If we all did it what a different world this would be."

Dr. Ring's own inspiration seems to have come from the combination of her very stubborn, very literal personality and the progressive values she learned from her parents. She decided to become a doctor simply to make herself useful. In dedicating her professional life to meeting the needs of the medically underserved, she recalls her early lessons in the potential effectiveness of activism. She met many strong role models along the way, many good doctors whose practice she admired. Still she did not aspire to follow in the footsteps of any one specific doctor. Instead, she made her own way, coming to her mobile medical practice in California in part simply because a friend from medical school was practicing in rural California. A deep sense of spirituality, as well as her personal ethics, guides her as she treats others with compassion and respect. By managing her practice in this way, she has been able to stay right with herself while also bringing medical care to the uninsured and underserved.

CHAPTER 15

The Kindest Cut: Surgery with Soul

Dr. William Schecter
with Dr. Gisela Schecter

Dr. William Schecter is professor of clinical surgery and vice-chair of the department of surgery at the University of California at San Francisco (UCSF), and chief of surgery at the San Francisco General Hospital. He is a past governor of the American College of Surgeons, a member of the Governor's Committee on Blood-borne Infections and Environmental Risks, and Chairman of the American College of Surgeons Committee on Perioperative Care. His clinical expertise is the field of general surgery, trauma surgery, and critical care. He has also served as the chief of surgery at the LBJ Tropical Medical Center, Pago Pago, American Samoa (1981–1983) and as a lecturer in surgery at the University of Natal, Durban, Republic of South Africa (1983–1984). Dr. Schecter's clinical interests include the surgery of poverty: trauma, soft tissue infections related to drug use and alcoholism, advanced malignancy related to poor access to health care, and the surgical treatment of HIV-infected patients.

He is a cofounder of Operation Access, a nonprofit organization that mobilizes a network of medical volunteers, hospitals, and referring community clinics to provide low-income uninsured people access to donated outpatient surgeries and specialty care that improves their health, ability to work, and quality of life. According to Bill Schecter, prior to the establishment of the organization, "It was easier for doctors to go to Guatemala or Southeast Asia than to provide free surgical services to the needy in their own communities." The initial partnership consisted of 15 medical volunteers, 1 hospital, and 7 clinics in San Francisco County. Today, the network has grown to include over 550 medical volunteers, 22 participating hospitals, and 60 referring community clinics in 6 Bay Area counties.

In 2004, Bill spent a sabbatical at the Shaare Zedek Medical Center in Jerusalem, Israel, studying civilian hospital response to mass casualty events. In 2006, he served in the Rebecca Sieff Hospital in Safed, Israel, caring for casualties from the 2006 Thirty Days' war with Lebanon. On the campus of UCSF, he is known to get involved in antiwar protests.

Dr. Bill Schecter is a graduate of Harpur College, the State University of New York, and the Albany Medical College. He completed a residency in anesthesiology at the Massachusetts General Hospital, a residency in surgery at UCSF, and a fellowship in hand surgery. He has published and lectured extensively on a wide range of issues relating to surgery, trauma, and disaster response.

Bill's wife, Dr. Gisela Schecter, works in public health and in infectious disease and internal medicine. She maintains a practice in Half-Moon Bay, California.

Terry Gross of National Public Radio's show *Fresh Air* once pointed out that the most fascinating people do not always make for the best interviews. Dr. William Schecter is a case in point. When I first contacted him to request an interview for this book, he seemed reluctant to participate—not because he was bashful or uncooperative, but because he just is not comfortable talking about himself. He warned me point blank. "I'm not a good story . . . I've had an easy life . . ." When he answered so many of my questions with, "You really should ask my wife," I decided that I did, in fact, need to recruit the help of Dr. Gisela Schecter, a specialist in infectious disease and internal medicine to whom he has been married 34 years. Also, Bill's wide-ranging interests and wealth of experiences have also made it possible to mine a number of third-party sources.

If by *easy life*, he means one in which he has never had to deal with personal financial hardships, that much is true. "My father was born in a tenement, but he became very successful," he said. "I didn't have to worry about money—I've had a silver spoon in my mouth my entire life. That's one of the reasons why I do the work I do. I've got to return all the privilege that I've received."

Born on the lower east side of New York, Bill's father began working at a very young age to help support his family. He had always wanted to become a doctor, but instead ended up in his own father's business. While he apparently passed on those aspirations to his son, it was Bill's mother who inspired her son's great respect not only for the field of medicine, but for the military as well. A combat surgical nurse at the Normandy invasion, she was caught behind German lines during the battle of the Bulge. She married late by the standards of the day—she was nearing 40 when she decided to wed—and had two children. Stateside, she was a psychiatric nurse, a job she loved, and worked at New York's Bellevue Hospital.

Respect for medicine is one thing, but choosing it as a profession is something else entirely. In college, Bill was planning a career with the military or as an intelligence operative. He read a short story, written (in Hebrew) by Israeli novelist Aaron Meged, in which a former freedom fighter who had given up his settled life in the kibbutz to work in Tel Aviv, reunites with his fellow soldiers and is revitalized by the memories of his idealistic youth. Bill realized that he wanted to do something truly significant with his life. While he holds that any government service as a career would be worthwhile, he was disheartened by the military policies emanating from Washington, District of Columbia, at that time, and was torn about whether or not to enlist in the armed services.

Gisela adds, "Bill grew up and became draft eligible right toward the end of the Vietnam War, when it was really very clear that what we were doing in Vietnam was terrible. He really couldn't support that." By 1972, when Bill took his physical exam to make him draft eligible, the war was drawing to an end, and the decision of whether to join became a moot point. He did not end up getting drafted. Had that particular war not been being waged at the time, he would almost certainly have enlisted, if only to fulfill his desire to contribute to society.

It is easy to picture William Schecter as a military man. Gisela described him as a man of tremendous self-discipline, and "very much of a straight arrow," and to this day he holds himself to a daily regimen of military calisthenics and walking. Tall, fit, and trim in the pictures I have seen, he embodies the stereotypical calm, distinguished gentleman doctor, an appearance that belies the fact that he is the head of trauma surgery at an inner-city hospital regularly beset with the bleeding, wailing, and often hysterical victims of car crashes, household accidents, and knife and gunshot wounds.

How is it, I wondered, that among all the other ways in which someone can do something significant in life, Dr. Schecter came to choose surgery as his specialty? He was heavily influenced by a medical emergency in his own family. While Bill was in his second year of medical school, his father's heart rhythm went into ventricular fibrillation, where the cardiac muscles contract irregularly rather than pump in a coordinated effort. Without immediate stabilization, this arrhythmia will halt circulation and cause death within minutes. A cardiologist resuscitated Bill's dad, who lived another 7 years.

This successful intervention strongly influenced Dr. Schecter to become a trauma surgeon. These surgeons generally work at those hospitals that have the equipment, specially trained staff, and spectrum of specialists on call to handle a wide range of emergencies—the highly sophisticated and certified emergency centers that never close. These "super ERs" are where the helicopters are heading when the news reports that people with life-threatening injuries—especially those injured in remote or inaccessible areas of the countryside—have been transported by medical evacuation.

Of course, not every patient sent to a trauma surgeon has been plucked off a mountainside or rescued from a fiery plane crash. Many of the cases come from ordinary misadventures—rollover car crashes, gas leak explosions, construction accidents, etc. Many of them come from acts of interpersonal violence, which is why so many trauma centers are located in the hearts of cities where the population is the most dense. The hospital where Dr. Schecter has served as head of trauma surgery is just such an inner-city hospital. Why would Dr. Schecter, a man whose curriculum vitae suggests he could have worked anywhere he desired, choose a public hospital?

"That's where I get the most satisfaction," he said. "Taking care of people who are disenfranchised—who don't have other options."

Gisela expanded, "Early on in his medical career, he decided that he wanted to take care of poor people. He wanted to train in a system that had a public hospital, and he wanted to work in that sector. Private practice never had any attraction for him. He wanted to work where he was most needed."

Bill was at the very top of his medical school class. During one of his residencies, he met a physician named Dr. Green whose style of practice influenced him; he always gave an hour to each patient, always did a full exam, and never took shortcuts. Dr. Schecter counts Dr. Green as one of his strongest supporters. This senior physician taught him, among other things, the value of listening.

> I get the most satisfaction in taking care of people who are disenfranchised—who don't have other options.

"Listening is 95% of the job," said Bill Schecter, adding that renowned physician Sir William Osler said it over 100 years ago. " 'Listen to the patient: he is telling you the diagnosis.' And often patients will tell you what the best course for action is, too. A lot of times there are different paths you can walk down therapeutically, and if you don't listen to the patient, you may choose the one that sounds right for you, but that may not be right for that particular patient."

Listening, as well as being thorough and paying attention to details, are three of the most important instruments in Dr. Schecter's medical bag. "He carried those lessons with him when he was working as an intern," Gisela told me, explaining how it had helped him solve many a medical mystery. "For example, he once found out that a patient who was placed in the psychiatric ward in fact had a sky-high serum calcium that was causing the problem. He discovered that because he was thorough and paid attention to details." Bill follows Dr. Green's example of not taking shortcuts.

That does not mean, of course, that Dr. Schecter lets his own instincts and education take a secondary role, only that he uses all five senses both to determine diagnoses and develop courses of treatment. "Sometimes I think something should be done, and the patients don't agree with me, but I listen because ultimately they're the boss."

I asked if he could recall a time when the best course of action, such as a treatment plan, was evident, but that for some reason he had been unable to follow through. He answered, "No," but curiously then recounted an example of just that. "One time we had a 14-month-old child with 40% burns. The child needed to go back to the operating room repeatedly for burn debridement and grafting procedures. After the first one, the mother declined to give permission. I spent hours trying to find the key to that mother's psyche, without success." It is telling that he chose first to exhaust all possibilities of communication and dialogue with the mother before pursuing the only avenue he could conceive of that would save the child. "I actually had to go to court to get permission. I consider that to be a personal failure, that somehow I was unable to cross the divide that separated me from that mother. My own personal view is that if something like that reaches the court, it's basically the doctor's fault," he asserts. "The fact that the mother has different views or there's a problem with the child—that's not the mother's fault. That's a problem, and I was unable to stop it. That's an example of a failure—a failure of communication on my part. But it wasn't for lack of trying."

When I asked about any other circumstances that may have caused similar regrets, Dr. Schecter chose an anecdote in which his failure was again not a typical surgical error, but another communication gone awry. "There was one patient we had committed to the hospital with an infected toe, which turned out to be an infected malignant melanoma. He was an older patient who turned out to have metastatic disease," said Dr. Schecter. "He had two daughters who were married, two young women, and they asked me what had caused the disease. I looked at them and said, 'We don't know what causes cancer. If I knew, I'd be a candidate for the Nobel Prize.' " He was not, he said, trying to be funny or make light of a serious situation, only expressing exasperation about the state of medical knowledge. "We're pretty ignorant about what causes cancer now; maybe in the next generation we'll know more." Unfortunately, the daughters mistook his frustration for sarcasm.

"They took that comment to be a joke at the expense of their father, and I actually didn't even know about it for 2 days, until one of the husbands told me," said Dr. Schecter. "I tried to explain it, and recoup, but I never really reestablished relations with those two daughters. I regret that. Here their father was in a terrible situation, and I unintentionally made it worse by just making a comment. . . . It may have been a cross-cultural complication, but at any rate, I didn't need to lay that on them." It seemed that he took as much responsibility for wielding words as he did for wielding a scalpel. "These kinds of miscommunications are technical business problems. It's my job to make sure that they don't happen, and I have to take responsibility for it when they do."

Shortly after finishing up their respective residencies, Gisela and William Schecter went overseas. He served as the chief of surgery at a hospital in

American Samoa in the early 1980s. Gisela recounted for me an incident that her husband may have considered a failure of sorts but that was, as it turned out, the key to many successful outcomes thereafter. "There was a patient there with esophageal cancer. That is a tough disease. Bill operated on the patient. Initially, the patient survived the operation, but he developed one complication after another. After 6 weeks—a very long course of treatment, 6 weeks in the hospital—he did die," said Gisela. "That case haunted Bill for a long time. He kept asking himself, 'Should I have not even done it?' You see, esophageal cancer is not that common in the United States, so he hadn't worked on that many cases or even seen them. One reason I think that case haunted him so is that there's no buffer in places like Samoa—you're the only doctor who's coming in every day. You have all the responsibility. There's no other colleagues right there for you to consult."

Following his assignment in Samoa, Dr. Schecter traveled to Durban, Republic of South Africa, where he spent a year as a lecturer in surgery at the University of Natal, Durban—it was the only Black medical school in South Africa in those days when Apartheid was still the law in that country. Gisela worked at a mission hospital. Because Dr. Schecter had completed a hand fellowship, he was asked to help the school set up a training program in hand surgery. However, his Samoan experiences were still fresh in his mind. Gisela explained that in return for setting up the program, Bill asked for time to be made available for him to study and learn everything he could about esophageal surgery—because esophageal cancer is the second most common cancer among Africans. He would have at least one day a week to do esophageal surgery with the University of Natal's expert, an excellent surgeon who had done hundreds of the procedures, and in return Dr. Schecter designed and implemented a comprehensive hand surgery and training program.

Gisela suggested that Bill's greatest success was another case he had in Samoa. A woman had come to him with the kind of breast cancer rarely

> Listening is 95% of the job. Physician Sir William Osler said it over a hundred years ago: 'Listen to the patient: he is telling you the diagnosis.' And often patients will tell you what the best course for action is, too. A lot of times there are different paths you can walk down therapeutically, and if you don't listen to the patient, you may choose the one that sounds right for you, but that may not be right for that particular patient."

seen in the United States anymore—an open, draining, fungating breast lesion. These types of lesions, with their ulcerations and even necrotized tissue, may occur with certain types of cancer (e.g., melanomas, squamous cell cancers, and breast cancer) in their greatly advanced stages and often give off a distinctly unpleasant odor. Such was the case with this woman's cancer; she had found herself isolated as other people could not bear the smell of the lesion. Dr. Schecter researched the options, and ultimately treated her with chemotherapy to shrink the tumor and a radical mastectomy to remove the cancer that had spread to the chest wall. She healed and was then able to return home, lesion and odor free.

All seemed a complete success until she returned 6 weeks after surgery for a follow-up examination. Dr. Schecter had just read an article about breast surgery and sexual function, so he was moved to ask her how relations between her and her husband were progressing now that the surgery was over and she was well again. The woman burst into tears. It seemed that she was afraid to have sex with her husband because of the surgery. Dr. Schecter reassured her, telling her that it was all healed and she had nothing to fear. The next time she came in, a month later, she was beaming. Things were much better at home, she told him, and she could 'fulfill her role as wife.'

> I have recited 'The Lord's Prayer' in the operating room prior to surgery with believing Christians, referred to God's will as Allah when discussing high-risk procedures with believing Muslims and occasionally asked God to protect the patient from the surgeon and his assistant before laying knife to skin in a particularly difficult case. . . . There are very few real atheists in foxholes or hospitals.

Bill had told Gisela that he learned much about courage from the woman and what people were willing to endure, but also about the importance of continually reading—of keeping current with everything possible. According to Gisela, Bill "always, always continues to read the literature. He never thinks 'I know it all,'" she said. "At the very least he will skim each journal article so he can continue to improve. He's never satisfied with what he already knows; he's always ready to learn more." If Bill had not just been reading the journal article, he may never have thought to have asked the question that ultimately healed this woman's psychic wound in addition to her surgical scar.

From the earliest days of the AIDS epidemic, Bill has led the way on the surgical treatment of HIV-infected patients. Although this focus has never wavered, Dr. Schecter expanded his clinical interests to include what could be called the "surgery of mass casualties." Living and working in the California region—known for earthquakes, wildfires, and mudslides—seems to have combined with current events worldwide to inspire Bill's interests in emergency medical response following disasters. "San Francisco hospitals will one day be challenged by mass casualties caused by an earthquake, an industrial or transportation accident, or an attack involving either conventional or unconventional weapons," he wrote. "Previously competing hospitals must then communicate with each other, share resources, and perhaps transfer patients between institutions."

Dr. Schecter did not merely extrapolate from his experiences at San Francisco General Hospital. Rather, in 2004 he spent his sabbatical at a hospital in Jerusalem, Israel. There he studied the civilian hospital's response to 31 separate terrorist multiple- or mass-casualty events and coauthored a piece about his experiences in the *Journal of Trauma-Injury Infection & Critical Care* in 2007. In a sense, he emulated the fictional commando in the Meged story that so inspired him during his college years. "Trying to help people and rescue them…that's how I wanted to spend my life," said Dr. Schecter. To that end, he took his lectures on the road, speaking in 2005, for example, at the University of Queensland Australia on terrorist mass casualty events in Israel, outlining the historical context and clinical management.

He then put himself in harm's way for two months in the summer of 2006 at the Rebecca Sieff Hospital in Safed, Israel, where he helped take care of casualties from the Lebanon Thirty Days' War. He shared some of his journals from that time with me and they make for fascinating reading. Here is an excerpt from August 8, 2006:

> In the early morning we received a tank commander that was shot in the face. The job of a tank commander is particularly dangerous as they like to have their torso outside of the turret in order to get a better view of the battle. Our patient was very fortunate. He lost the soft tissues of his upper lip and upper teeth but his life is not in danger. . . . The two attending surgeons who cared for him are Israeli Arabs. The resident scrubbed on the case is a Jew. . . . I just took a break from writing because of two air raids and just heard the distant explosion of a landing Katyusha. . . . Last night while I was waiting to do a case, one of the OR nurses gave me dinner—lentils and vegetables that she had brought from home. . . . while I was eating, a huge explosion from a Katyusha landing close to the hospital occurred. The nurses were quite shaken. I kept on eating as the dinner was quite delicious."

His letters home from that time reflect his irrepressible spirit and deep love of humanity. In view of Dr. Schecter's upbringing in a close-knit Jewish family and neighborhood, and his intensely personal visits to Israel, I wondered if he would speak to a spiritual component to his work. When I asked him about this, Dr. Schecter said, "I'll answer that question by quoting Ambroise Paré, a 16th-century military physician" and royal surgeon for several French kings. "[Paré] said, '*Je le pansai, Dieu le guérit,*' which means 'I dressed him, and God healed him.'"

A 2006 article in the *San Francisco Chronicle* about the SFGH emergency room quotes Dr. Schecter as saying, "Doctors, nurses, social workers, psychologists and technicians are all there because they choose to serve the poor, the afflicted, the ignored, and the forgotten" (Weiss, 2006, p. A-1). Half the trauma surgeries performed there are the result of penetrating trauma—stabbings or gunshot wounds. It could be said that the trauma team handles casualties from the battlefields of hopelessness, defeatism, and neglect, including victims of "acts of violence, complications of drug addictions, alcoholism, and cigarettes, and treatment of advanced malignancies due to lack of access to medical care" (Weiss, 2006, p. A-1).

Yet Dr. Schecter still seems unwilling to take primary credit for saving lives. He repeats, " 'I dressed him, and God healed him.' I think that is just as true today as it was in the 16th century," said Dr. Schecter. "But I'd never admit it in public." In fact, Dr. Schecter did not speak directly about his spiritual beliefs at all, despite the obvious fact that his approach to life is deeply colored by his sense of morality and ethics. In fact, when I asked Bill who he thought had taught him his respect for humanity, he answered, simply, "My culture." His writings and references are filled with commentaries on social ills, the state of health care in the United States, and pervasive worldwide violence:

> A gunshot wound is just a vector of a disease, like a mosquito carrying malaria. If you got rid of the bullets, you wouldn't have a disease. Our society is totally out of control, and I'm sort of like a social worker with advanced training. Some kid gets shot in Jerusalem, it's on the front page of every newspaper in the world. But a kid gets shot in San Francisco, and it probably doesn't even make the newspaper. You know why? Because fundamentally nobody gives a shit. (as cited in Weiss, 2006, p. A-1)

Whereas several of our exemplar physicians are vocal about their faith and interspersed many of their answers with references—and deferences—

to God, Bill has always made it a point to focus on what his patients believe, and to be culturally sensitive. "I have recited the Lord's prayer in the operating room prior to surgery with believing Christians, referred to God's will as Allah when discussing high-risk procedures with believing Muslims, and occasionally asked God to protect the patient from the surgeon and his assistant before laying knife to skin in a particularly difficult case," said Dr. Schecter in his convocation speech at the graduation ceremonies of the University of California San Francisco School of Medicine class of 2007. He adds: "There are very few real atheists in foxholes or hospitals" (Schecter, 2007).

Bill says that there are two basic principles that guide him, which are, "Don't do anything to anyone that you wouldn't do to yourself, and love your neighbor as yourself." Both rules speak directly to Dr. Schecter's nonprofit organization, Operation Access, as well. Operation Access came about after a fortuitous meeting between Dr. Schecter and Dr. Douglas Grey, chief of thoracic and vascular surgery at Kaiser Permanente Medical Center. The two surgeons had both happened to attend a meeting at which a professor from the University of California, Davis spoke about the difficulties of getting health care to the uninsured. The speaker pointed out that while medical personnel in some areas of health care—for example, family practice, general practice, or internal medicine—have a number of outlets for volunteerism, there was no such venue for surgeons inside the United States, which meant that the uninsured who needed operations had nowhere to turn. He asked the rhetorical question of the audience, "Why have surgeons not been able to organize an infrastructure that would allow people to volunteer and provide simple surgical services to some of the 40 million uninsured in this country?"

> Don't do anything to anyone that you wouldn't do to yourself, and love your neighbor as yourself. The technical parts and the knowledge—that's going to change with time, but those principles won't.

Drs. Schecter and Grey moved forward and founded the Ambulatory Surgery Access Coalition. The purpose of the private, nonprofit corporation was to develop the resources and infrastructure that would allow volunteers to deliver free surgical care to uninsured, low-income patients in San Francisco. They secured a grant from the Robert Wood Johnson Foundation and began a pilot program to work out the bugs. The pilot program ended in 1995, but the full-scale program, Operation Access, continues to flourish.

The doctor duo enlisted the aid of Paul Hofmann, DPH, who provided invaluable administrative experience and expertise. "It was like the *Field of Dreams* movie—every time we would come up with a problem, the problem's solution would come to us within a week, by some random force," said Dr. Grey (2008) in an interview at Stanford University. "If we had no funding, then we'd get an unsolicited letter in the mail the next day, offering money. It was the weirdest thing I've ever seen."

As Gisela pointed out, success was hardly a foregone conclusion. "The problem is getting something set up in such a way that people feel it's safe to participate," she said. "It's very different from donating money. If you donate money and something goes wrong, so what? But if you donate yourself . . . there really are some issues that have to be addressed, particularly in the United States."

The nature of the specialty dictated that the organization could not consist of simply a list of willing volunteers. The planning required to establish the organizational structure suited Dr. Schecter's thorough, methodical, detail-oriented nature. Provisions had to be made not just for the actual surgeons, but also for surgical support teams (e.g., anesthesiologists, operating room nurses, etc.), operating rooms, equipment, instruments, supplies, and medications. Business and legal issues such as malpractice protection had to be completely worked out before the first scalpel-to-skin contact. "This is so representative of Bill," said Gisela. "Get a group together that has some business experience, some foundation experience. They spent quite a while making sure that when they launched it, there wouldn't be glitches, there wouldn't be people with regrets."

Setting up Operation Access required, among other things, negotiating with area hospitals. Thanks to the high standing in the medical community of both Dr. Bill Schecter and Dr. Grey, the surgeons' proposal was received with respectful consideration, and ultimately, after months of what Gisela called "networking and selling," they were able to secure the cooperation of some local practitioners.

The program continues to grow. According to its Web site, in 2007, "662 surgical services were donated, a 32% increase over 2006" (Operation Access, 2007).

As more and more hospitals became interested, and more and more surgeons said, "Yeah, I want to be a part of that," momentum has built, not just regionally but statewide and nationally as well. Both Drs. Bill Schecter and Grey, who have spoken extensively about Operation Access, receive frequent requests from doctors all around the country who want to learn more about how they could implement a program of their own.

I wondered if all the notoriety had affected Bill, but Gisela confirmed my impression that although the publicity helped open doors, he continues to focus on those actions that would serve his patients rather than himself. "It's very hard for him to talk about himself in any other way than, 'Oh, I'm just a country doctor,' " she said.

That came through clearly in a 2006 *San Franciso Chronicle* article: "A safe surgeon leaves his ego at the door," Bill Schecter told the reporter. "You have to beware of the surgeon with misplaced confidence. Obviously, to do this work you have to have a big ego—you can't cut people open unless you think you're pretty good—but nobody's totally mastered this. It's a constant struggle to avoid error" (Weiss, 2006, p. A-1).

I asked Bill how, with so much going on, he managed to avoid getting burned out. He laughed. "Well, how do you know I'm not burned out? Basically, I just try to get up every morning and do the very, very best I can, and go home to my wife," he said. "What I want them to put on my tombstone is, 'He did the best he could under the circumstances.' That's how I resist burnout: I have realistic goals."

It was clear that he also genuinely enjoyed the work. "He enjoys the challenges of surgery," said Gisela. "Every day, you don't know what you're going to find; that makes life interesting. He's very competent. That probably counts, too, because he feels like there are some things that he can do that most surgeons can't do, and that's motivating."

Nevertheless, since Bill had undergone bypass surgery himself not too long ago, it might be reassuring to think he would cut back. I asked Gisela why he did not simply rest on his laurels. "That's just not part of Bill. He really wants and needs to contribute. That's very important to him," she said. "He is 60 now, and age takes its toll on surgeons—they get back problems, for example, from the positions they maintain for long periods of time. He isn't able to work as many hours and stay up as many nights and function the next day as well as when he was 40—there's no doubt about that. In that sense, he has cut back."

That did not mean, apparently, working less than full time, however, although Gisela pointed out that Dr. Schecter no longer answered routine night calls as he once did. "If they have a difficult case down at the hospital, and they call him, of course he'll go," she explained, "but he doesn't do it on a routine basis, so that was a concession. At a certain point, you know, you have to take care of your own body, too. But to give it all up? No. Not Bill."

Another minor concession has been that Dr. Schecter's daily regimen of military calisthenics and running is now still the same daily regimen of military calisthenics but walking instead. "I exercise regularly every day," he said.

One of the main ways he has kept balance in his life is through spending time with his family. "Family is very critical to him. He's very devoted to us," said Gisela. "Doctors often make their vacations 3 days added onto a meeting, and do it three or four times a year, and the family will fly out for those days. Not Bill. He made a point that we take a summer vacation, a real vacation, that had nothing to do with meetings, every year. The longest one we ever took was 6 weeks," she said. "This was when my son had his bar mitzvah, my daughter was almost 10, and we shipped our bikes over to France. We bicycled through France for 5 weeks; it was just fantastic. A couple of other times he was able to take a month. Usually it was 2 weeks, but it was always every year. It really makes a huge difference in terms of the relationship you have with your children."

Sometimes doctors make the worst patients. I asked Gisela how her husband had handled having to place his life in the hands of another surgeon. "He really very much appreciated the care that he got from the surgeon and the hospital. He made it a point to bring gifts to people who took part in his care. Every year he writes a letter saying 'I'm doing fine.' He knows it's hard to take care of patients, and he really appreciated the care they gave."

I closed my interview with Dr. Schecter by asking what he would like to see as his lasting legacy. He remained humble and understated to the end. "My lasting legacy? I don't think anyone's going to remember me, unfortunately. I would have liked to have had a life like Winston Churchill, or something like that, but it didn't happen," he said. He did not sound particularly disappointed. "My legacy is going to be my children and my residents." And what would he leave behind with those residents? "Don't do anything to anyone that you wouldn't do to yourself, and love your neighbor as yourself. The technical parts and the knowledge—that's going to change with time, but those principles won't. They shouldn't change, at any rate. I hope not."

CHAPTER 16

A Summation of What Was Shared

"My grandfather was a physician during the Civil War, and several of my children are physicians today. I think we would all agree that my children, because of the enormous amount of dollars earmarked for medical research this past century, know a hundred times—perhaps a thousand times—more about the human body than my generation did. But I have always wondered: *Why is it we know so little about the human spirit?*"

Sir John Templeton (1912–2008)

John Templeton was a philanthropist who funded an ambitious research agenda on medicine and spirituality. His foundation sponsors a prestigious annual award for progress on spiritual realities that counts Mother Teresa and Aleksandr Solhenitsyn among past winners. To follow up and build on Templeton's words we can rightly ask, why is it that we know so little about physicians who attempt to minister to the mysterious spirit along with tending the human body?

What stands out as the most indelible impressions of the Pride in the Profession Award honorees?

In the course of coming to know the fine physicians profiled in this text, I was struck by the fact that the thickest common thread woven between them was an enduring interest in spiritual and sometimes religious concerns. At times I even wondered about the dozen physicians who were invited into the conversation but who did not respond. Was that cluster the atheist and agnostic subgroup? Or have almost all of the doctors who have ever been honored with the Pride in the Professions Award shared proclivities toward faith-based living and work? Certainly I knew that I had planned to inquire about their belief systems, but I had no idea that the emphasis on their relationships with God's work would be so strong. Friends and family would say "How is that book on physicians coming along, Helen?" and I would joke in response, "Actually I'm writing a book on spiritual leaders, I just didn't know that when I started." I endured the quizzical looks and continued to ponder the collective take-home message.

To illuminate the driving force behind the honorees' life's work, I needed to look at both why they applied themselves so diligently and at how they might be guided by a sense of noble purpose. J. D. Salinger (1951) once said that the mark of immaturity is the willingness to die nobly for a cause, but true maturity brings the desire to live humbly for one. Perhaps Parker Palmer, a truly inspiring educator, put this most succinctly: "We project either a spirit of hope or a spirit of despair, either an inner confidence in wholeness and integration or an inner terror of life being diseased and ultimately terminal . . . Consciousness precedes being, and consciousness can help deform, or reform, our world" (Palmer, 1994, p. 27).

The physicians profiled here share an unusually high level of self-awareness. They are very conscious of leading from a deep source of hopefulness and trust. They seem to understand that if they fail to use their spiritual resources to fortify their inner beings that their outreach to the external world will be diminished as well.

As I joined in conversation with the honorees, I confirmed my prior speculation that they would come across as self-actualized people in the sense that humanistic psychologist Abraham Maslow defined them. Since a key quality of the actualized is humility, I am sure a few will wince as they read this comparison. Still, Maslow's portrait of fully functional, psychologically healthy individuals bears a striking resemblance to the group assembled here. Professor Maslow noted that such rare people share a group of characteristics such as detesting duplicity, manifesting an acceptance of reality more than a neurotic worry about circumstances. They are spontaneous and genuine, enjoy creativity in solving problems, and like their solitude as well. Additionally, the actualized are independent, sustain a fresh appreciation of even repetitive tasks, and are touched by good humor, which certainly is helpful in maintaining feelings of kinship with the human race and significant others. Self-actualized people are comfortable with their own value system and feel certain that they know right from wrong. They long ago moved past a focus on any felt deficiencies and are now more motivated by such values as truth, goodness, and justice.

So when I hold Maslow's ambitious list of attributes side by side with the characteristics displayed by our exemplars, I see more than a few parallels. This summary chapter will extrapolate from their stories and anecdotes to highlight the qualities developed through their early influences, sustained by their sense of mission and elevated by their spiritual and ethical foundations.

As I characterize the qualities of this elite but not elitist group in this chapter, I suspect that I will feel like developmental psychologists Larry Kohlberg and Abe Maslow often reported feeling—happy that such people exist, but wishing that there were more of them in our world.

As a former graduate student of Kohlberg's, I think about his research on people who have advanced to what he called "post-conventional" reasoning. These individuals are guided by an enlightened conscience. Kohlberg was very influenced by the philosophy of Immanuel Kant and his concept of a categorical imperative. In this vision, moral action is defined as that which would be the right thing to do for any human in a similar situation. Kant and Kohlberg's precepts always include a notion of universality.

Likewise, the honorees cannot go along with a passive acceptance of the prevailing societal norms in the delivery of health care. In fact, they are actively working toward a world in which everyone is given full and equal respect. The honorees take action simply because it is right, not because it is expected or expedient.

Professor of psychiatry Kay Redfield Jamison cites this passage from an Anglican prayer in her book on exuberance: "Shield your joyous ones," the line enjoins (2004, p. 3). With most prayers focused on alleviating pain and suffering, those people who manage to live their daily lives in a bright light are not joined by many other spiritual cheerleaders. Although that lack of strength in astronomical numbers is not ideal, as the honorees have made clear in sharing their stories here, their passion for their own lives is still and always will be its own reward. And as Jamison might add, they are incapable of being indifferent. This means we can count on them to keep on keeping on.

What are the early influences that contributed to the honorees' character?

In considering the unifying themes that emerge as the physicians talk about their important early influences, I hear recurrent images of caregiving as a crucial influence from their earliest memories onward. Their interests and hobbies, fed by books, movies, and media, gravitated towards tales of rescue and healing. The role models and mentors they most valued demonstrated real-life versions of these endeavors. Bill Schecter's mom serving as a nurse in Normandy is one of the more obvious examples. Parents or nurturers who were great humanitarians figured heavily for most, both in showing the possibility of making a real difference in others' lives for good and in embodying the joy of doing so.

A few of these doctors had markedly negative role models as well, against whose influence they developed and exhibited the beginning of personalities shaped by the attributes of resilience and persistence. Their ability to rebound from and reject negative input may have to do with the fact that at some point, most of them spent long periods of time around people who were faced with significant challenges and responded to them proactively. These physicians, as young people, saw and absorbed habits critical to developing resilience.

Persisting until a solution was found was a skill expressly modeled and taught by many of their early role models. The idea that solutions should benefit all involved was conveyed. Satisfaction and self-worth came from how well they could use problem-solving skills—especially if the resolution would benefit those with the least power in society. The interviews reveal that the honorees' early caretakers impressed them with the idea of serving others, often through physical healing in particular.

What experiences with parents or nurturing figures had the most substantial long-term effects?

The influence of parents and nurturers—or the lack of nurturing—on emotional development and personality is an extensive area of study in psychology. But are there certain kinds of parents who are more likely to raise healers? Do physicians of this caliber grow from a particular kind of environment or nurturing, or do they perhaps react against the absence of support by becoming exquisite caregivers themselves? These questions are of course not fully answered in the brief interviews, but some of what the doctors themselves think was important and most of what they say about the kind of homes they were raised in comes across in a positive light.

It is certainly notable that the majority of the doctors in this book had parents for whom humanitarian concerns and action were central to their lives. Pride and gratitude for the influence of these parents characterizes their children's descriptions. A great many of the subjects spoke of their parents in glowing terms, not only as parental authority figures and role models, but as simply great human beings (words like *kind*, *generous*, *sweet*, and *beautiful* were offered frequently). They earned their children's respect through their love, fortitude, and commitment to doing right. Several said that going the extra mile for another human being simply defined their parents' way of being in the world, the young doctors observed that their parents practiced a high degree of courage and selflessness. This selflessness was sometimes directly and explicitly connected to the family's understanding of religion, but not always. Gary VanderArk's father was a minister who attempted every day to live his creed. He wanted his son to be a pastor, and Dr. VanderArk feels that he is a pastor of sorts, ministering through his practice of medicine instead of theology.

However, the clear—and, notably, embodied—dedication of these parents to a code of ethics that demanded justice, generosity, and compassion towards all and some of the joy with which that code was lived is evident in the subjects' vivid memories and language. Mark Asperilla's grandfather was a surgeon, and Mark remembers seeing fresh produce left by grateful patients on the steps outside as their way of saying "Thank you," and providing payment. Michael VanRooyen's father had been a resistance fighter in World War II and survived a concentration camp during the Holocaust, but somehow never allowed any of the darkness of that past to taint his son's childhood. Jeannette South-Paul, whose family ran a rescue mission in downtown Philadelphia for almost 35 years, recounts the ways they helped the poor. She also remembers that by watching them facilitate and gather resources for their clients, she became aware that while she was awed by their diligence, she wanted to be the one who could take direct, quick, and effective action.

Threaded through these accounts is the repeated sense of generous and careful attention to people, a listening for *all* of their human needs—not just those expressed in words, and not only the immediate needs of their bodies. Several of the subjects also mentioned their parents' lack of regard for gender, race, wealth, or position in their behavior towards other human beings, declaring that they treated everyone equally and with respect and compassion. Implicit within those parents' behavioral codes was the appreciation that self-worth, dignity, and respect are as much primary human needs as food, shelter, and clothing are. The doctors who had positive parenting witnessed this overall attention in their parents' treatment of others.

Furthermore, the parents who served as charitable role models gave their children a functional knowledge of how to serve human needs. Their commitments went beyond abstraction or espoused theories into daily behavior. Jack McConnell gives the example of his father asking his children at the dinner table each night what they had done for someone else that day. If someone had an idea, his father would enlist the other children's support for the project, along with their further ideas, and ask them to find resources to help bring the idea to fruition. Here again, altruistic plans were quickly moved through the conceptual stage to be enacted. Thus many of the doctors had their parents as guides in dealing with obstacles. Not content to let their children merely think about or envision how to help, they saw them through the process of implementing goals and plans.

Among the honorees whose relationships with their parents were in some ways problematic, almost all report a long-term, meaningful, and positive relationship elsewhere in their young lives. For Dr. Sister Brooks, it was the nuns at the convent where her father brought her as a child. They provided a safe and loving holding environment for her. Seeing and believing that the daily happiness she observed in them was possible and identifying that sense of joy in life as a goal became key to her own identity. For Coleen Kivlahan, whose father's alcoholism cast a shadow over her family life at home, it was within the warm, demonstrative and loving extended family of a childhood friend, where hugs and open expression of emotion were the norm. This is a stark contrast to the dynamics of an alcoholic family where "walking on eggshells" to avoid provoking outbursts is more typical.

Those who had nurturing parents benefited from their support of education and the learning process, formal and otherwise. Even the honorees who were not well nurtured at home relate in their stories that a connection was made for them between becoming educated and their ability to maximize their own potential. Almost all report having someone in their young lives directly affirm their potential as an individual with words that expressed the idea that you can do anything you want to do.

In their younger years, the award honorees may have sensed that service to others was directly or indirectly expected by their caregivers. It is clear that care for others became a cornerstone of the physicians' own lives as they grew older. Whether this began as a tribute made out of respect or as an outgrowth of their own passion and curiosity, they ended up emulating those who had nurtured them in character and deed, if not directly in a choice of profession.

The parents and nurturers of the honorees in this book clearly had a profoundly formative effect on the children they raised. Their dedication to caring for others' needs helped crystallize the intents of the young physicians-to-be towards the value of nurturing health and happiness in others. The physicians' responses to their own first caregivers helped them form a sense of mission and became their initial preparation toward a path helping others as a vocation.

How was caregiving modeled for the young physicians?

The concept of caregiving as both a primary function and a vocation was unavoidable in many of the early lives of the honorees. Most found themselves in situations where it was an absorbing dynamic in their childhoods. Their responses to the idea of caregiving, however, were and continue to be notably positive, even in cases where they might not have been. Many had their own early exposure to suffering or felt the lack of attention they might have known due to someone else's suffering. In light of this, the children who became these doctors might have understandably shied away from the necessity for caregiving and rebounded away from it in their lives and careers. On the contrary, though, most found a deep passion and inspiration for human service instead.

Many of the honorees discuss the fact that members of their families had serious illnesses. Some became the main caretakers of a loved one literally, emotionally, or both. As a result, several saw the positive effects of medicine and healing work done by medical professionals. A few recount a specific moment in their childhoods when they witnessed a particular intervention and saw how critical it was in making the difference to someone's quality of life or very survival. These observations planted the idea that protecting people's health and well-being through medicine was a worthy path. For example, as the youngest child in a large family, Jack McConnell derived self-esteem from learning to help his mother treat her illness. Sylvia Campbell saw a brother rescued from drowning and later herself rescued an injured friend after a boating accident. Michael VanRooyen helped at an accident with farming equipment. Bruce Gould talks about his eye injury being healed by a pediatrician.

The memories of the physicians reveal a strong quality of observation coupled with analysis, even from an early age. Within their recollections I find a high level of attentiveness to and specificity about the details of particular events and important moments of learning. Many of them evidence a profound curiosity about how things work. Coleen Kivlahan talks about her fascination with the natural world. In her case, she reports that curiosity as being intense enough to overcome what might be considered, for a child, a certain natural squeamishness about death and the more icky elements of anatomy, etc. So many of the honorees seemed predisposed to concentrate on, speculate about, and figure out the why and how of things. For most, this early mental engagement with their surroundings translated fairly rapidly into an assertiveness toward the physical and natural worlds.

Experiencing the pain and confusion of loss due to the lack or limitations of medical care figures into several of the honorees' accounts. Mark Asperilla, for example, had one sister with meningitis, another with cerebral palsy, and lost a third sister with a congenital heart defect when she died from a post surgery infection. Alcoholism, an implacable and confounding illness that until recently had few effective treatment options, affected some of the families as well. This struggle with drinking and addiction appears a few times as an example of a challenge in the physicians' later lives.

None seem to characterize the caretaking dynamic as a negative influence in their formative years. On the contrary, most appear to have found within it the bedrock of an identity that suited them. It provided an environment in which their interests, fascination, and nascent talents could combine, as well as a forum in which to live out the admired values they were absorbing from the significant heroes, mentors, and role models of their childhood and young adulthood. The importance of care for others' needs and seeing others give and receive it became primary. As such, caregiving may have provided another means to immediately implement the espoused values of their role models, such as respect for humanity, taking them from abstract principles into fundamental daily practice. This may also contribute, for many of them, to their adult understanding of principles as being inseparable from action. Many of the doctors express feelings of indebtedness not only to the caregivers of their youth, but also to their own medical caregivers as adults and to partners and family members who make their work possible by nurturing and supporting them in their homes and professional lives today.

The acceptance of caregiving as a positive and life-sustaining dynamic meant that the doctors saw the adoption of the role of caregiver as one that held some of life's greatest potential. Far from seeing it as a draining role, they found within it a source of identity and an exciting world of anticipated exploration. The respondents often mention feeling grateful to be involved in the field of medicine, finding in it a synthesis of their intellectual interests and their spiritual beliefs. In short, from their early experiences with caregiving, the doctors drew positive conclusions about its validity as a life path, from which they did not stray as they grew older.

Toward what types of narratives, media, and communities were the young physicians drawn?

Along with the examples of caregiving that the doctors absorbed in their early lives, they appear to have sought role models in stories, true and fictional, that exalted the role of the caregiver as a rescuer and hero. Since many of these stories were based on factual accounts, the honorees were able to get some sense of the reality of their idols' lives. Again we find a place where aversion could have been a natural response or merely being content to learn of the exciting accomplishments of their heroes without ever wanting to emulate them. Instead, many of the physicians report beginning to articulate their goals in response to the admiration they felt for some of these medical heroes.

Reading was seminal to most of the doctors in their younger lives, particularly in helping them begin to articulate a sense of personal goals and mission. Stories of inspirational figures made lasting impressions on most of them, and themes of rescue, bridging two disparate worlds, or offering second chances predominate. Several mentioned the name of Albert Schweitzer as someone whose accomplishments impressed and inspired them. The book, *Fire on the Mountain*, and the work of Dr. Tom Dooley was very influential for Coleen Kivlahan. Jeannette South-Paul indicates that reading Paul Brand's book on working with lepers and studying history texts on the Holocaust led to her articulation of questions such as, how can you be civilized and knowingly allow others to suffer without doing anything about it? Bill Schecter talks of reading a short story in college about a man who, after a brief weekend of engagement with the world of idealism and action, deliberately leaves his dreams of an adventurous life behind and goes back to his humdrum job. That story convinced him to try to find an exciting career in which he could rescue people and make a real difference in society. Mark Asperilla says that from reading Hemingway, particularly *The Old Man and the Sea*, he derived the value of persistence and never giving up. Wendy Ring remembers listening to her father reading her Dr. Dolittle books and deciding she wanted to be like the kindly animal doctor. Jerry Jampolsky credits a book called *A Course in Miracles* with teaching him to look at the world in a spiritual way.

Bill Schecter also mentions the television characters of Dr. Kildare and Ben Casey from their respective shows—both smart, kindly doctors who cared and got involved as being heroes in their patients' lives. Gary VanderArk's role model, found after an active search, inspired a novel and a movie all at once; the man he names as his mentor, Eddie Kahn, served as the inspiration for the book and film entitled *Magnificent Obsession*. One of its themes is that happiness comes from doing good for others, since the giver ends up benefiting by feeling more blessed than the receiver.

Several belonged early on to youth, religious, and service organizations that sharpened their awareness of the need and the opportunity to serve humanity. Wendy Ring, for example, links her first experiential learning about social justice through the United Farm Workers to her current work. Michael VanRooyen says he made a connection between his father's heroism during World War II and the service opportunities he encountered as a member of the Boy Scouts. Bruce Gould was shaped by his Scout experiences as well.

The idea that giving blesses the one who gives was presented in numerous ways to the doctors in childhood and young adulthood. The cultivation of a desire to be like the celebrated heroes of the media, literature, and community groups paved the way for real-life mentorship experiences with other admirable figures.

How did having a mentor figure into the formation of the honorees' life's work?

It may be that the idealism instilled in the honorees by early experiences gave them a certain level of faith that allowed them to find and respond to strong mentors later. Most of them depended absolutely at one time or another on the guidance of an older, experienced medical veteran, and most found placing themselves in the hands of those mentors a trust-inspiring experience.

Almost all of the doctors are able to cite at least one person who played a vital mentorship role in their young adult lives. The contributions of these mentors cannot be overstated. Many of the doctors benefited greatly from an opportunity or series of opportunities they provided. For most, their mentors were older physicians or teachers who took them under guidance at crucial junctures in their lives and exerted a decisive, formative, and positive influence. Some are directly responsible for the career path of the honoree. They provided advice, teaching, hands-on experience, and often employment. In many instances they also provided a kind of parental supervision to a young student or practitioner. That oversight apparently included a great deal of psychological affirmation as the eventual doctors undertook their first major educational and career challenges. For these doctors, their path was made clearer by mentors, who often became lifelong supports and influences. To this day, several of the honorees keep a picture of their mentor in view at their offices.

However, not all the doctors in the book received mentorship of a straightforward positive kind. Some of them, especially those from minority groups, got what might be considered antimentoring, in the form of discouraging input that ironically spurred them onward to achievement in spite of it. Some cobbled together learning apprenticeships from the best aspects of various experiences. For one, a major developmental turning point came when he decided to go in another direction than that recommended by an influential mentor. For at least one, the knowledge that she would have to be her own best champion became a guiding principle.

The ways that the doctors were able to respond to and maximize their mentorship experiences demonstrate the following principles: first, that many simply felt lucky to receive positive nurturing from experts in the field; second, that they were able to accept direction and guidance and follow it in creating a path for themselves, and third, that regardless of the places they found it, the doctors showed they intuitively and very quickly understood the need to use what mentorship they could find in positive ways. In this way, even the negative people in their lives ultimately became positive contributors.

What did the physicians do about obstructionists along the way?

Turning negative experiences into the basis for acquired wisdom is a hallmark of resilience, and all the honorees' descriptions of how they responded to negativity show this trait. While their answers are not Pollyanna-ish, some clearly still expressed the hurt and indignation they felt when confronted by the obstructionists in their past. Their responses nonetheless show their belief in their own strength. Some who are naturally more fiery in temperament use their reaction to that unfairness to develop a philosophy that in some way acknowledges the need to compartmentalize negativity in order to have a productive life.

Interestingly, several of the honorees were unable to identify any memorable naysayers on the way to their goals. Wendy Ring says there were none for her, Leonard Morse describes terrific support from friends and family, and Mark Asperilla explains the lack of opposition in his environment by saying that most of the people around him were educated.

Several people in underrepresented categories in medicine—women, persons of color, or both—reported encountering prejudice along the way to college and medical school. This seemed to inspire some to work harder, both as a way of improving themselves and of distracting from the destructive input.

Additionally, those who encountered strong resistance, rather than giving up, developed self-nurturing, resilient habits, including positive self-talk, returning to inner resources, and seeking other supporters. For Coleen Kivlahan, a school principal made the difference by offering words of encouragement that negated a teacher's defeatist message. Sylvia Campbell had a physician tell her to be a nurse instead of a doctor because as a woman she could not go to medical school. But her response seems to imply that she has learned to expect some opposition and is prepared for some resistance. "If you listen to those who tell you no, you'll never do anything," she says.

For some, including Michael VanRooyen, the negative force was not so much an overt opposition as the lack of information or active support. For them, finding their way to medical school and envisioning a career was initially much more a lone search and a process of trial and error, until they found a niche much later on.

The physicians' stories of coping with naysayers in their lives each had their own particular sting, but the responses of the doctors to those negative elements carried some similarity. It is obvious now, although it certainly was not a foregone conclusion, that none of the doctors was stopped from moving ahead. Upon bumping up against opposition, whether in the form of derision (e.g., a professor suggesting that Jeannette South-Paul need not work hard since she was only there as a token representative of her race and sex anyway) or discouragement (being told medical school was not a possibility at all), the physicians describe different emotions but similar responses. Even while feeling greatly demoralized, most indicate that their course of action shifted fairly rapidly to looking for alternative means—a way around their challenges, a different path to the same goal, enlisting another opinion or more support, or in some way amassing strength in order to push through. None seem to have internalized the premise of the opposition (i.e., "You simply cannot do this"), and that can be considered remarkable. Another common response to adversity was to decide and believe that one blocked opportunity on a pathway gives way to a better one. Jack McConnell still thinks wistfully about what he might have done on an overseas mission had he not contracted tuberculosis. Still he avows deep satisfaction with what did transpire.

Those who consider themselves loners to some degree may have relied substantially on their own strength, others on support networks of various kinds, but none decided to abandon their goals, even temporarily. Most do not indicate that they spent much time even considering it as a reasonable option. A notable resilience along with determined persistence thus characterizes these award-winning doctors. It is also characteristic of their optimism that they did not spend much time analyzing any obstacles they encountered, but rather immediately sought to push onward. To this day, the forward-moving energy of the honorees is remarkable.

It could be that it is not as interesting to the physicians to spend time recalling negative opposition as it is to examine what came of it later that was positive. In general the stories they tell of encountering naysaying lead to stories of persistence, not tales of defeat.

What was the sum effect of the early influences?

Though the physicians' sense of mission in life focused and narrowed as they grew older, the effects of their early influences remained relatively unchanged. The values that emerged early in their lives evolved but did not essentially vary. Whether their early influences were so strong and formative as to provide the basis for a lifelong practice, or whether those influences simply drew out and strengthened the impulses of a nascent healer, most of the doctors can identify key moments dating from childhood when they identified with the role of caregiver. Each found in that role a sense of recognition and vocation that he or she carried forward into the notable careers that followed.

How does a sense of mission provide meaning to the honorees' work?

Finding and articulating a unique sense of mission and purpose is no doubt a critical task for those who undertake work of the magnitude of these physicians. Certainly not calling themselves heroes, and not thinking of themselves as heroic (a few even say they see themselves as average people), the doctors nonetheless achieve extraordinary things on a daily basis. How they are able to maintain the quality and quantity of work they do is linked to the sense of vocation most of them discovered early on, and that serves them in their daily activities and decision making by providing a constant reference point. The interviews reveal the many ways in which a strong sense of personal mission has become the navigational tool they rely on to guide their careers.

The interviews also helped me understand how some of the physicians have found their way to positions in which they feel not only distinctively engaged and rewarded but exquisitely utilized; in other words, they feel that their skills and talents are maximally utilized. Some do indicate that through their influence and ability they have found their way to positions they did not anticipate, and sometimes wonder about whether they should be doing more or using their skills in a different way. However, their words reflect the sense that fate, as the honorees understand it, has brought them to the places they are most needed.

What makes these physicians so willing to take on enormous amounts of responsibility?

What is especially notable in the doctors' relationship to responsibility is how they define it; less a burden than a gift. Responsibility is seen as simply a fact in life. It is not only what we owe to other humans as well as ourselves, but also the very way that all life works. Being able to meet responsibilities with skill and resources is a cause for celebration, not an invitation to fatigue.

In the interviews, the word *responsibility* occurs again and again. Another repeated theme is that though so much to do sometimes felt as a burden, it was more often a spur or a driving incitement to action. Jeannette South-Paul makes a great point of asserting the value of each person's contribution, explaining that even when you feel you have little power, there is still always someone with less power than you whose life you could affect positively. The people portrayed in this book by and large take it as a fundamental premise that although there is so much yet to do—issues to be confronted politically, forces to be mobilized within a community, quality of lives to be improved—they should be on the front lines of getting it done.

It is not just that many of them have been raised to think that from those to whom much has been given, much is expected. Beyond that adage, there appears to be an unquestioning pragmatism at the core of each doctor's individual philosophy regarding the necessity for all humans to care, demonstrate compassion, and seek justice for each other. It seems obvious to them that human survival, civilization, and social evolution—all progress depend upon it—and several utter words that reflect the belief that we are all responsible for each other. Without a trace of self-consciousness or overstatement, Leonard Morse avows straightforwardly that he is responsible for every college student in his community of Worcester, Massachusetts, and that every member of that metropolitan population (177,000 people) is important to him. Gary VanderArk explains that he recruits others for service to the poor by reminding them that if everyone does a little, no one individual will feel the burden of responsibility is too heavy to bear. This principle may be self-evident, but the underlying notion of collective responsibility for humanity is not necessarily obvious to all, even those in the helping professions.

Most look at the issue of responsibility through multiple lenses—political, spiritual, social, and personal. Several of the doctors offer the opinion that while taking on huge amounts of responsibility is not always desirable, it is a duty, and because they live by a personal ethical code, that duty is an unshirkable one. Then again, that deeply felt duty to act is also expressed as a vocation, and at times, a benefit. Michael VanRooyen says that being in a position where one is capable of alleviating suffering is a great privilege. For many of the doctors, not being able to help seems the worst form of suffering. When they talk about what has influenced or continues to influence them, the times when they were unable to effect change seems to remain a burden in their memories. In addition to the assumption that all humans are responsible for each other, the doctors share the perspective that not having the chance to act on that belief is a worse fate than bearing its burdens.

The doctors' relationship to responsibility is almost never expressed as an adversarial one, even when they feel that they are the only ones who could fill the shoes they currently fill. They seem to understand responsibility to be as much a part of the natural order of things as gravity or the need to breathe oxygen. Since taking responsibility is a given in life, not just for those in medicine, but for all humans, it makes sense that the honorees found ways to cultivate and enjoy their capacity for it. A spirit of both humility and adventure is communicated when the honorees talk about their obligations.

How do the physicians engage with the inevitable obstacles they encounter?

Learning how to engage with obstacles creatively so that the honorees do not exhaust themselves fighting useless battles has been a key lesson. In this method of engagement, an obstacle is not dwelled on for its own sake, but it is made to become part of the fabric of work. Some of the physicians enjoy the challenging process of confronting an unyielding system and finding creative, win-win solutions. Others seem to have a selective memory in that they only concentrate on what strategies succeed. Pessimism as a state of mind that inhibits action does not come into the picture often, although many of the obstacles they describe are huge, institutionalized, and unwieldy.

Most interviewees felt in some way hindered by institutional structures, whether that was in the particular organizations they worked in or by the fact that their projects followed different timelines than grant-making foundations or institutions would acknowledge or effectively support. Jack McConnell finds his mission hampered by regulations and struggles with the overall infrastructure of health care in the United States. Those physicians in positions of advocating for change felt frustrated by their inability to get sufficient access to people who make decisions and set policy. They often felt hindered by legislators, rigid guidelines, or elitist sentiment and attitudes in those with whom they need to collaborate within the various institutions. Jeannette South-Paul has felt this frustration in trying to get funding to move the agenda on teen pregnancies in this country.

Many of the honorees are at the forefront of a medical program that they founded or that they now run. Most provide services, improved care or access to care, often for the underserved. The existence of their programs, some extremely collaborative and innovative, is testimony to the fact that they continue to find ways around the obstacles that stand in the way of their mission. Most have found a way to step outside of the system, to varying degrees, to get that mission fulfilled. Some feel perfectly suited to multitasking, but a few express frustration with the daily need for it. Several indicate that they are in positions they could not have imagined they would end up in, and while for some it seems like an adventure, for others it is a source of perplexity. Wendy Ring says she thinks she does not really have the kind of organizational mind or detached emotions necessary for her job, but she feels the call to serve along with the awareness of a lack of anyone else to currently fill her role.

A few of the doctors say they have often chosen not to engage with the politics at work in their environments, although those politics, or inequities and unfairness, were personally troubling. Without ignoring such dynamics, they chose rather to deal with the parameters of each situation in a less global way. Several assert that there are ways to get around obstacles in the system without confronting them directly, in the interest of keeping their focus on the work of healing rather than getting caught up in conflict. Others report moments when they felt confrontation was urgently required. Of those, most describe those incidences as not simply bickering, but times when they took the opportunity to try to change another's point of view or at least behavior, usually with some success.

Almost all of the physicians told stories of meeting resistance when trying to rally resources or encourage disempowered people to utilize their own strengths. This was especially difficult when the needed resources involved time, staff, and money to local and community projects. Often that barrier came from authorities in government or the healthcare system itself. There is some irony here that in responding to such resistance, many of the doctors had to become political without doing so on the surface, in that they had to engage in creative bargaining tactics or implement new ways of navigating within an existing structure.

In the area of dealing with obstacles, most of the honorees' replies showed that they have come to apply great emotional intelligence to the process, and this is doubtless one reason why they successfully avoid burnout. Creativity, acceptance, compartmentalization and quiet or noisy persistence are some of the ways they have found to cope. These strategies sometimes help them completely reframe the problem at hand in a way that helps generate solutions.

What keeps the honorees from collapsing under the weight of their own agendas?

Surely there is a critical necessity for self-protection and self-care in a profession that involves such great risk and loss, not to mention its current crisis state both politically and economically. Without developing a conscious strategy to avoid burnout, these doctors undoubtedly could not keep up their enthusiastic contributions to the field. Yet in some ways, the interviews reveal less a planned strategy on the part of each honoree than fortuitousness in how they have *discovered* ways to keep themselves recharged. Not surprisingly, these personal habits seem organically linked to their belief systems and senses of vocation. This is not to say that they have not given conscious thought to self-care, and in the transcripts they exhibit their understanding of its importance.

"I love my life! I love my job! I love what I do!" the interviewed doctors asserted. When these honorees talk about their work, it is most often with enthusiasm and always with vitality. Almost all acknowledged that they had been blessed or gifted with more than average amounts of energy, and that they virtually had no time to be despairing since there is always so much to do. They respond to obstacles as incentives to keep working and problem solving within a field they love. In addition, several felt that their lives have been so easy that there would be virtually nothing to be burned out over. In their estimation, they had been extraordinarily privileged by being able to do what they love and they expressed a great amount of joy, daily satisfaction, and gratitude for their lives.

Even those in underrepresented groups who had perhaps experienced more frustrating situations than others did not evidence bitterness. Furthermore, several said they were too busy to be focused on negativity. Experience had taught them to dwell in the realm of the positive, that negative emotions harm only the one harboring them, and they do not support change in the external situation. If they did not evidence the same level of happiness and satisfaction as those who perceived that the way had been relatively easy, they do share the emotion of gratitude for the opportunity and the ability to do the work they do. Several of the doctors continued to comment on the need to be conscious of how they use their energy and what they choose to spend it on. The importance of strategizing when and where to exert one's will for maximum gain is a theme many of the physicians touch on when they talk about conserving strength and wielding influence.

In their interviews, most deplored the current American healthcare system for its inadequacies and mismanagement while still offering nothing but praise, respect, and admiration for their own caregivers and colleagues within that system. Almost all concur that the state of American healthcare is awful, broken, and in need of a complete overhaul. Several bring up other countries that have succeeded in doing better, providing all citizens with insurance and guaranteed health care in spite of ostensibly fewer resources.

Those doctors who have been in the position of serving as advocates for poor or underprivileged patients or relatives within the system confess that they needed to be tireless and vigilant about getting them adequate care, and about keeping aspects of that care from falling through the cracks. The snarl of bureaucracy, red tape, the inability to ensure that all necessary parties have adequate information, and the lack of centralized systems are cited as endemic and toxic. In spite of the ways that they feel hindered, however, they all still feel that they are making a marked impact for good both within the system and without. That strong sense of mission overrides any disenchantment. Many decades into their careers, none express anything even remotely like a temptation to give up.

What is probably more important in examining how they inoculate themselves against burnout, though, is that despite this disillusionment with our own system, most evidence a very high level of trust in medicine itself and in peer medical practitioners. Perhaps not surprisingly, those who had a spouse who was a patient or who themselves experienced being a patient when their status as a doctor was known report that their care was exemplary, and their memories nothing but positive. What is striking is the effusiveness, gratitude, and humility with which these doctors praise the care they themselves received. In these instances, they seem to primarily identify as patients, not practitioners, and certainly no trace of competitiveness or judgment for a colleague comes across. Finally, whatever inequities and problems exist in American health care, the field of medicine itself and the opportunities to make it better and more accessible are continually rewarding to these practitioners.

Overall the doctors indicate that they have used both self-knowledge and the accumulated wisdom of years to know how and when to exert their energy. Because they feel their work gives back to them in the form of literal and intellectual energy, this is not as difficult as it might be for others who do not feel that same sense of mission. Furthermore, at the risk of oversimplification, there is a general consensus in my discussions with the honorees that there is far less chance of burning out when work does not feel like work. Because the physicians are doing what they love and feel both qualified and privileged to do it, they simply move forward rather than retreat.

How has the practice of effective listening come to be incorporated in the physicians' daily professional style?

As I reread the transcripts of the interviews, *listening* became a category of focus unto itself because it figured so prominently in the physicians' descriptions of what is most vital in their work. Far from being only a method for dealing with patients, it represents a significant and particular orientation to all relationships and to treatment of other people in general. As described by the doctors, listening forms the very essence of compassion, revealing it in many moving dimensions.

Almost every honoree went far beyond what the surface definition of the word listening might evoke. Instead, they each described a holistic, multi-sensory process involving much more than ears and hearing. Many talked of the importance of listening for what is not being spoken—of both intuiting and analyzing the circumstances around what each patient might have to say. Some said touch was a necessary part of accurate listening. Several also mentioned that there are patients who will express very little verbally, and really seeing them—their appearance, expression, and body language—becomes a strong component of listening.

Most said there was nothing more essential to being able to provide superior care, or even adequate care, than truly listening on many levels. Another facet of this deep listening is that it invokes the resources of the listener on both conscious and unconscious levels. The listener describes a process of having to empty the mind of distraction and assumption, of creating an open and neutral place both externally and internally. In this way the listening process becomes a primary example of selflessness that is not just an orientation, but an actual de-selfing, in which the listener deliberately pushes his or her own experience temporarily aside in order to be available to fully enter the patient's model of the world. Several doctors referred to the need to push preconceived notions as well as time restraints aside in order to get to the heart of what is going on with a patient. They use words such as *relaxed* and *unhurried*. More than one describes this quality of listening as being one of the most impressive things they saw exhibited by a role model or mentor.

Most of the physicians decry the patient care model imposed by managed care in that it does not allow time or recognition for what they see as this essential tool. Michael VanRooyen reiterates that listening is a responsibility one has to train oneself to do impeccably. He stresses that it is important not only to listen, but also to develop habits that allow you to listen.

It is clear that these physicians regard receptiveness, characterized by deep, unbiased listening and observation, as a crucial technique to be learned, developed, and continually practiced. It also demonstrates the commitment to a mindset in which the patient, not the doctor, has the essential answers. Their words show that this commitment to receptivity and bilateral dialogue with the patient forms the basis of their practices.

It does not mean, however, that these physicians do not offer advice, direct, cajole, or express opinions. The style of practice described by most of the practitioners demonstrates an eclectic blend of detachment and involvement. The practitioners respect the discrete parameters and the uniqueness of each patient's life and path. In other words, they know enough to know that they do not know as much as the patient does about the totality of the patient's experience and health. On the other hand, the doctors tell many stories in which they describe themselves taking a personal interest in their patients well beyond the scope of the mere examination, procedure, or clinical hour. In fact, the patient's quality of life overall may be of greater interest to the practitioners than any one medical condition. Their investment in the patient's well-being does seem to be a personal one inasmuch as it is central to each doctor's own sense of purpose.

Within the doctor–patient relationships that they describe, they do not always use the traditional skills of empathic listening. They evidently feel free to scold, reward, monitor, entice, and continually exhort their patients, in one way or another, towards greater health. All describe the necessity on the patients' part of feeling cared about in addition to being cared for, and of having their human dignity as well as their healthcare regimens reinforced and upheld. Quite often, this particular kind of attention as it is described by the doctors translates into these unusual time commitments: time spent listening to patients, time spent investigating patients' backgrounds, time spent following up, or ensuring adequate follow-up beyond the specific time allotted to be spent under the doctors' auspices.

This need to spend a decent amount of time with patients is obviously not part of the United States managed care model. It would seem to put the physicians on somewhat of a collision course with the prevailing medical structure in this country. Because of this, it is interesting to consider that these are demonstrably maverick doctors, engaged in overtly or covertly tweaking, challenging, and critiquing American health care by their very daily actions, and yet they are those whose practices have nonetheless been deemed most worthy of commendation. It is a telling representation, perhaps, of where American medicine stands in relation to its own standards at this point in history.

The kind of listening advocated by the doctors may be the most concise image and representation of compassionate practice that this book offers. In reviewing their words about what listening asks of them, I can appreciate how radical the physicians' orientations are within the current medical establishment and yet how simply this listening personifies the healing relationship. It is the same listening described and modeled by Carl Rogers and other major figures in humanistic psychology. It demands that the practitioner listen for the pulse of the patient's whole life, not only mind or body, but the total experience of it. These doctors believe only this kind of unselfish attention can yield the information and the relationship they need in order to implement healing.

What can we conclude about the honorees' sense of purpose?

Like Bill Schecter, most of the doctors interviewed express the idea that there can be no alternative to doing what they do, and for the most part they mean it positively—that they are where they need to be to make their maximum contribution. They make meaningful personal connections with both coworkers and patients and express that sense of personal commitment daily. Gratitude comes across in large measure when they talk about doing their very particular jobs, towards which they feel both great responsibility and great privilege.

What are the spiritual and ethical principles articulated by the physicians?

In looking at the role of spirituality in the honorees' lives, I found that all build their raison d'etre around some notion of it. Most belong to some organized religion, but it is not doctrines but certain elements of spirituality—most often something approximating the golden rule—that unifies the doctors with each other. In many instances their words about it are practically identical. When Bruce Gould says, "I guess I would say that God is, in many ways, that interaction in helping another human being," he might be speaking for all of the honorees. Whatever else they may think about God, the principles of serving others with a nonjudgmental compassion and a practical holism emerge as the cornerstones of their lives and practices. In their work as healers, religion functions as a nondenominational toolbox from which may be drawn whatever symbols and rituals that help people most. It is the helping and service that is central, not adherence to any particular creed or law. The importance of feeling and expressing gratitude for the gift of life and for their own blessings and talents is central and mentioned frequently by the honorees.

The quality of relationship to everyone in their lives, from patients to coworkers to family, is a constant consideration for the doctors interviewed. They believe that their spirituality is best reflected in their connection to others, and they ask of themselves that those relationships with others be characterized by mutual dignity, respect, and true caring. In the interviews, peak moments and memories usually involve not high-profile events, such as getting certain jobs or awards, but a strong moment of connection with another human being. Many talk about being touched by a simple thanks. In general they view their lives as a systemic whole—work practices not separate from the values expressed at home with family, and vice versa. Their ideas of what is courageous, what represents a success or a failure, and what constitutes a life well lived are all viewed in the light of how well other human beings were served.

Virtually all the honorees evidenced a spirituality that encompassed but was more inclusive than religion. Though a particular physician may be a strong adherent of a given religion or belief system, the honoree still felt that compassion was the key to a life well lived and expressed the need to extend that gift to all patients regardless of their religious orientations. When they talk about their beliefs, many directly reference this inclusiveness as a prominent feature of how they practice their faith. Most share the belief that there are many truths and many paths to truth in the universe and that they exist independently of each other—one does not cancel another out. Several say that it is not at all important that others believe as they do or even agree with them—they sound as if they accept diversity of opinion as simply another manifestation of the diversity in the natural world. One who is Catholic says he prays for his patients regardless of their own denomination or religion, and he cites studies that have shown that patients who are prayed for heal faster. One from a Christian background has a partner she playfully calls "a closet Buddhist," and says she looks to him as a role model for practicing authenticity and tolerance.

Most of the honorees expressed a commitment to social justice as a natural outgrowth of their understanding of spirituality. For some this was specifically political—work must be done to establish equal access to health care, for example—and spoken of in those terms. For others it was the recurrent idea that as human beings we are all equal and equally vulnerable, regardless of our degree of privilege, and that those who find themselves in a position of abundance are bound by ethics and honor to try to share what they have.

Some describe feeling and believing in a personal connection to or direct relationship with God. Sylvia Campbell says that in prayer she asks God what to do. She also talks about learning from her mother the importance of faith and having a supportive faith community. In those who have a church or religion, it is central to their lives and identities, and they refer to it occur frequently as they talk about how they make choices and navigate the difficult areas of their lives. Even those who do not describe involvement in a congregation or religion acknowledge spirituality as a sustaining force.

But evangelism, at least in the realm of religion, is not generally a part of these physicians' lives. While many go after their patients and colleagues in the hopes of influencing them to better service or better self-care, they generally do not express an interest in converting anyone to their own beliefs. Jerry Jampolsky specifically states that he does not feel it is his role to try to change anybody. Given the emphasis all the doctors seem to place on nonjudgmental listening, it might be inferred that religious proselytizing of any kind simply does not fit into their idea of the doctor–patient relationship. Certainly it was not explicitly spoken of in the interviews. However, some of the honorees share their patients' religious orientations if not backgrounds, and it may be easier in that context to include a particular vision of God in the medical consultation without it seeming to interfere or distract from the focus of physical healing. Perhaps, too, the doctors use whatever notion of God they have elicited from the patient as a way to talk about the role of religion in healing. Though many of the doctors consider the idea of God as implicitly guiding their own mission, none say they make or require any avowals of God in their interactions with patients.

A few of the honorees talked about some kind of larger life force guiding them, but do not necessarily ascribe to the notion of that something being a personal God. Whether that force is fate, responsibility, or guiding principle, however, all the doctors express humility before the miraculous forces of life that are much larger than their personal concerns or egos. More than any explicitly religious ideal, basic respect for humanity links the doctors ethically to one another, and again the example set by mentors early on continues to resonate through their lives and work. However, even with many of those mentors having been religious people, it is still the basic ethical practice of treating people according to the golden rule that echoes through all the interviews.

How do the honorees keep their external and inner lives in balance?

Perhaps the most essential skill required by physicians whose careers are as demanding as these is that of finding personal balance. How they practice that skill in view of their responsibilities is described in simple terms that are, at times, hard to imagine. The honorees use the time-honored methods of taking vacations, of not taking work home, of having engaging hobbies and activities outside of work. These are not new ideas or suggestions, but the fact that they are utilized by people with such crowded days and critical work is what is important to note. Too often, it may seem that conventional methods for dealing with stress are only available to those whose lives are not stressful. My conversations with the honorees defied the idea that only the idle rich get to seek respite.

Several mention their relationship to anger and talk about how they have learned to use or reframe it. For some of those who identify themselves as having fighter-type personalities, it transforms into a motivational fuel. Several used to get angry and frustrated but now find it an ineffective use of energy.

A number of the physicians assert that they have found a way to be entirely focused on whatever experience is at hand without letting concerns from one area of their lives enter into another. This compartmentalization is particularly linked to the ability to enjoy family life and relaxation time unspoiled by work stresses. For example, Scott Morris remarks that when he is taking a dance lesson with his wife he will not be thinking about work issues, but only about where he is going to put his foot down next. Several discuss this ability as being essential to keeping emotional balance in their lives of multitasking and convey the sense that it is something they are both proud of for cultivating and grateful for finding within themselves.

Despite their compartmentalization, there seems to be a common pattern of perception in how the doctors regard the different categories of their lives. Many describe all the aspects of their life—work, home, mentorship, volunteering—as feeding and strengthening each other, and they cannot imagine one fully functioning without the other. This perception may be critical in that a jam-packed life is instead experienced as an organic whole in which one set of experiences revitalizes another, so the doctors do not feel as though they are overcommitted or being spread too thin. Instead of feeling drained by their aggregate experiences, the honorees understand them as a circuit that is continually recharging.

Family life, humor, exercise, outdoor adventures and religion or spirituality come up most often when the doctors reflect on how they are able to keep mental and physical balance in their lives. It is surprising and perhaps unusual that doctors who are invested in as many compelling projects as the honorees are seem to keep loved ones in the forefront of their minds. Most of the physicians describe setting aside large chunks of time to share with friends and relatives, and they have many positive things to say both about the people closest to them and about the beneficial effects of simply being together. Mark Asperilla refers to his three children as "my elixir" because spending time with them restores him.

The majority of the honorees describe being active physically in their recreational time, through sports, hiking, camping, and travel. Several mention nature as restorative. For some, art and music also supply diversion, engagement, and restoration. Almost all the doctors allude directly or indirectly to the importance of self-care and maintaining their own physical health.

They all say they could not keep balance without humor and laughter, and, as with other positive habits, they are proactive about finding it. One mentions keeping a joke book nearby, another mentions going back to the work of comedian Henny Youngman. Another shares humor she finds on the Internet with friends and colleagues and says, "You gotta laugh so you don't cry." Bruce Gould talks about cultivating an active sense of the absurd and attributes some of his appreciation for that to his Jewish culture. Within the interviews most of the doctors expressed themselves with humor and circumspection even while being passionate about their ideas and experience. The joy, or at least affirmation, that most of them say they feel in their day-to-day functioning is fed by seeing the larger picture of events as moving in a positive direction. They laugh rather than despair over the contradictions of humanity as a way to keep that positive perspective.

As frenetic, demanding, and engaging as these physicians' careers are, most have found ways to relate to those demands without making them the total sum of their lives. The doctors identify caring for others as their primary objectives, but they realize they need to include compassion for themselves. The interviews reveal that they have given thought to the need for treating themselves well so that they can be available to others. This is one way in which a healthy holism prevails in their lives.

What constitutes failure to these physicians?

"I just block it out!" one of the honorees frankly acknowledges in response to my question about failure. Though not all the doctors are this direct, there is a demonstrated tendency towards optimism in their behavior, if not their words. Failure is defined in terms of being unable to extend themselves enough to effectively relieve suffering.

In grappling with the question of failures, the doctors in this book are much more alike than dissimilar. For many the sensation of regret seems a little difficult to access at first. Further exploration begins to reveal why; most of them have created deep and useful learning from past misfortunes. The lessons they absorbed are still being deliberately and consciously applied to their lives every day. Being able to apply that learning, with results that are measurably different from the original experience of failure, seems to considerably redeem it. It is as if these failures had rolled off their backs and disappeared, or as if the values and lessons acquired, which now serve them in a positive way, had replaced the explicit memory of the failure itself. Each honoree's value of all of their life's history, positive and negative, comes across. Experiences another person might have left labeled as failures have been reframed in their psyches as earned and essential wisdom.

When they do focus on an experience of failure, it is remarkable that, without exception, the sense of falling short is connected to not having done enough to help others, whether because of an inability to mobilize resources or simply not having the realm of influence to effect the necessary change in a particular environment. G. Scott Morris, like many of the others, finds little to regret except in occasions where he was unable to prevent suffering. William Schecter expresses regret for failures of communication or judgments that caused others pain. Jerry Jampolsky gives an example of a time when he wished he had been able to offer more comfort to the dying. Michael VanRooyen's regrets were in not having found his career path sooner; he thinks he could have done more if he had.

Many of the physicians reiterate the idea of being blessed and of wanting to offer more strength and solace to those who are, in some ways, living more day-to-day on the front lines. Dr. VanRooyen describes a persistent sense of guilt every time he leaves the doctors who are working full time in other countries where there are inadequate resources and supplies. Almost all mention a patient whose suffering or death they wish they had prevented. Many of these were patients over whose care and treatment they were able to exert a measure of control, but whose fate was nonetheless ultimately out of their hands. Some of them were nonadherent patients, those who did not follow doctors' recommendations, or patients who chose not to opt for certain life-preserving procedures. One of Dr. Asperilla's patients, a Jehovah's Witness, who for religious reasons rejected the blood transfusion that would have saved her life, subsequently died. Her death is obviously still hard for him, especially because in medical terms it was unnecessary. Dr. McConnell had a very similar heartbreaking case with a Jehovah's Witness.

Several physicians reiterated their knowledge, both intellectual and practical, that you cannot make people do things for their own good. Most feel emotionally invested in respecting their patients' distinct life paths and choices. But coupled with that knowledge is the strong relational aspect of their practices. The interviews reveal a deep level of personal connection with patients. Many describe actively liking their patients and being interested in their lives beyond their immediate medical needs. They also regard that interest as not exceptional, but basic to the kind of care they want to provide. Given this dynamic, it is not surprising that they would feel personal loss, at least temporarily, when a patient suffers or dies.

Most of the honorees regret how problems in the current healthcare system have hampered them, as well as their inability at times to function as skillfully as they would like. This was especially the case in the face of institutionalized bureaucracy and in situations where finance and political economics have seemingly trumped good patient care. Some are angrier about it than others, but they all seem to view complacency within the system, or giving in to the temptation to despair over it, as equally perilous and antithetical to the ongoing work that is necessary for change. Many express that they are disappointed when their efforts and projects are not as effective as they had hoped, but often the interviews reveal them beginning to analyze the difficulties and strategize for future improvements in the next breath.

For people whose trajectory is founded on optimistic principles, failure is not part of their daily vocabulary. To consider a regretted action as permanent and unredeemed by subsequent learning would render them incapable of moving ahead. Because they believe that salvation for all lies in continued positive and pragmatic action, the demoralizing effects of calling something a failure are minimized.

How do the honorees recall their moments of extreme courage or cowardice?

It is evident from their accomplishments and the overall arcs of their careers that the physicians have often exhibited great courage. Getting them to identify bravery where and when it happened and defining it in a way that resonated for each of them personally took a little time. Most of the doctors did not seem to respond immediately to the question regarding courage and cowardice. It is as if they were not used to thinking in those terms. Maybe it is because the terms are quite broad. Several of the doctors said they make a point of taking things one day, one problem, one instance at a time, both to focus in the face of multiple responsibilities, and often quite likely in order to avoid feeling overwhelmed. A few also consider it part of their spiritual discipline to stay in the present moment as much as possible.

It could be said that the physicians in this book are on the whole more concerned with verbs than nouns. It may also be that the word *courage* has faintly heroic connotations, and perhaps they are subconsciously familiar with the truism that, as G. Scott Morris quoted, "Pride goeth before the fall." However, on reflection, most found a way to view the question of courage through the lens of other experiences and associations.

Several describe situations in which they upheld a holistic view of patient care, although it was not the prevailing ethic; for example, Leonard Morse persisting in using only two antibiotics to combat certain infections when the trend among some younger doctors was to attack them more aggressively with four. He defends this decision on grounds that more antibiotics can cause bacterial overgrowth resulting in new systemic imbalances and complications. This taking into account the patient's whole long-term quality of life in situations and environments where it is not the norm is implicit in almost all the anecdotes the honorees share.

It is also evident from these stories that a common function of their courage is their flexibility under duress. Sylvia Campbell specifically talks about developing adeptness at moving in and out of the mind-set of clinical detachment that is necessary to function in the face of emotionally upsetting or particularly stressful emergency trauma surgery cases. Although the other doctors may not make that connection verbally, many of their stories also carry the theme of moving back and forth between analysis and emotion, between a brave decisiveness in the moment and feeling a flood of emotions later, when the crisis has passed. In nonclinical settings, many mention the necessity for creativity in getting around obstacles in the system as well as in terms of analyzing, reenvisioning, and thinking about problems in unconventional ways. A leap of faith toward trying many novel approaches and refusing to let go of a problem until it is solved are part and parcel of one another.

But several of the physicians also questioned their own courage in not always speaking up, challenging the system, or using all the tools they may have learned to circumvent bureaucracy. Many said that they fight little battles of one kind or another all day long and that they must choose when and where to especially exert themselves, since they cannot always effect the results they would like. Several mentioned a scrupulous examination of conscience over the times they chose to press forward and the times they decided they had gone as far as they could.

"Each of those decisions in a day, when you either pursue something and push it to its end point, or choose not to for whatever reason, are either acts of optimism and acts of courage, or cowardice, or fatigue," says Bruce Gould. He further alluded to the need for a physician to ask the difficult question of whether a particular course of treatment or procedure is being undertaken more for the sake of the patient or for that of the physicians who are treating him or her. In the same vein of self-inquiry, Jeannette South-Paul also wondered if she was challenging authority often enough, even though she acknowledged the necessity of a measure of compromise in order to remain effective within her own sphere.

It might be that courage is simply a too grand-sounding word in contemporary life. It might also be that the thought of what evokes courage leads one to contemplate fear, if only momentarily. For those used to moving through or reframing fear in the course of their lives, to think about courage in the abstract may not be useful. The actions that reflect courage may also be part of their larger commitment to improving lives, and that idea stays more present than any discrete idea about bravery per se.

What do the honorees hope will be their lasting legacy?

Not surprisingly, what the honorees hope to leave behind is connected to demonstrating what is possible. Most believe that extending compassion to someone makes it much more likely that the recipient will do likewise. For the honorees, this principle is of course inclusive, extending well beyond medicine, but many hope that their medical work will be continued and improved upon by virtue of their having modeled the possibility of a new paradigm. A great example of this is in the community center that grew out of the clinic started by Dr. Sister Brooks. The momentum she started now reaches into people's lives in so many additional areas such as education and social support. Supporting human needs in every respect possible defines the honorees' hopes.

Almost all the doctors who are parents mention their children as being their most important legacy. Relationships with family and dear ones, including being a role model for them and subsequent generations, are paramount.

Some of them reference, directly or indirectly, their contributions to public health in the form of information, access, or means. Several state that it is not the big victories nor necessarily even one's newsworthy contributions that become important as one matures, but the appreciation of precious small moments. Most say that they have built into their lives new ways of ensuring that they remain receptive to and enjoy moments of personal value. Memories and words of a particular patient, friend, or family member are frequently noted.

Several honorees keep diaries or notes and participate in formal or informal meditation, and almost all say they take time to consciously attend to that for which they are grateful. In the interest of practicing the vital spiritual task of staying in the present, a few resisted my question by saying they cannot let themselves think about something as far reaching as a legacy. G. Scott Morris and others envision a time when wellness will consist of treatment for emotion and spirit as well as body and hope their work is contributing to the understanding of the mind–body relationship.

Gary VanderArk offers this biblical quote: "Act justly, love mercy, and walk humbly with God." But he is not the only one whose concept of an important human legacy includes, but stretches well beyond, the world of hospitals and health care. Sister Anne Brooks and Jerry Jampolsky as well as others mention that they hope their legacies, even outside the medical realm, include being remembered simply as people who treated others with love, who helped those in need, and who were able to inspire others to demonstrate caring by their actions in the world. Simply put, they wish to leave things and people a bit better than they found them. For several, and specifically for Sylvia Campbell, this means treating everyone with respect and dignity regardless of their status, and specifically her peers who do not happen to be holding the knife, but whose work is equally significant in the larger scheme of patient care. She also adds that she hopes she will have helped people realize that it is only by reaching out to heal others that we ourselves are healed.

Many honorees allude to how much work is still to be done and frame the breakdown of the healthcare system in this country as a possible prerequisite to its rebirth. Several state the hope that they will see universal access to health care soon, or at least nationwide in the United States, and that they have done something to increase its likelihood. Along with their measurable contributions to medicine in terms of numbers of people treated, money raised, programs inaugurated, etc., many of the practitioners describe their legacies in language that evokes the experience of contributing to a transformation in health care. In other words, much of their lasting impact has been in getting people to change how they view a medical predicament or situation and as a result, change their thinking, theories, and behavior, to effect a structural change within the healthcare system. Through a fairly continuous challenge to the status quo as far as accepted treatment protocols, conventional business practices, beliefs about economic necessity, or most fundamentally, common understanding about what is possible, the majority of these physicians have initiated paradigm shifts that have the potential to modify the essential nature of health care in their respective areas. Several spoke of their legacy in terms of training others, to do not only what they do, which they see as critical, but also to think as they think.

This involves finding and encouraging students and younger peers to learn from them on several levels. It means passing on an ability to understand the complexities and flaws of the current medical system, as well as understanding the needs of human beings through a model more inclusive than any models American allopathic medicine has recently provided. Those who mention this kind of mentoring as part of their desired legacy make it obvious that they do not bear its responsibility lightly. In conceiving of themselves as role models, they feel not only the importance of handing on the work to competent and compassionate people, but also the need to keep themselves above discouragement—or at least from expressing negativity indiscriminately—lest others be dissuaded from following in their footsteps in advocacy or in some valuable aspect of healing practice within the medical field.

In general, the honorees' wishes regarding their legacies have much to do with their own mentorship of others. Their wish is that they have demonstrated the values they espouse in such a way as to make them compelling, attractive, and achievable for others. They hope that by example and encouragement they have taught both the means and the spiritual basis by which a very high standard of care for medical clients as well as humanity in general will come to predominate and prevail.

What is at the core of the life force that drives the honorees?

The concept of human service as the basis of spiritual life emerges with great clarity in reviewing the elements that contribute to the honorees' worldviews. It is the common theme appearing throughout their reports of early influences and their evolving sense of purpose. Most of the physicians express the importance of happiness and comfort in life for themselves as well as their patients and they do not seem to advocate martyrdom in the sense of enduring suffering for its own sake. Rather, they believe that the greatest joy and meaning in a lifetime can be found in improving the lives of others by helping to relieve *their* pressures and suffering and increasing *their* joy. In fact, their images of spiritual life are indelibly stamped with many impressions of serving others. For those who have an experience of a personal God, this is how they serve God as well. If they can be said to share a collective spirituality—it is one that is imminently practical in that it is inexorably linked to and measured by them in constant action on behalf of others and in positive, mutually beneficial relationships with humankind.

What have been the lessons learned from these leaders in medicine?

Sherwind Nuland, distinguished professor of surgery at Yale, wrote in 2008, "The expanding 'scientation' of medicine has led more and more to the dehumanization of medicine." Yet in listening to the honorees, I was left with images of doing medicine the old fashioned way. Dr. Sister Brooks is well past an age when most people retire and yet when awakened in the middle of the night, she troops out to the back seat of the car that pulled up in her yard and delivers twins with little more than her years of experience to help. Dr. Brooks is incapable of saying "call an ambulance for that woman—I need some sleep before tomorrow's shift." Her community knows she is nothing if not reliable. Like her peers in this volume—she offers her hands and her heart and is quite simply incapable of being inhumane.

Physician Rachel Naomi Remen believes that the theory of karma means that life itself is always both educational and healing, and that the undergirding wholeness in every being is continually being drawn out, clarified, and strengthened through lived experiences and challenges. There are always disappointments along the way for people who set ambitious goals (Remen, 1994). I greatly appreciate the fact that the honorees continue to persevere rather than perseverate. As they evolve across their life spans, they exhibit a marked capacity to marshal their resources in new and more effective ways. I got the distinct impression that there was an increasing joy as the honorees looked back on their sequence of successes.

All the honorees are highly respected and recognized as true leaders, but even at this pinnacle of success, they rely on peers, patients, coworkers, and trusted colleagues as sounding boards. This habit helps them preserve an openness and enables them to avoid stagnation by reinventing themselves without abandoning their core mission.

Without a true love for their call to service, the physicians would be drained of energy. Instead, they consistently consider their primary purpose to be showing up to help meet the human needs at hand. They understand that the abstract values of dignity, respect, charity, and love are only valuable if they are manifested in action. There is a single-mindedness exhibited by the physicians that is reflected in their zeal. The compelling beliefs that keep them so committed emanate from a deep and abiding faith, sometimes formal, but other times more like a personal notion of a transcendent ideal.

It is my hope that by spending time appreciating the distinguishing traits that the honorees embody, both new and experienced healthcare providers will feel motivated to reflect on their own evolving personal and professional stories. More than any other quality, they share an abundance of caring. In an era where I hear more people in medicine speaking about compassion fatigue, it has been uplifting to listen to a group of physicians who manage to resist giving in to that downward spiral. Perhaps above all else, this group of honorees can help their peers adhere to the most basic principles. As the first entry in the code of medical ethics, endorsed by the American Medical Association, states, "A physician should be dedicated to providing competent medical care, with compassion and respect for human dignity and rights." I hope that the profiles of the honorees in this volume will inspire more healthcare providers to continue to grow in wisdom and kindness.

Acknowledgments

It seems that the phrase *it takes a village* has gotten overused and a bit worn out. Unfortunately, I cannot think of a better way to express how many kind souls in my life have supported me through the process of finishing this book. First and foremost, I would like to thank the people in my home community at Bentley University. All of the faculty and staff in the Department of Natural and Applied Sciences have been characteristically supportive. In particular, Fred Ledley, Greg Hall, and Martha Keating have been truly wonderful in letting me know that they were pulling for me and helping in any way possible. Also, Joe Nezuh and Kim Morin provided their formidable technical skills to my benefit on many occasions. Tony Buono guided me through the Institutional Review/Human Subjects Protection Process. Additionally, the faculty affairs committee awarded me a grant to to hire a transcriptionist for the data obtained in the interviews.

The staff at the American Medical Association Foundation were wonderful from the first point of contact. Dina Lindenberg, the program officer for the awards, ably assisted by Alexis Koran, have been responsive and informative.

Over the years I have had the privilege to work with professionals in the healthcare industry who hold the highest standards of integrity. In particular, there are some professionals with Pfizer Pharmaceuticals who have been very forward thinking in their sponsorship of educational programming in the medical humanities and the behavioral sciences. Michael Flesher at Pfizer headquarters in New York has worked closely with the AMA to publicize the work of outstanding physicians. In the field, Brian Denton, Susan Donnelly, Farsh Fadaifard, Tom Radice, Ann Glasser, Donna Florio, Mike Barone, Marie Roache, Kent Staver, Del South, Kay Seekamp, Nora Tsivagas, Sheila Aldermen, Carmen Caggiano, and Kurt Zackrison all come to mind as stewards of innovation in healthcare practice.

Additionally, I am a very lucky person in that I have quite a few friends who are professional writers, copyeditors, and data gurus. I have prevailed upon all of them for input at some point in the process. Just to name a few: M. Wolf, J. Field, A. Hamavid, G. Benkert, K. Lake, A. March and M. Gordon. The group assembled at Jones and Bartlett is impressive and helpful. Thanks to Maro Gartside, Jill Morton, Lisa Gordon, and Dave Cella.

I come from a very supportive family who had to hear me say that I was not available for fun for the entire calendar year of 2008. Finishing this book meant that I missed out on spending more time with Brian, Beth, and Michael, as well as Anne and Phil. Similarly, I have a fantastic group of friends whom I have put on hold way too many times while I tried to finish this project. Karen Sontag, Susan Lindsay, and Peg Walsh all come to mind as good sports.

I feel like I would be remiss if I did not mention Mary Hardy, MD, a truly gifted physician from whom I have learned so much. I am grateful, too, for my years on the faculty of the Massachusetts College of Pharmacy and Health Sciences. So many professionals there, especially Mike Montagne, taught me about significant issues in health care today.

About the Author

Dr. Helen Meldrum is an Associate Professor of Psychology at Bentley University in Waltham, Massachusetts. She is a member of the Department of Natural and Applied Sciences and is an advisor to the Program in Health Sciences and Industry. Prior to coming to Bentley, she was an Associate Professor of Communication and Psychology at the Massachusetts College of Pharmacy and Health Sciences where she also coordinated the program in Health Communication. Dr. Meldrum has taught in graduate programs at Babson College, University of Rhode Island, and Northeastern University. Areas of expertise include, interpersonal and group dynamics, medication counseling and adherence, special patients, customer service, psychology of adulthood, telephone triage, communicating about clinical pathway guidelines, dealing with difficult people, mental health services, communicating about sensitive issues, conflict management, and presentation skills. Helen has a particular strength in "teaching skills," having facilitated many train-the-trainer programs in the United States, Canada, Europe, and Israel.

Helen received her Doctorate from The Hiatt School of Psychology and Education at Clark University in Worcester, Massachusetts. She holds a Masters in Counseling and Consulting Psychology from Harvard University, where she also did advanced graduate work in Human Development. Her B.S. is from Emerson College in Boston where she concentrated in Communication Education and Psychology.

Dr. Meldrum has addressed the wide variety of groups across the country and internationally. Her articles, interviews, editorials, and reviews have appeared in many publications, including *USA Today, The Wall Street Journal, Patient Care,* and *The Journal of Therapeutic Communication.* Her book *Interpersonal Communication in Pharmaceutical Care* has been widely adopted. Another text, *Provider–Patient Partnerships* was written with Mary Hardy, MD, and addresses the dilemmas faced by healthcare practitioners working in an era defined by managed care policies.

Active as a consultant, clients have included many pharmaceutical companies, hospitals, group practices, clinics, and professional associations. Dr. Meldrum has coauthored over 20 media scripts for nurses, physicians, pharmacists, and healthcare professionals and has appeared as an expert commentator in several educational videos and CDs. Academic presentations include addresses on treatment protocols for the American Pharmacists Association (APHA), communicating about risk for the United States Pharmacopia and teaching physicians to talk about care plans for the conference on Communication and Medicine at Oxford University, UK. She recently gave a presentation on communicating with patients to The International Listening Association in Frankfort, Germany.

Helen is a member of several professional associations including the National Communication Association. She frequently volunteers her time to animal welfare and rescue organizations.

References and Resources

PREFACE NOTES

1. Schweitzer, A. (1965). *The teaching of reverence for life* (R. Winston & W. Winston, Trans.). New York: Holt, Rinehart, and Winston, Inc.
2. To read more about Albert Schweitzer, I recommend: Brabazon, J. (2000). *Albert Schweitzer: A biography* (2nd ed.) Syracuse, NY: Syracuse University Press.
3. Irwin, A., Millen, J., & Fallows, D. (2003). *Global aids: Myths and facts*. Cambridge, MA: South End Press.
4. To read more about Paul Farmer, I recommend: Kidder, T. (2003). *Mountains beyond mountains*. New York: Random House.
5. Damon, W. (2003). *Noble purpose: The joy of living a meaningful life*. Philadelphia, PA: Templeton Foundation Press.
6. Colby, A., & Damon, W. (1992). *Some do care: Contemporary lives of moral commitment*. New York: Free Press.
7. Eliason, C. B., Guse, C., & Gottlieb, M. S. (2000). Personal values of family physicians, practice satisfaction, and service to the underserved. *Archives of Family Medicine, 9,* 228–232.
8. To read more about the origin of "Yes, Virginia, there is a Santa Claus," see www.newseum.org.

CHAPTER 1: INTRODUCTION

Adams, T. D. (1990). *Telling lies in modern American autobiography*. Chapel Hill, NC: University of North Carolina Press.

Allison, J., & Gediman, D. (Eds.). (2006). *This I believe: The personal philosophies of remarkable men and women.* New York: Henry Holt Publishers.

American Medical Association. (2006). *Physician characteristics and distribution in the U.S.* Chicago. Retrieved February 20, 2008, from http://www.ama-assn.org/ama/pub/category/12912.html.

Aquinas, T. (1273). *Summa theological: Secunda secundae* (Fathers of the English Dominican Province, Trans.) New York: Benziger Brothers. Original work published 1265–1274.

Bateson, M. C. (1989). *Composing a life.* Worth Publishers: New York.

Belsky, J. (2007). *Experiencing the lifespan.* Worth Publishers: New York.

Bolt, M. (2004). *Pursuing human strengths: A positive psychology guide.* New York: Worth Publishers.

Bowker, G. (1993). *The age of biography is upon us.* January 9, London, U.K. *The Times* Higher Education Supplement, pp. 8, 19–20.

Bronson, P. (2002). *What should I do with my life?* New York: Random House.

Brown, D. (2002). *Career choice and development.* San Francisco: Jossey-Bass.

Chirban, J. (2004). *True coming of age: A dynamic process that leads to emotional stability, spiritual growth, and meaningful relationships.* New York: McGraw-Hill.

Clausen, J. A., & Jones, C. J. (1991). Predicting personality stability across the life span: The role of competence and work and family commitments. *Journal of Adult Development, 5,* 73–83.

Colby, A., & Damon, W. (1992). *Some do care: Contemporary lives of moral commitment.* New York: Free Press.

Coleman, P. G. (1999). Creating a life story: The task of reconciliation. *The Gerontologist, 39,* 133–139.

Coles, R. (1993). *The call of service: A witness to idealism.* Boston: Houghton Mifflin Company.

Coombs, R. H., May, D. S., & Small, G. W. (Eds.). (1986). *Inside doctoring: Stages and outcomes in the professional development of physicians.* New York: Praeger Publishers.

Csikszentmihalyi, M. (1997). *Finding flow: The psychology of engagement with everyday life.* New York: Basic Books.

Csikszentmihalyi, M. (2003). *Good business: Leadership, flow, and the making of meaning.* New York: Viking Penguin.

Dan, B. (1988). *A piece of my mind.* New York: Alfred A. Knopf, Inc.

Erikson, E. H. (1950). *Childhood and society.* New York: Norton.

Erikson, E. H. (1959). *Identity and the life cycle.* New York: International Universities Press.

Erikson, E. H. (1968). *Identity: Youth and crisis.* New York: W. W. Norton.

Erikson, E. H., & Evans, R. I. (1967). *Dialogue with Erik Erikson.* New York: Harper & Row.

Farley, M. A. (1986). *Personal commitments: Beginning, keeping, changing.* New York: HarperCollins.

Foos, P. W., & Clark, M. C. (2003). *Human aging*. Boston: Allyn and Bacon.
Fowler, J. W. (1981). *Stages of faith: The psychology of human development and the quest for meaning*. New York: Harper & Row.
French, C. (2007). *What is anomalistic psychology?* Anomalistic Psychology Research Unit, Department of Psychology, Goldsmiths, University of London, New Cross, London. Retrieved November 11, 2007, from http://www.goldsmiths.ac.uk/apru/what.php.
Gawain, S. (1994). Work and play. In C. Whitmeyer (Ed.), *Mindfulness and meaningful work: Explorations in the right livelihood* (pp. 125–130). Berkeley, CA: Parallax Press.
Goodley, D., Lawthom, R., Clough, P., & Moore, M. (2004). *Researching life stories: Method, theory, and analyses in a biographical age*. New York: RoutledgeFalmer.
Gordon, R. (1999, February 11). A heart doctor with an extra big heart. *Harvard University Gazette*.
Groopman, J. (2000). *Second opinions: Stories of intuition and choice in the changing world of medicine*. New York: Viking Penguin.
Groopman, J. (2003). *The anatomy of hope: How people prevail in the face of illness*. New York: Random House.
Groopman, J. (2006). Foreword. In S. Pories, S. H. Jain, & G. Harper (Eds.), *The soul of a doctor: Harvard medical students face life and death* (pp. xvi–xviii). Chapel Hill, NC: Algonquin Books.
Groopman, J. (2007). *How doctors think*. Boston: Houghton Mifflin.
Halberstam, J. (2000). *Work: Making a living and making a life*. New York: Berkley Publishing Group.
Hill, O. W., Pettus, W. C., & Hedin, B. A. (1990). Three studies of factors affecting the attitudes of blacks and females toward the pursuit of science and science-related careers. *Journal for Research in Mathematics Education, 27*, 289–314.
Hopke, R. H. (1997). *There are no accidents: Synchronicity and the stories of our lives*. New York: Riverhead Books.
Jung, C. G., Jaffe, A., & Saint-John, P. (1979). *C. G. Jung: Word and image*. (A. Aniela, Ed.). Princeton: Princeton University Press.
Kail, R. V., & Cavanaugh, J. C. (2007). *Human development: A life-span view*. Belmont, CA: Thomson/Wadsworth.
Kaplan, A. G., Jordan, J. V., Miller, J. B., Stiver, I. P., & Surrey, J. L. (1991). *Women's growth in connection: Writings from the Stone Center*. New York: Guilford Press.
Lee, E. V., Bryk, S. A., & Smith, B. J. (1993). The organization of effective secondary schools. In L. Darling-Hammond (Ed.), *Review of research in education* (pp. 171–267). Washington, DC: American Educational Research Association.
Levoy, G. (1997). *Callings: Finding and following an authentic life*. New York: Three Rivers Press.

Lown, B. (1996). *The lost art of healing*. New York: Houghton Mifflin.
Maslow, A. H. (1954). *Motivation and personality*. New York: Harper and Row, Inc.
McAdams, D. P. (2003). Identity and the life story. In R. Fivush & C. A. Haden (Eds.), *Autobiographical memory and the construction of a narrative self: Developmental and cultural perspectives* (pp. 187–208). Mahwah, NJ: Lawrence Erlbaum Associates.
Menninger, K. (1963). *The vital balance: The life process in mental health and illness*. New York: Viking Press.
Milligan, M. A., & More, E. S. (1994). Introduction. In M. A. Milligan & E. S. More (Eds.), *The empathic practitioner: Empathy, gender, and medicine*. New Brunswick, NJ: Rutgers University Press.
Muirhead, R. (2004). *Just work*. Cambridge, MA: Harvard University Press.
Murakami, S., Otsuka, K., Kubo, Y., Shinagawa, M., Yamanaka, T., Ohkawa, S., et al. (2004). Repeated ambulatory monitoring reveals a Monday morning surge in blood pressure in a community-dwelling population. *American Journal of Hypertension, 17*(12), 1179–1183.
Nakash, O., & Brody, L. (2006). The effects of social roles and personal motives on autobiographical memory. *Sex Roles: A Journal of Research, 54*(1–2), 39–56.
Neher, W. W., & Sandin, P. J. (2007). *Communicating ethically: Characters, duties, consequences, and relationships*. Boston: Allyn and Bacon.
Poris, S., Jain, S. H., & Harper, G. (Eds.). (2006). *The soul of a doctor: Harvard medical students face life and death*. Chapel Hill, NC: Algonquin Books of Chapel Hill.
Richmond, L. (1999). *Work as a spiritual practice*. New York: Random House.
Robin, V., & Dominguez, J. (1992). *Your money or your life: Transforming your relationship with money and achieving financial independence*. New York: Viking Penguin.
Rogers, C. (1961). *On becoming a person: A therapist's view of psychotherapy*. London: Constable.
Schor, J. (2007). *Employees working harder and longer*. Retrieved October 29, 2007, from http://www.fishervista.com/statistics.htm.
Sigelman, C. K., & Rider, E. A. (2006). *Life-span human development*. Belmont, CA: Thomson/Wadsworth.
Snyder, C. R. (1994). *The psychology of hope: You can get there from here*. New York: Simon & Schuster.
Subotnik, R. F., Stone, K. M., & Steiner, C. (2001). Lost generation of elite talent in science. *Journal of Secondary Gifted Education, 40*, 33.
Vaillant, G. E. (1993). *The wisdom of the ego*. Cambridge, MA: Harvard University Press.
Weiten, W., & Lloyd, M. A. (2006). *Psychology applied to modern life: Adjustment in the 21st century*. New York: Thomson/Wadsworth.
Williams, N. (1999). *The work we were born to do*. Shaftsbury, Dorset, England: Element Books Limited.
Zuckerman, H. (1997). *Scientific elite: Nobel laureates in the United States*. New York: Free Press.

CHAPTER RESOURCES

Chapter 2: Dr. Sister Anne Brooks

Catholic Online. (2003). *Sister Anne Brooks marks 20 years as a doctor; Catholic extension helps brooks open doors to new health care.* Retrieved July 5, 2008, from http://www.catholic.org/prwire/headline.php?ID=613.

Humane Health Care. (2005). *Wounded healer: Sister/doctor in the Delta.* Retrieved July 5, 2008, from http://www.humanehealthcare.com/Article.asp?art_id=349.

Kelly, K. (2001). Sister runs Mississippi clinic on 'Pearly Gates' plan. *The Catholic Key,* Retrieved July 5, 2008, from http://www.catholickey.org/index.php3?gif=news.gif&mode=view&issue=20021206&article_id=2163.

National Health Service Corps. (2008). *Success stories: Mississippi: Melody of hope in the birthplace of the Delta blues.* Retrieved July 5, 2008, from http://nhsc.bhpr.hrsa.gov/about/success_stories/ms.asp.

Tutwiler Clinic. (2008). *Tutwiler Clinic: Community health plan.* Retrieved July 5, 2008, from http://tutwilerclinic.org/index.html.

Chapter 3: Dr. Michael VanRooyen

Asa, R. (1998). *Michael Vanrooyen: Physician spans the globe, bringing relief to others.* Retrieved July 7, 2008, from http://www.uic.edu/depts/spha/about/healthpr/hlpro98/vnrooy.htm.

Harvard Humanitarian Initiative. (2008). *Michael Vanrooyen, MD, MPH, FACEP.* Retrieved July 7, 2008, from http://www.hhi.harvard.edu/index.php?option=com_content&task=view&id=22.

VanRooyen, M. & Leaning, J. (2005). After the tsunami—facing the public health challenges. *New England Journal of Medicine, 352*(5), 435–438.

Chapter 4: Dr. Sylvia Campbell

American College of Surgeons. Operation Giving Back (2007). *2007 Domestic Volunteer Award—Sylvia D. Campbell.* Retrieved July 8, 2008, from http://www.operationgivingback.facs.org/content1607.html.

Judeo Christian Health Clinic. (2008). *History of the clinic.* Retrieved July 8, 2008, from http://www.judeochristianhealthclinic.org/english/history.htm.

WWWDesign. (2008). *Uninsured: Part of the solution.* Retrieved July 8, 2008, from http://wihwod.org/uninsured.htm.

Chapter 5: Dr. Jack McConnell

AARP. (2007). *Impact: Awards 2007 honorees.* Retrieved July 10, 2008, from http://www.aarpmagazine.org/people/impact_awards_2007_mcconnell.html.

Alliance for Aging Research. (2000). *Dr. Jack McConnell: Transforming health care, his community, and himself.* Retrieved July 10, 2008, from http://www.agingresearch.org/content/article/detail/936/.

Bartleme, T. (2004). *Jack McConnell, MD: "What have you done for someone today?"* Retrieved July 9, 2008, from http://findarticles.com/p/articles/mi_m0843/is_6_30/ai_n8563545.

Caring Institute. (2007). *Honorary board of trustees & board of directors.* Retrieved July 9, 2008, from http://www.caringinstitute.org/trustee_JBMcConnell.htm.

Loma Linda University. (2001). *LLU news: Schools of medicine and dentistry will hold graduation ceremonies Sunday, May 28.* Retrieved July 9, 2008, from http://www.llu.edu/news/today/may1100/llu.htm.

Volunteers in Medicine Web site. (2008). Retrieved July 9, 2008 from http://www.vimclinic.org/history.

Chapter 6: Dr. Bruce Gould

Area Health Education Center. (2008). *Kids into health careers: Area health education centers.* Retrieved July 11, 2008, from http://bhpr.hrsa.gov/KIDS CAREERS/ahec.htm.

Faculty Bio: Associate Dean for Primary Care, Medicine, University of Connecticut Health Center Director, Connecticut Area Health Education (2008). Retrieved July 11, 2008, from www.chip.uconn.edu/dirbio/GouldBruce.

Shaskan, J. (2004). *Primary care specialist honored by American Medical Association.* Retrieved July 11, 2008, from http://advance.uconn.edu/2004/040419/04041904.htm.

Chapter 7: Dr. G. Scott Morris

Alpha Epsilon Delta. (2004). *Tentative convention program.* Retrieved July 12, 2008, from http:// www.jmu.edu/orgs/nationalaed/1html/agenda.htm.

Church Health Center. (2008). *Our story.* Retrieved July 11, 2008, from http://www.churchhealthcenter.org/default.aspx?pid=2.

ReachMD. (2008). *G. Scott Morris, MD, MDiv.* Retrieved July 12, 2008, from http://www.reachmd.com/xmradioguest.aspx?pid=7487.

The Society of Entrepreneurs. (2006). *G. Scott Morris; the Church Health Center, executive director.* Retrieved July 12, 2008, from http://www.societyofentrepreneurs.com/members/bio.asp?ID=40.

Chapter 8: Dr. Coleen Kivlahan

Doctors of the World—USA. (2008). *Philanthropy careers: Employer profile.* Retrieved July 13, 2008, from http://philanthropy.com/jobs/profiles/14979.htm?pg=i.

Florence Project. (2008). *The Florence Immigrant and Refugee Rights Project.* Retrieved July 12, 2008, from http://www.firrp.org/index.asp.

Henderson, N. (2001). *Coleen Kivlahan, MD, MSPH, receives AAMC Humanism in Medicine Award.* Retrieved July 12, 2008, from http://www.aamc.org/newsroom/pressrel/2001/011103e.htm.

La Linea. (2007). *Conversation with Coleen Kivlahan, MD, MSPH: Appointed to the Florence Project board of directors in December 2007,* p. 2. Retrieved July

12, 2008, from http://www.firrp.org/documents/newsletters/LaLinea Spring 08.pdf.
Little, R. (2007). Feel-good diplomacy. *The Baltimore Sun*. Retrieved July 12, 2008, from http://www.baltimoresun.com/news/health/bal-te.comfort28oct28,0, 6410019.story?page=4&coll=bal_tab01_layout.
Schaller Anderson, Incorporated. (2008). *Senior executive staff Coleen Kivlahan, M.D., M.S.P.H.* Retrieved July 12, 2008, from http://www.schalleranderson.com/StaffKivlahan.aspx.
Trible, L. (1991). *Appointment—Coleen Kivlahan.* Retrieved July 12, 2008, from http://www.hhs.gov/news/press/pre1995pres/910213.txt.

Chapter 9: Dr. Mark Asperilla

Doctor's Digest. (2007). *Doctors Digest on emergency planning.* Retrieved August 25, 2008, from http://www.doctorsdigest.net/content/board.php.
Filipino Image. (2007). Marianito "Mark" Asperilla, MD. *Filipino Image* magazine. Retrieved August 25, 2008, from http://www.filamimage.com/2008_TOFA/asperilla_mark.html.
Semon-Krauss, N. (2008) *Two men and a Clinic: St. Vincent DePaul community healthcare's clinic fills a vital gap, thanks to Drs. Asperilla and Klein.* Retrieved August 25, 2008, from http://www.harborstyle.com/2008-07/2-men.html.
USA Freedom Corps. (2003, November 11). *President Bush to recognize Florida doctor for dedication to volunteer service* [press release]. Retrieved August 25, 2008, from http://www.usafreedomcorps.gov/about_usafc/newsroom/local_vols_dynamic.asp?ID=242.

Chapter 10: Dr. Gary VanderArk

Colorado Neurological Institute. (2008). *Tribute to CNI founder: Gary D. VanderArk, MD.* Retrieved July 19, 2008, from http://www.thecni.org/vanderark.htm.
Doctors Care. (2008). *Doctors Care.* Retrieved July 20, 2008 from http://www.drscare.org/.
University of Colorado Department of Neurosurgery. (2008). *Team profiles: Dr. Gary VanderArk, MD—Clinical professor.* Retrieved July 20, 2008, from http://www.cuneurosurgery.com/team-profiles-dr-gary-vanderark.htm.
University of Michigan Medical School. (2001). *Class notes—Medicine at Michigan fall 2001: The 1960s: Gary VanderArk.* Retrieved July 19, 2008, from http://www.medicineatmichigan.org/magazine/2001/fall/classnotes/default.asp.
VanderArk, G. (2001). *A magnificent obsession: Classic novel should resonate with neurosurgeons.* American Association of Neurological Surgeons Bulletin, *10*(4), 36.

Chapter 11: Dr. Gerald G. "Jerry" Jampolsky

ICAH. (2008). *The International Center for Attitudinal Healing: Jerry Jampolsky, M.D.* Retrieved July 18, 2008, from http://www.attitudinalhealing.org.
Jampolsky, G. (2004). *Love is letting go of fear.* Berkeley, CA: Celestial Arts; Ten Speed Press.

Serinus, J. V. (2005). *Common ground: Heal thyself, heal the world.* Retrieved July 18, 2008, from http://commongroundmag.com/2005/10/healing0510.html.

Stanford University Medical Center. (2005). Gerald Jampolsky, MD '50 wins Pride in the Professions Humanitarian Award. *SUMC Alumni Association Newsletter.* Retrieved July 17, 2008, from http://smstaging.stanford.edu/alumni/newsletter/05_05.html.

Wakan Films. (2000). *Attitudinal healing* [documentary with Jerry Jampolsky]. Retrieved July 17, 2008, from http://www.wakan.com/Documentary/Attitudinal%20Healing.html.

Chapter 12: Dr. Jeannette South-Paul

Clark, V. (2004). *In the spotlight: Dr. Jeannette South-Paul.* Retrieved July 16, 2004, from http://www.aamc.org/members/facultydev/facultyvitae/sept04/spotlight.htm.

National Library of Medicine. (2008). *Changing the face of medicine.* Retrieved July 16, 2008, from http://www.nlm.nih.gov/changingthefaceofmedicine/physicians/.

University of Pittsburgh Medical Center. (2008). *UPMC: Jeannette E. South-Paul, M.D.* Retrieved July 16, 2008, from http://www.upmc.com/Communications/MediaRelations/UPMCExperts/BySubject/M/Minority+Health+Disparities/SouthPaulJeannetteE.htm.

Chapter 13: Dr. Leonard Morse

Dayal, P. (2007). Needle disposal effort set: Collections foster a cleanup for city. *Worcester Telegram and Gazette News.* Retrieved July 15, 2008, from http://www.telegram.com/article/20070907/NEWS/709070762/1116.

The FAIR Foundation. (2008). *Board of Directors.* Retrieved July 15, 2008, from http://www.fairfoundation.org/Board/board.htm.

UMass Medical School. (2008). *NIAID director Anthony S. Fauci, MD, to deliver UMass Worcester commencement address.* Retrieved July 15, 2008, from http://www.umassmed.edu/Content.aspx?id=46110.

Chapter 14: Dr. Wendy Ring

California Health Care Foundation. (2008). *CHFH health care leadership class of 2007–2009.* Retrieved July 19, 2008, from http://www.chcf.or/press/view.cfm?itemID=133475.

Humboldt Del Norte Medical Society. (2003). *Wendy Ring, M.D., California Medical Association Plessner Award recipient.* Retrieved July 19, 2008, from http://humboldt1.com/~medsoc/Awards.html#wendy.

Mobile Medical Office. (2008). *Health care in motion.* Retrieved July 19, 2008, from http://www.mobilemed.org.

Chapter 15: Dr. William Schecter

Avidan, V., Hersch, M., Spira, R., Einav, S., & Schecter, W. (2007). Civilian hospital response to a mass casualty event: The role of the intensive care unit. *Journal of Trauma-Injury Infection & Critical Care, 62*(5), 1234–1239.

Emergency Medical Services Authority. (2007, July). *Designated trauma centers,* p. 8. (Ref. No. EMSA 90B, April 1987). Sacramento, CA: State of California.

Grey, D.(2008). *Stanford School of Medicine, models and mentors: In conversation with Douglas Grey, M.D.* [Interview transcript; L. Cochran, interviewer]. Retrieved July 20, 2008, from http://med.stanford.edu/community/models-mentors/doug_grey.htm

Harlow, C. W. (2002). *Firearm use by offenders: Survey of inmates in state and federal correctional facilities.* (U.S. Department of Justice, Bureau of Justice Statistics, Publication NCJ 189369). Washington, DC: U.S. Government Printing Office.

Hertzler, J. O. (1936). *The social thought of the ancient civilizations.* New York: McGraw-Hill. Retrieved July 15, 2008, from http://www.questia.com/PM.qst?s=o&d=62057311.

Operation Access. (2004). *Grant: Operation Access in San Francisco coordinates free surgeries for low-income and uninsured people.* Princeton, NJ: Robert Wood Johnson Foundation.

Operation Access Newsletter. (2008, Spring/Summer). Retrieved July 15, 2008, from http://www.operationaccess.org/pdf/newsletterspring08.pdf.

Operationaccess.com. (2007). *History.* Retrieved July 15, 2008, from http://www.operationaccess.org/html/history.htm.

Paget, S. (1899). *Ambroise Paré and his times, 1510–1590.* New York: G.P. Putnam's Sons.

Schecter, W. P. (2007, May). Convocation speech from graduation ceremonies, University of California San Francisco School of Medicine, class of 2007 [transcript].

Schecter, W. P. (2008). *Curriculum vitae.* Department of Surgery, San Francisco General Hospital, University of California, San Francisco. Retrieved July 20, 2008, from http://surgery.ucsf.edu/faculty/william-p-schecter-md.aspx.

Schechter, W. P., Grey, D., & Hofmann, P. B. (1994). The Ambulatory Surgery Access Coalition: Creating a program of elective surgeries for the uninsured. *San Francisco Medicine, 67*(7), pp. 23–24.

Schechter, W. P., & Wilder, L. (2005). Preparing for the inevitable: Notes from the San Francisco General Hospital disaster committee. San Francisco Medical Society. Retieved July 15, 2008, from http://www.sfms.org/AM/Template.cfm?Section=Home&SECTION=Article_Archives&TEMPLATE-/CM/HTMLDisplay.cfm&CONTENTID=2417.

Singer, I., & Adler, C. (Eds.). (1906). Hillel. *The Jewish Encyclopedia.* New York: Funk and Wagnalls. Retrieved July 20, 2008, from http://www.jewish encyclopedia. com/view_page.jsp?artid=730&letter=H&pid=0.

Staudenmayer, K., & Schecter, W. P. (2007). Civilian hospital response to mass casualty events: Basic principles. *Bulletin of the American College of Surgeons, 92*(8), pp. 16–22.

Weiss, M. (2006, December 10). General, life and death at San Francisco's hospital of last resort: For trauma team, saving lives is both a social and medical mission. *San Francisco Chronicle,* p. A-1. Retrieved July 20, 2008, from http://www.sfgate.com/cgi-bin/article.cgi?f-/c/a/2006/12/10/MNGVOMT3NL1DTL.

Chapter 16: A Summation of What Was Shared

American Medical Association. (2001). *History of the Principles of Medical Ethics.* Retrieved December 20, 2008, from http://www.ama-assn.org/ama/pub/category/2512.html.

Jamison, K. (2004). *Exuberance: The passion for life.* New York: Vintage Books/Random House, Inc.

Nuland, S. (2008). *The uncertain art: Thoughts on a life in medicine.* New York: Random House, p. 3.

Palmer, P. J. (1994). Leading from within: Out of the Shadow, into the Light. In J. A. Conger, (Ed.), *Spirit at work: Discovering the spirituality in leadership* (p. 27). San Francisco: Jossey-Bass.

Remen, R. (1994). *Kitchen table wisdom.* New York: Riverhead Books/G.P. Putnam's Sons

Salinger, J. D. (1951). *The catcher in the rye.* Boston: Little, Brown, and Company.

Templeton, J. (2005). Foreword. In C. R. Snyder & S. Lopez (Eds.), *Handbook of positive psychology.* New York: Oxford University Press.

Index

A

A Course in Miracles, 157
ACCESS Care Inc., 127
Adams, Timothy, 6
Aetnal Medicaid, 115
AIDS Hotline for Kids, 154
Alliance to Defend Health Care, 2
Ambulatory Surgery Access Coalition, 213–214
American Academy of Family Physicians Exemplary Teaching Award, 166
American Board of Family Practice, 165
American College of Surgeons Humanitarian Award (2007), 62
American Foundation Pride in the Profession Award, xiii
American Friends Committee Peace Center, 193
American Medical Association code of medical ethics, 251
American Medical Association Council on Ethical and Judicial Affairs, 179
American Medical Association Foundation, xiii
American Medical Association Journal, 81
American Samoa, 208–210
Anderson, Warner J. "Butch," 39
Aquinas, Thomas, 24
Arapahoe Medical Society, 141, 147, 152
Archives of Family Medicine, xiv
Area Health Education Center (AHEC), 97
Aristotle, 27
Asperilla, Mark, 127–140, 228
  ACCESS Care Inc., 127
  allocating resources for the Philippines, 136
  aunt's respect for humanity, 131
  Belgian nuns, influence of, 130–131
  books that influenced him, 131, 226
  burnout, ways of coping, 135–136
  commitment to service through medicine, 130
  courage, 137
  discrimination, 130
  education and professional life, overview, 127–128
  failure, 136, 244
  family life in the Philippines, 128–129
  keeping his life in balance, 135–136, 242
  learning about persistence, 131
  legacy, 139–140
  listening to and understanding your patients, 133
  mother's illness, 131–132
  motivation, 133
  obstacles to his goals, 135
  opens pharmacy after Hurricane Charlie, 134–135
  outside community projects, 134
  parents' influence, 129–130, 132, 221
  partnering with Volunteers in Medicine (VIM), 135
  personal ethics, 134
  quality of his clinical practice, 136–137
  reflection on his parents, 132
  regrets over healthcare system in the United States, 138
  resources, 263

Ryan White funding for the uninsured, 134
spiritual component in his work, 138–140
when the best course of action cannot be taken, 137–138
Association of American Colleges' Humanism in Medicine Award, 116

B
Bateson, Catherine, 18
Bayfront Medical Center, St. Petersburg, FL, 39
Bean, Orson, 158
Belsky, Janet, 25
Berrigan, Daniel, 59
Berrigan, Phil, 59
Blessed Teresa of Calcutta, 32, 33, 34
Body and Spirit, 108
Bosnia, 55, 59
Boston Medical Library, 179
Bowker, Gordon, 6
Brand, Paul, 170
Brigham and Women's Hospital, Boston, 53, 56
Bronson, Po, 24
Brooks, Anne, 35–47
  burnout and despair, resisting with prayer, 42
  confidence, development of, 44–45
  convent boarding school, 37
  education and professional life, overview, 35–36
  family life, 36–37
  "I am not a healer, I am a facilitator," 40–41
  joins Sisters of the Holy Name of Jesus and Mary, 37
  legacy, 46–47, 247, 248
  legal problems, 45
  lessons we have learned from her, 250
  listening to the patient, 39–40
  loving what she does, 40–41
  medical degree, 38–39
  personal ethics and goals, 42
  resources, 261
  spiritual component in her work, 45–46
  support from other sisters, 43, 222
  teaching, 37–38
  Tutwiler Clinic, 35–36, 42–44
  a White person caring for Black people, challenges, 41
Brown, Duane, 11
Bush, George H.W., 128
Bush, George W., 83–84

C
Campbell, Sylvia, 61–73, 68
  activities outside of medicine, 67
  American College of Surgeons Humanitarian Award (2007), 62
  birth of her stillborn child, 64
  burnout and despair, resisting, 67
  Caribbean trauma system, 69
  community involvement, 68
  courageous events, 69–70, 246
  education and professional life, overview, 61–62
  events that influenced her career direction, 62–63, 224
  family life, 67–68
  in Haiti, 66, 68–69
  healing the spirit as well as the body, 71
  health care and the insurance system, 66–67
  helping a girl from Uganda, 68
  her moral compass, 66
  husband's support, 63
  importance of a faith community, 64, 240
  judgment calls, 70
  legacy, 72, 248
  lessons in communication, 70–71
  listening to and touching patients, 65
  mother's Alzheimer's disease, 65
  mother's influence, 64
  negatives, refusing to focus on, 65–66
  opposition to her life's plan, 63, 228
  prayer, 67
  resources, 261
  sexism, 66
  state of the medical profession, worries about, 72–73
  Vietnam War, impact of, 63–64

INDEX **269**

Caring Institute, Washington, D.C., 36
Center for International Emergency, Disaster, and Refugee Studies (Johns Hopkins U.), 50
"Changing the Face of Medicine: Celebrating America's Women Physicians," 166
Charles Donnegan Award for Volunteerism, 128
Charlotte County HIV Clinic, 127, 138
Chirban, John, 10
Christie, Agatha, 9
Church, Francis, xv
Church Health Center Clinic, (Memphis, TN), 103–104, 107, 110–114
Circuit, The, 100
Cirincione, Diane, 153–154, 156–157, 160, 162
Clearwater free clinic, 35
Colby, Anne, xiv
Coles, Robert, 18, 19, 20
College Youth Health Service Corps, 99
Colorado Coalition for the Medically Underserved (CCMU), 141, 152
Colorado Neurological Institute (CNI), 141–142
Colorado Physician Insurance Company, 148
Commitment, 18–19
Connecticut Youth Health Service Corps, 89, 98–99
Continuing Medical Education (CME), 36
Course in Miracles, A, 157, 159
Creedmoor State Hospital, Queens, N.Y., 90–91
Csikszentmihalyi, Mihaly, 24–26

D
Damon, William, xiv
Darfur, genocide in, 49
De Kruif, Paul, 184
Debos, Rene, 183
Democratic Republic of the Congo, 50
Distinguished Physician Award, 104
Doctors Care program, 141, 147–149, 152

Doctors of the World, 116, 118
Doctors Without Borders, 125
Dolittle, Dr., 193–194
Dooley, Tom, 116, 117, 225
Douglas, Lloyd C., 143
Durban, South Africa, 209

E
Empathy, 29–30
Erikson, E.H., 11–12
Ethics, 26–31

F
FAIR foundation, 179
Faith and spiritual beliefs, 31–34
Falchuk, Myron, 27–28
Family Practice Research Journal, 116
Farley, Margaret, 18
Farmer, Paul, xi, xv
Federal Emergency Management Agency (FEMA), 134–135
Fire on the Mountain, 225
First, do no harm, 31
Florence Project board of directors, Arizona, 116
Flow, 24–26
Foley, Mark, 135
Fowler, James, 33

G
Gary VanderArk award, 152
Gawad Kalinga homeless program, 127
Gawain, S., 24
Gerber, Lane, 119
Gilligan, Carol, xiv
Gould, Bruce, 89–101
  Area Health Education Center (AHEC), 97
  being there for his patients, 91–92
  Boy Scouts, 90, 95, 226
  College Youth Health Service Corps, 99
  Connecticut Youth Health Service Corps, 89, 98–99
  courage or cowardice, 246
  cultural competence, 95
  Dr. Van Tienhoven (Dr. V.), 91
  education and professional life, overview, 89–90

epidemics at the camps, 98
ethical constructs, 100, 101
failure, of the healthcare system, 92–93, 95–96
failure, personal, 95–96
Francisco Jimenez, inspiration of, 99–100
friend's health crisis, 92
going the extra distance, 94–95
intention to become a doctor, 90–91
legacy, 97
Lisa, 91
listening and being in the moment, 94
migrant program, 97–98
National Health Service Corps, 99
National Youth Health Service Corps, 99
nutrition in medicine, 93
parents' influence, 96
Rabbi Sokobin, 91
regrets, 97
resources, 262
sense of humor, 96, 242
setting boundaries, 94
spiritual component in his work, 99, 239
taking his children with him when he works, 100–101
underserved communities, introduction to, 93–94
Greater New Bedford Community Health Center, 179, 185
Green, Dr., 207
Grey, Douglas, 213–215
Groopman, Jerome, 23, 28, 30–31, 33–34
Gross, Terry, 204
Guided imagery, 21–22

H
Habitat for Humanity, 42, 89, 136
Haiti, 62, 66, 68–69, 122–123
Halberstam, John, 16, 19
Harrity, Tricia, 98
Hartford Department of Health and Human Services, 89
Harvard Humanitarian Initiative, 50, 55
Harvard University and Brigham and Women's Hospital, 53
Healthcare system in the United States, 1–2, 92–93, 95–96, 138, 201
Hemingway, Ernest, 131, 226
Hepatitis outbreak, 1969, 189
Hoffman, Paul, 214
Holocaust, 50, 221, 225
Hope, 31
Hotel Rwanda, 59
How to Start a Church-Based Health Clinic, 105
Human Genome Project, 75
Hurricane Charlie, 134–135
Hurricane Katrina, 62, 192

I
I Am the Lord Who Heals You, 104
I Don't Know If I'm Good Enough, 156
Institute of Genomic Research, 75
International Center for Attitudinal Healing, 153–154
International Physicians for Prevention of Nuclear War, 2
Introduction and overview, 1–34
  choosing the profession, 4–13
    approach to physicians' personal histories, 6
    career choice, 10–11
    collecting and analyzing life stories, 4–5
    Dr. Bernard Lown, 1–2, 13
    healthcare system in the United States, 1–2
    personality and psychoanalytic theory, 8–10
    questioning, direct, 8
    questioning, general area of, 3–4
    role models and mentors, 11–13
    selective memory of the interviewees, 6–8
  professional and personal identity, 14–22
    burnout, 20
    commitment, 18–19
    doctors' reasons for entering the medical field, 14–15

emotional and physical energy of participants, 19–21
job dissatisfaction, 15–17
medicine as a calling, 15
myths pertinent to this book, 21
personal malaise, 19
positive thinking, 21–22
professional recalibration, 17–18, 20
resources, 257–260
the wellspring, 22–34
  empathy, 29–30
  faith and spiritual beliefs, 31–34
  first, do no harm, 31
  flow, 24–26
  holding out hope, 31
  joy in the job, 23–25
  listening to the patient, 27–28
  love, 34
  mindfulness, 24
  self-actualization, 21, 28–29
  true calling, concept of, 32–33
  virtue ethics, 26–31

J

Jack B. McConnell, MD Award for Excellence in Volunteerism, 76
Jamison, Kay Redfield, 219
Jampolsky, Gerald G. "Jerry," 153–163
  AIDS Hotline for Kids, 154
  asking for help, 160
  burnout, 160
  A Course in Miracles, 157, 159, 226
  desire to make a difference, 154–155
  Diane Cirincione (wife), 153–154, 156–157, 160, 162
  early work with children with AIDS, 157
  education and professional life, overview, 153–154
  financial difficulties, 158
  International Center for Attitudinal Healing, 153–154
  learning from the past, 161
  legacy, 162, 248
  listening to the patient, 158–159
  living authentically in the moment, 162
  love, the essence of our being, 162–163
  maintaining personal balance, 162
  moral dilemma, 161
  parents, 154–155
  personal illness, 158
  philosophy, 159, 160
  practical principles, 162
  practical spirituality, concept of, 157
  psychiatry, path toward, 155
  purpose of his ministry, 159
  resources, 263–264
  spiritual component, 162, 240
  "sticking his neck out," 155–156
  suicide of patient, 160
  Vietnam War, opposition to, 156
  view of himself, 156
  writes *Love is Letting Go of Fear,* 157–158, 159
Jeanne Schmit Free Clinic (Herndon, VA), 116, 120
Jerusalem, Israel, 211
Jimenez, Francisco, 99–100
Job dissatisfaction, 15–17
John Paul II, Pope, 32
Johns Hopkins, 52–53
Johnson & Johnson Laboratories, 75
Journal of Family Practice, 116
Journal of Trauma-Injury Infection and Critical Care, 211
Joy in the job, 23–25
Joy McCann Foundation Award, 166
Judeo Christian Health Clinic, 61–62
Jung, C.G., 21–22

K

Kahn, Eddie, 143, 144, 152, 226
Kefalides, Nicholas, 168–169, 172
Kegan, Robert, xii
King, Martin Luther, 19
Kivlahan, Coleen, 115–126, xv
  burnout, 121–122, 123, 124
  challenges of her childhood, effects of, 124, 222
  challenging patients, 124–125

clinical work, 120–121
Doctors of the World, 118
Doctors Without Borders, 125
education and professional life, overview, 115–116
empathy and kindness, 124
encouragement from high school principal, 118–119, 228
family life, 124
future path in medicine, indications of, 116–117
legacy, 126
listening to the patient, 120
Medicaid policy role, 120
medical care as a child, lack of access to, 117–118
medical school, choice of, 119–120
network of physicians, education on child abuse, 123
parents' influence, 117, 119
personal and professional successes, 123
personal ethics, 121–122
Project Hope trip to Haiti, 123–124
resources, 262–263
Sexual Assault Forensic Examinations (SAFE), 115
spiritual component in her work, 125–126
Tom Dooley, 116, 117, 225
uncle's support, 117
Koans, 32
Kohlberg, Lawrence, 219, xiv
Kosovo, 55
Kyasanur Forest disease, 183

L

Leaning, Jennifer, 55
Lederle Laboratories, 75
Levoy, Gregg, 32–33
Lost Art of Healing, The, 2, 13
Love, 34
Love is Letting Go of Fear, 154, 157–158, 159
Lown, Bernard, 2–3, 13

M

Magnificent Obsession, 143–144, 226
Making a Difference Award (2006), 90

Maslow, Abraham, 21, 28, 218–219
Massachusetts Medical Society award, 180
McAdams, D.P., 7
McConnell, Enoch Luther, 77–79, 81, 222
McConnell, Jack, 75–87, 135
  Albert Schweitzer as role model, 80
  burnout, 84–85, 87
  courage and cowardice, 85–86
  education and professional life, overview, 75–76
  failure, 244
  father's influence, 77–79, 81, 222
  helping a former teacher, 79–80
  home life, 76–78
  joins the pharmaceutical industry, 81
  legacy, 87
  malpractice insurance for volunteers, 86
  mother's influence, 223–224
  moves to Hilton Head, 81
  Navy V-12 program, 79
  obstacles to his goals, 83–84, 232
  opens clinic at Hilton Head, 82
  resources, 261–262
  spiritual component in his work, 86–87
  tuberculosis, recovering from, 80–81, 229
  Volunteers in Medicine Clinic, 76, 78, 82–83, 86
  wife's influence, 85
McNeil Laboratories, 75
Medically Indigent Committee, 151–152
Medicine as a calling, 15
Meged, Aaron, 205, 211
Meldrum, Helen, profile, 255–256
Menninger, Karl, 22
Mindfulness, 24
Missouri Department of Health, 115
Mobile Medical Office (MMO), 191–192
Morris, Scott, 103–114
  attends seminary, 104–105
  awards, 107
  Body and Spirit, connecting, 108, 113–114

INDEX 273

burnout, 111–112
courage or cowardice, 245
disappointing himself, 112–113
divinity school courses that made a difference, 108
divorce, 111
education and professional life, overview, 103–104
encouragement toward his goal, 107
explaining the rules to patients, 112
failure, 244
fund raising, 110
a hands-on ministry, 105–106
legacy, 114, 248
listening to the patient, 109–110
maintaining balance, 112
medical school at Emory U., 109
medical school at Yale, 105, 108–109
mother's death, 109
Pastor Granger Westberg, 105
personal ethics, 110–111
personal medical crisis, 109
resources, 262
talking to patients, 110
William Coffin, 106–107, 112, 113
Morse, Leonard J., 179–190
Alexander P. "Johnnie" Johnstone, 180–181
army career, 182–183
books that influenced him, 183–184
burnout, 186–187
childhood during the Depression, 180
commissioner of public health in Worcester, 185–186
decision to retire from practice, 188
Dengue virus first isolated while he was in Thailand, 183
develops Kyasanur Forest disease, 183
education and professional life, overview, 179–180
efforts to degregulate syringes and needles: Operation Yellow Box, 186
family, 188
Greater New Bedford Community Health Center, 179, 185
hope, 187–188
infectious disease fellowship at U. of Maryland, 183
Internist of the Year, 180
legacy, 189–190
listening to the patient, 184–185
maintaining balance through love of nature, 188
marriage, 182
Massachusetts Medical Society award, 180
Merrill Snyder, 181
movies, effects on children today, 188–189
obstacles in his work, 186
parents, 180, 181
people who influenced his choice of career, 181
persistence and realistic optimism, 190
personal ethics and goals, 186
personal medical emergency, 184
regrets, 187
resources, 264
responsibility to others, 186, 231
retaining a sense of fun, 188
spiritual component, 189
support from friends and family, 228
Theodore Woodward, mentor, 181–182, 184, 187
at U. of Maryland Medical School, 181–182
at Walter Reed Army Institute of Research, 182
William McD. Hammond, 183
Movies and TV
effects on children today, 188–189
role models from, 11, 226
Muirhead, Russell, 9
Murrow, Edward R., 5
Myths pertinent to this book, 21

N

National Advisory Council on Migrant Health, 90
National Health Service Corps, 35, 99
National Youth Health Service Corps, 99
New England Journal of Medicine, 55
Night They Burned the Mountain, The, 116
Noble Purpose: The Joy of Living a Meaningful Life, xiv

Nuland, Sherwind, 250

O
Okafor, Martha, 98
Olam, Tikun, 100, 101
Old Man and the Sea, The, 131, 226
Operation Access, 203–204, 213–215
Operation Crosswords, 115
Operation Yellow Box, 186
Osler, William, 28, 190, 207

P
Paré, Ambroise, 212
Pasteur, Louis, 189
Peale, Norman Vincent, 21
Personal malaise, 19
Personality and psychoanalytic theory, 8–10
Pfizer Medical Humanities Initiative, xii
Pfizer Pharmaceuticals, xiv
Physicians for Social Responsibility, 2
Plessner Award, Rural Physician of the Year, 192
Positive thinking, 21–22
Power of Positive Thinking, The, 21
Presidential Service Volunteer Award, 128
Pride in the Professions award winners, 12, 120
Project Hope, 115, 122–123

R
Rebecca Sieff Hospital, Safed, Israel, 211
Recalibration, professional, 17–18, 20
Relief for the Body, Renewal for the Soul, 104
Remen, Rachel Naomi, 250
Researching Life Stories: Method, Theory, and Analyses in a Biographical Age, 6
Ring, Wendy, 191–202, 228
    American Friends Committee Peace Center, 193
    becomes a United Farm Workers organizer, 192, 226
    being authentic at work, 199
    burnout and despair, difference between, 198–199
    courage, 200
    Dr. Dolittle books, 193–194, 226
    education and professional life, overview, 191–192
    engaging with obstacles, 233
    fathers' influence, 193
    first interest in medicine, 194
    goals for her practice, 196
    healthcare system in the United States, 201
    husband's heart attack, 199
    improving her administrative abilities, 197
    influence on patients, 201
    inspiring and helpful people, 194–195
    integrity and empathy, 196–197
    legacy, 201–202
    listening to the patient, 195
    Mobile Medical Office (MMO), 191–192, 200
    parents' values and respect for humanity, 193, 202
    perseverance, 195–196
    Plessner Award, Rural Physician of the Year, 192
    Quaker beliefs, 200–201
    regrets, 199–200
    remarks on her amazing staff, 196
    resources, 264
    spirituality and personal ethics, 202
    teaching and mentoring other people, 197
Robert Wood Johnson Foundation, 213
Rogers, Carl, 238
Role models from movies and TV, 11, 226
Rwanda, 49, 55, 58, 59
Rwandan Ministry of Health, 49
Ryan White funding, 134

S
Salinger, J.D., 218
San Francisco General Hospital (SFGH) emergency room, 203, 211, 212
Sane/Freeze, 106
Schecter, Gisela, 203–216
Schecter, William, 203–216, 226

Ambulatory Surgery Access Coalition, 213–214
in American Samoa, 208–210
basic principles that guide him, 213
being thorough, paying attention to details, 207
burnout, 215
convocation speech, U.C. San Francisco School of Medicine, 213
decision to become a trauma surgeon, 206–207
Dr. Green, support of, 207
in Durban, South Africa, 209
early life, 204–205
education and professional life, overview, 203–204
Gisela, 203–216
greatest success, 209–210
in Jerusalem, Israel, 211
legacy, 216
listening, 207, 209
Operation Access, 203–204, 213–215
parents, 205, 206, 220
personal failures, 207–208, 244
personal health problems, 215–216
at Rebecca Sieff Hospital, Safed, Israel, 211
resources, 265–266
role models, 226
self-discipline, 205–206
sense of purpose, 238
SFGH emergency room, 203, 211, 212
spending time with family, 216
spiritual component to his work, 212–213
"surgery of mass casualties," 211
taking care of people who are disenfranchised, 206–207
treatment of HIV-infected patients, 210–211
Schweitzer, Albert, 80, xi, xv
Self-actualization, 21, 28–29
Sexual Assault Forensic Examinations (SAFE), 115
SFGH (San Francisco General Hospital) emergency room, 203, 211, 212

Sisters of the Holy Names of Jesus and Mary, 35, 37
Snyder, Charles R., 5
Somalia, 55
Some Do Care: Contemporary Lives of Moral Commitment, xiv
South-Paul, Jeannette, 165–177
American Academy of Family Physicians Exemplary Teaching Award, 166
burnout, 171–172, 175
career in the U.S. Army, 165
challenges, 173–174
decides to become a physician, 167
Dr. Nicholas Kefalides, role model, 168–169, 172
Dr. Paul Brand, role model, 170, 225–226
education and professional life, overview, 165–166
failure, 175
family, 166, 167
first job in a research lab, 168
grant funding, 173
greatest personal achievements, 175
greatest professional success, 174
Joy McCann Foundation award, 166
keeping her balance and focus, 175–176
legacy, 177
listening to patients, 176
medical care for father and brother, 171
medical school, 169–170
mission, 177
mother's support, 167–168
motivation, 172–173
parents' influence, 171, 221
personal ethics and goals, 173
personal philosophy, 172
racial prejudice and misunderstandings, 169
regrets, 177
relationship to responsibility, 231
resources, 264
respect for humanity, 170–171
self-advocacy, 176–177
style with patients, 176

USUHS Distinguished Service Medal, 165
St. Francis/U. of Connecticut Medical School Primary Care Center, 89
St. Vincent de Paul Charity Clinic and Pharmacy, 127
St. Vincent de Paul Clinic (Phoenix, AZ), 121
St. Vincent Hospital, Worcester, MA, 184
Steinbeck, John, 66
Sudan, 56
Summation of what was shared, 217–251
  concept of caregiving, 223–225
  early influences, effect of, 220–223, 229–230
  engaging with obstacles, 232–234
  failure, 243–245
  indelible impressions of the honorees
    guidance by an enlightened conscience, 219
    as self-actualized people, 218–219
    sense of noble purpose, 218
    spiritual and religious concerns, 217–218
    taking action because it is right, 219
  influence of parents or nurturers, 221
    dedication to their code of ethics, 221–222
    descriptions of their parents, 221
    mentors and other positive relationships, 222
    parents' treatment of others, 222
    sense of caring, 223
    support of education and the learning process, 222
  keeping external and inner lives in balance, 241–243
  legacy, 247–249
  lessons we have learned from them, 250–251
  life force that drives them, 249
  listening, 236–238
  mentors, 226–227
  moments of courage or cowardice, 245–247
  narratives, media, and communities, seeking role models there, 225–226
  obstructionists, 228–229
  relationship to responsibility, 230–232
  resources, 266
  self-protection and self-care, 234–236
  sense of mission and purpose, 230, 238
  spiritual and ethical principles, 238–241

T

Templeton, John, 217
Teresa, Mother, 32, 33, 34
Terkel, Studs, 5
This I Believe, 5
Thompson, Tommy, 83, 84
Tillich, Paul, 31, 108
True calling, concept of, 32–33
Tutwiler Clinic, 35–36, 42–44

U

U. of Colorado Health Sciences Center, 142
U. of Connecticut Medical School, 89
U. of Natal, Durban, 209
U. of South Florida College of Medicine, 61
U.C. San Francisco School of Medicine, 213
Uganda, 62, 68
UIC School of Public Health, 50
United Farm Workers organizer, 193
University Hospital, Columbia, Missouri, 115
Upledger, John, 35, 38
USUHS Distinguished Service Medal, 166

V

Vaillant, George, 12
Van Tienhoven (Dr. V.), 91
VanderArk, Gary, 141–152
  Arapahoe Medical Society, 141, 147
  burnout, 147
  Colorado Coalition for the Medically Underserved (CCMU), 141, 152

Colorado Neurological Institute
  (CNI), 141–142
courage, 150–151
cowardice, 150
Doctors Care program, 141, 147–149,
  152
early commitment to be a doctor,
  142–143
Eddie Kahn, mentor, 143, 144, 152,
  226
enthusiasm for his work, 145
exercise, 149
father's role, 143, 221
Gary VanderArk award, 152
goal: help the medically underserved,
  146
legacy, 152, 248
listening to the patient, 144–145
Medically Indigent Committee,
  151–152
mother's encouragement, 142, 143
patients' choices, when not in their
  best interest, 151
personal ethics, 145–146
personal illness, 144
prayer and meditation, 149, 151
relationship to responsibility, 231
relationship with his patients, 150
resources, 263
U. of Colorado Health Sciences
  Center, 142
VanRooyen, Michael, 49–60, 228
  Boy Scouts and the value of service,
    51, 226
  burnout, 56
  education and professional life,
    overview, 49–50
  events that turned him toward medi-
    cine, 51–52, 224
  facing the issue in Rwanda, 58
  failure, 56, 244
  father's influence, 50, 51, 60, 221
  goals and medical ethics, 54
  humanitarian education, 55–56
  identity, 54–55
  imprisonment in Zaire, 57–58
  legacy, 59
  listening to the patient, 53, 237
  move to Harvard University and
    Brigham and Women's
    Hospital, 53
  move to Johns Hopkins, 53
  persons with medical challenges,
    52–53
  question of cowardice, 59
  regretful experience, 58
  relationship to responsibility, 231
  religious views, 58–59
  resources, 261
  Somalia, Bosnia, Rwanda and Kosovo,
    55
  style, 57, 59
  synthesizing from different experi-
    ences, 57
  talking to people at home, 59–60
  value of family and keeping a sense of
    humor, 56
  views about his "calling," 54
Vietnam War, impact of, 63–64, 156
Virtue ethics, 26–31
Vital Balance, The, 22
Volunteers in Medicine Institute, 76
Volunteers in Medicine (VIM), 76, 78,
  82–83, 86, 127, 135

W
Westberg, Granger, 105
William Coffin: charity and justice,
  106–107, 112, 113
Winter of Our Discontent, 66
Worcester District Medical Society schol-
  arship fund, 190

Y
Yale Divinity School, 105, 108
YMCA camp, New Hampshire, 180–181
Youngman, Henny, 188, 242
Your Money or Your Life, 23–24

Z
Zaire, Dr. VanRooyen's imprisonment in,
  57–58
Zen moment, 25

www.ingramcontent.com/pod-product-compliance
Lightning Source LLC
Chambersburg PA
CBHW071859290426
44110CB00013B/1205